BIHAR AND ORISSA DISTRICT GAZETTEERS

Patna/ **L.S.S. O'Malley**
Shahabad/ **L.S.S. O'Malley**

BENGAL DISTRICT GAZETTEERS

Burdwan/ **J.C.K. Paterson**
Darjeeling/ **L.S.S. O'Malley**
Howrah/ **L.S.S. O'Malley**
Hooghly/ **L.S.S. O'Malley**
Santal Parganas/ **L.S.S. O'Malley**

BIHAR AND ORISSA DISTRICT GAZETTEERS

PATNA

BIHAR AND ORISSA DISTRICT GAZETTEERS

PATNA

BY

L.S.S. O'MALLEY, I.C.S.

REVISED EDITION

BY

J.F.W. JAMES, I.C.S.

LOGOS PRESS

New Delhi-110 002

Cataloging in Publication Data—DK
Courtesy: D.K. Agencies (P) Ltd. <docinfo@dkagencies.com>

O'Malley, L. S. S. (Lewis Sydney Steward), 1874-1941.
Bihar and Orissa district gazetteers : Patna / by L.S.S. O'Malley. — Rev. ed. / by J.F.W. James.
p. cm.
Reprint. Originally published: Patna : Supt., Bihar and Orissa Govt. Print., 1924.
Includes bibliographical references.
Includes index.
ISBN 8172681216

1. Patna (India : District)—Gazetteers. I. James, J. F. W. II. Title.

DDC 915.412 003 21

ISBN : 81-7268-121-6
First Published 1924
Reprinted 2005

Printed and Published by
LOGOS PRESS
Building No. 4788-90, Street No. 23, Ansari Road, Darya Ganj,
New Delhi-110 002 (India)
Phone : 23272187

PREFACE TO THE FIRST EDITION (1907).

I DESIRE to acknowledge my obligation to Mr. J. G. Cumming, I.C.S., formerly Collector of Patna, for materials which have been used in compiling this volume. I am also indebted to Mr. W. R. Bright, I.C.S., C.S.I., Opium Agent, Bihar, and Mr. W. B Thomson, I.C.S., Collector of Patna, for the ready assistance they have given me.

L. S. S. O'M.

PREFACE TO THE REVISED EDITION.

THIS is the second of the revised District Gazetteers of the Bihar and Orissa series. A great part of the present edition reproduces Mr. O'Malley's work; but much rewriting and revision has been rendered necessary by changes and developments since 1907. A complete record-of-rights has been prepared for the district; the cultivation and manufacture of opium, formerly so important, has been abolished; and Patna itself has become the capital of a Province. The Archæological Department of the Government of India has been busy in the district during these years; and local archæological and historical research has been encouraged by the Bihar and Orissa Research Society, with the result that it has been necessary to revise or amplify much of what was written in the original Gazetteer regarding Rajgir, Nalanda, and Pataliputra. As the publication of the separate statistical appendix has been discontinued, some statistical matter has been included in the Gazetteer itself, which Mr. O'Malley relegated to the B volume of the original edition.

I desire to acknowledge my obligations to the local officials of Government and the District Board, and to all who have given assistance in the preparation of this book, of whom some are mentioned in the book itself. Those who have contributed or revised complete chapters or articles are Lt.-Col. H. R. Dutton, I.M.S. (chapter V); Mr. G. E. Fawcus (chapter XV); Mr. V. H. Jackson, (the article on Rajgir, and much in chapters II and XVI); and Mr. J. A. Page (Nalanda). I should also thank Mr. H. L. Henderson, Fellow of New College, Oxford, and the distinguished author who writes under the pseudonym of Sydney C. Grier, for assistance rendered.

J. F. W. J.

TABLE OF CONTENTS.

CHAPTER I.

PHYSICAL ASPECTS.

CHAPTER II.

HISTORY.

CHAPTER III.

THE PEOPLE.

CHAPTER IV.

RELIGIONS.

CHAPTER V.

PUBLIC HEALTH.

CHAPTER VI.

AGRICULTURE.

CHAPTER VII.

IRRIGATION.

CHAPTER VIII.

NATURAL CALAMITIES.

CHAPTER IX.

RENTS, WAGES AND PRICES.

CHAPTER X.

OCCUPATIONS MANUFACTURES AND TRADE.

CHAPTER XI.

MEANS OF COMMUNICATION.

CHAPTER XII.

LAND REVENUE ADMINISTRATION.

CHAPTER XIII.

GENERAL ADMINISTRATION.

CHAPTER XIV.

LOCAL SELF-GOVERNMENT.

CHAPTER XV.

EDUCATION.

CHAPTER XVI.

THE CAPITAL OF BIHAR AND ORISSA.

CHAPTER VII.

GAZETTEER.

APPENDICES.

MAPS.

GAZETTEER

OF THE

PATNA DISTRICT

CHAPTER I.

PHYSICAL ASPECTS.

PATNA, the smallest of the districts of Bihar, but by no means the least interesting or important, is bounded on the north by the river Ganges, on the south by Gaya district, on the east by Monghyr, and on the west by the river Son, which separates it from Shahabad. It is eighty-two miles in length from east to west, and from twenty-eight to forty-two miles in breadth. The area of the district is 2,114 square miles; and its population, according to the census of 1921, is 1,574,287 souls. The district takes its name from its principal town, the capital of the province of Bihar and Orissa, which stands on the site of the ancient capital of Magadha, (25° 37′N and 85° 10′E). **GENERAL DESCRIPTION.**

With the exception of a small area of hill and jungle in the south-east, Patna district consists of an alluvial tract, sloping gently to the Ganges on the north, and intersected by several rivers and artificial irrigation channels. Along the southern bank of the Ganges there is a strip of high ground about four miles broad, which diverts eastward the rivers flowing north from the Gaya district; and in consequence of this obstacle to the natural drainage, the low-lying country on the south of Patna City, Barh, and Mokameh is under water in the rainy season. In the south-east the district is **Natural configuration.**

for thirty miles divided from the district of Gaya by the Rajgir Hills, which run in a south-westerly direction from Giriak.

Scenery.

With the exception of the Rajgir Hills and a solitary hill rising from the open plain near Bihar town, the general aspect of the district is that of an unbroken level diversified only by groves of mango and palm trees. The greater part of this tract is singularly fertile, being watered by the streams which descend from the Hazaribagh plateau to join the Ganges; and no jungle is left except in the Rajgir hills and in the flooded country towards the mouth of the Son. The north and west of the district, with its shady roads and frequent mango groves, is a pleasant country, though it contains no striking scenery. On the east of the district is the great plain, bare of trees, which is known as the *tal*. The description of this country which was given thirteen centuries ago by Hiuen Tsiang applies to it now; the village houses are huddled together on large mounds which become islands during the monsoon rains, when the whole *tal* is one great lake, and boats are used for communication between village and village. In the dry season this region suffers from lack of shade; and in May or early June, when the crops have been cut, and the burning wind blows unchecked across the dusty plain, it is as unpleasant a country for the traveller as can be found in this part of India. There is no such monotony in the irrigated area in the south of the district; but here, except during the driest season, communications are greatly obstructed by private canals and their distributaries, with steep sloping sides and soft and treacherous beds. In the extreme south-east of the district, the country is of a very different description. Here the rugged line of the Rajgir Hills stretches away to the south-west, a long range breaking into many detached spurs and peaks, clothed with thick low jungle and interspersed with masses of rock.

Hill system.

The Rajgir Hills are the only hills in the district. They form part of a long range extending from Bodh-Gaya north-eastwards for a distance of forty miles until they terminate abruptly at Giriak, where their base is washed by the Panchana river. At Handia hill, on the boundary of the district, they rise to a height of 1,472 feet; but elsewhere they seldom attain an altitude of more than a thousand feet.

Their sides are rugged and precipitous, and are mostly covered with thick low brushwood, broken only by irregular pathways strewn with rocks.

Starting from Giriak, two parallel ranges of hills stretch away to the south-west, enclosing a narrow ravine, through which a rivulet called the Bawan Ganga rushes down in cascades and rapids to join the Panchana. To the south of the village of Rajgir the two ranges broaden out and enclose a valley, in which the ancient city of Rajagriha was built. The northern range here rises into a peak of inconsiderable height known as Ratnagiri, from which two spurs diverge at right angles, one descending southwards across the defile leading to Giriak, while the other strikes off to the north-west and joins the Vipulagiri peak. To the west of the latter peak is a narrow ravine, through which the Saraswati stream forces its way into the low country at the foot of the hills. The range then pursues a south-westerly direction for three miles till it attains a considerable elevation at the Baibhar hill, where the southern range again approaches it. The south-eastern corner of the Rajgir valley is marked by the Udayagiri peak which throws out a spur to the north to meet that coming southwards from Vipulagiri. To the west the hill sinks into a defile, beyond which is a high hill called Sonagiri, opposite the Baibhar hill. At this point the two ranges again resume their south-westerly course, and again enclose a narrow ravine overgrown with jungle.

Pirpahari.

Besides these hills there is a small isolated hill, called Pirpahari, rising abruptly from the plain on the north-east of Bihar town. The southern slope is gradual, covered with boulders, which form a natural staircase; but the northern side consists of a precipitous cliff with numerous rocks scattered along it

RIVER SYSTEM.

The Ganges forms the northern boundary of the district, while the Son forms its boundary on the west. The other rivers intersect the district from south-west to north-east. They all flow northwards from the Gaya district, and take a sharp turn towards the east soon after crossing the boundary: with the exception of the Punpun, none of them join the Ganges within this district, being driven eastwards by the high land on its southern bank. None of them are of any great size, and the greater part of the water brought down is diverted into irrigation channels and reservoirs, and distributed among the fields, so that their main channels are mere dried-up beds for the greater part of the year: in fact, only the Punpun, Morhar and Panchana contain any volume of water. This is particularly the case in the south-east of the district, where the streams and rivers are used up in a network of *pains* or artificial channels, expending themselves before reaching the Ganges or mingling in the *tal* in the Barh subdivision. The whole of the country to the south of Barh is very low, but the strip of high land along the Ganges prevents any of these streams from entering the main river. They meander about in a confusing manner, known by different names till the necessities of irrigation and the dryness of the season leave nothing but tortuous sandy beds to mark the direction of their courses. Their beds are sandy, and the banks in general low and sloping, so that when they come down in flood during the rainy season, the adjacent country is inundated, but part of the water finds an exit by the Maithun or Kuluhar river.

Ganges.

The Ganges most sacred of rivers to the Hindu, forms the northern boundary of the district from the confluence of its waters with the Son on the west up to the village of Dumra on the east, its total length in Patna being ninety-three miles. The river at Patna is about six hundred yards wide in the cold season, and the stream is then sluggish until it is joined by the Gandak; but from June to September under the combined effect of the melting Himalayan snows and the monsoon rains it becomes a mighty stream several miles wide. It is at this season that changes occur in the course of the river. The main stream comes down with great violence; and if it takes a course which impinges upon high land on either side, that land is in danger of being cut away. There has sometimes been ground for uneasiness in Bankipore and Patna city, though the southern bank is here generally protected by revetments: and a journey past Patna by boat will show many broken columns which have collapsed under the pressure of the flooded river. While the main stream is impinging upon one bank, the stream on the other side is comparatively gentle, so that before the flood subsides it ordinarily deposits a certain amount of the detritum with which the water is heavily loaded. The heaviest portion of the detritum is deposited first; but much of the sand has

District
PATNA

Scale 1 Inch = 8 Miles

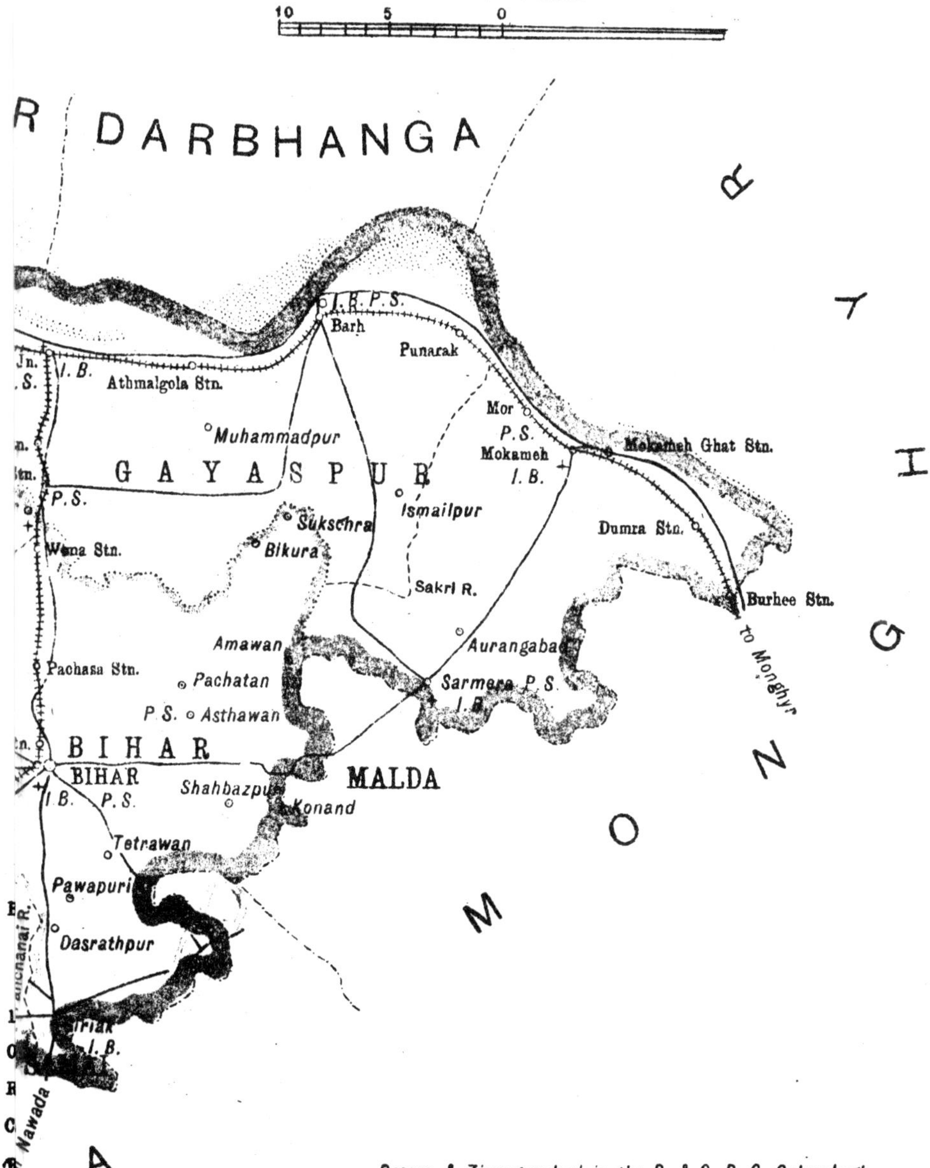

Drawn & Zincographed in the B. & O. D. O. Gulzarbagh

Facing Page No. 4

already been deposited before the river reaches Patna district, so that the *chars* and *diaras* thus created in this district quickly become covered with the highly fertile silt which is brought down by the river. When silt is deposited, these formations produce magnificent crops; and many of the *diaras* are very valuable Government estates. They are unfortunately the cause of many disputes, with frequent riotous struggles for possession, owing to the fact that land-marks are apt to be washed away in the annual flood. In extensive *diara* areas there is usually a part which is covered with a deposit consisting chiefly of sand, on which a low scrub jungle appears which gives shelter to wild pig. The pig do much damage in the cultivated portion of the land; so that the Dinapore Tent Club is a popular institution with *diara* cultivators. The best grounds for the Tent Club in this district of late years have been the *diaras* of Bakhtiarpur, where the going is comparatively good, and the neighbourhood of Gangahara, which is favoured chiefly for its convenience of access.

At present the confluence of the Ganges with the Son is near the village of Hardi Chapra, whence the river flows in a single stream to Digha. Here a side channel of the Son, the last remnant of its ancient easterly course, enters the Ganges. The Patna-Gaya canal joins the Ganges by this side stream; but in some years there is not enough water to render it navigable, and the double lock of the canal is liable to be left high and dry after the monsoon flood subsides. Digha is a commercial station of some importance, where a number of steamers may always be seen, the large stern-wheelers which come up from Goalundo, and the smaller steamers which start from here for Buxar and the Gogra. Immediately below the moorings of the steamers the Kurji school is prominent on the Patna side. From here to Bankipore the Patna bank is an almost continuous brickfield. The river flows at present (1923) close under Bankipore past Patna city; this most interesting portion of it is described in chapter XVI. From Patna city branches of the Gandak join it from the north, swelling its stream, and forming great *chars*, for many miles. The Punpun joins the Ganges at Kurtha. At Barh the river turns to the north in a horse-shoe curve, and at present the town is away from the main stream.

Son.

The Son, the Erannoboas of Megasthenes, forms the boundary between Patna and Shahabad. At Parao, a few miles south of its confluence with the Ganges, it is crossed by the bridge of the East Indian Railway. Since the anicut was built at Dehri, there has ordinarily been little water in the river except during the rains; but however low the water may be, it is dangerous to cross except at the known fords, since its bed abounds in quicksands. The Son drains a very large hill area; and after heavy rain in the Central Provinces it is apt to come down in sudden and violent flood; but its floods are of short duration. The name which is given to this river by the ancient Greek writers on India is apparently a corruption of the Sanskrit Hiranyabahu, or golden-armed, derived, like the name Son, from the golden colour of the sand which it brings down in flood. It formerly flowed far to the east; and the Punpun now flows in its ancient bed. After being joined by the Morhar, it pursued a north-easterly direction as far as Chilbil, thence turned east, running south of the present site of Patna city, finally joining the Ganges at Fatuha. There is a long tract of low ground in this last direction, destitute of trees, which is known as the dead Son, clearly marking the ancient bed of the river. The courses of the Ganges and the Son were thus nearly parallel for many miles; and in the narrow tract lying between the two rivers was situated the famous city of Pataliputra. The Son gradually worked westward, until its lower course closely approximated to the present alignment of the Patna-Gaya canal as far as Phulwari; and it is probable* that the Son burst across the narrow neck of land which divided it from the Ganges at that place before the year 750 A.D. The confluence with the Ganges was afterwards at Sherpur; and even in 1772 it was at Maner. At the beginning of the nineteenth century Maner was three miles south of the union of the two rivers; and now the Son joins the Ganges six miles north of Maner.

Punpun.

The Punpun enters Patna district near Shahzadpur, and flows in a north-easterly direction until it approaches Naubatpur. Here it turns sharply to the east, and joins the Ganges at Fatuha, after flowing for fifty-four miles in the district. The Punpun is joined by the Morhar and Dardha, about nine miles from its junction with the Ganges; but

* Reports of the Archæological Survey of India, Vol. VIII.

shortly before its confluence with that river some of its waters diverge along a channel, called the Dhoa, which runs nearly parallel to the Ganges. This river retains water throughout the year, but except in the rains is useless for purposes of navigation owing to the number of irrigation channels which it supplies with water in this district as well as in Gaya, where a large dam intercepts the stream. So much of the water is thus diverted that, except in times of high flood, only a small portion reaches the Ganges. At the point of junction the river attains a width of about a hundred yards enclosed within high steep banks. The Punpun is a sacred river, and it is the duty of every pilgrim to Gaya to shave his head on its banks and bathe in its waters on his way to the holy city.

Morhar and Dardha. To the east of the Punpun are the Morhar and Dardha, two branches of the same river, which bifurcates in the Gaya district. Both streams follow a north-easterly direction, and join the Punpun near the same spot; and both are nearly dry during the greater portion of the year, as the cultivators build dams across them, and the water is dispersed among the fields or stored in artificial reservoirs.

Phalgu. The Phalgu enters the district a short distance to the south of Telarha, but soon loses its identity, as its waters are almost entirely expended in irrigation channels. Near Telarha it bifurcates, one branch, known as the Sona, striking due north, and the other, the Kattar, taking a north-easterly direction. Both branches eventually fall into the Maithun river, but are practically dry after the end of the rainy season.

Maithun. The Maithun or Mithwain, which is formed by the confluence of the Dhoa and Sona, flows parallel to the Ganges throughout the entire length of the Barh subdivision. Near Chero it is joined by the Jamuna river, and at Tirmohani by the Dhanain; and thence the united stream flows, under the name of the Kuluhar, into the Monghyr district.

Panchana. In the Bihar subdivision the Panchana is formed by the confluence of five streams debouching from the Gaya district, which unite near Giriak and thence flow northwards to Bihar town. Here five small streams branched off to the west, intersecting the town in different places, but all have long since dried up. A great sand bank has formed in the bed of the river below Bihar, which forces its water into the irrigation channels on the east; and the result is that, except in times of flood, only a feeble stream trickles along its sandy bed. After leaving Bihar, it pursues a north-easterly direction and then deflects to the east, eventually joining the Sakri or Mohana.

Sakri.

The last river of any importance is the Sakri, which enters the district to the south-east of Bihar town. This river flows to the north through the Bihar subdivision and then takes a sharp turn to the east through the south-east of the Barh subdivision, from which it enters the Monghyr district. Like the Panchana, it fails to attain any great volume, owing to the demands made upon it for the purpose of irrigation, nearly all its water being carried away by two large channels constructed on its left bank twelve miles south-east of Bihar. These two *pains* have widened and become large streams, with the result that the greater part of the supply of this river, which extends as far as Lakhisarai in the Monghyr district, has now been diverted. The lower portion of the Sakri below the offtake of these channels is also silting up rapidly as a continually decreasing supply of water passes down it.

Geology.

The greater part of the district is composed of Gangetic alluvium, *i.e.*, of silt brought down for ages past by the Ganges. During the rainy season, the Ganges and its tributaries increase enormously in volume, carrying down vast quantities of silt or mud, with the result that they overflow into the adjacent country. When the water subsides again, the rivers in their retreat leave some of the silt, which they have brought with them, spread over the once flooded land as a thin soil deposit. This process has been repeated during thousands of years, and the land has thus been gradually growing and the surface of the land gradually raised. The excavations which have been made at Patna indicate that there has been a deposit of about twenty feet in the course of a thousand years.

In the south-east of the district the Rajgir Hills present an entirely different geological formation. These hills, which are more or less isolated in the alluvial plain, belong probably to the Purana group of metamorphic schists and slates with a layer of massive quartzite. The beds strike ENE.—WSW., corresponding to the general trend of the hill ranges; they have been much folded by earth movements, and lie at high angles dipping NNW. and SSE. To the north-west of the main range the more thinly-bedded rocks are interbanded with several trap-dykes, and still further in that direction, near Ghunsura, there are a few isolated little knolls of archæan crystalline granitic rock, presenting an intrusive habit among the schists. It is probable that the Purana group of schists and quartzite is of Bijawar age.

In the alluvial country which forms the greater portion of the Patna district, rice, wheat, pulses, sugarcane, and a great variety of other crops are extensively grown; and the area under cultivation is bare or dotted over with clumps of bamboos and mango orchards. In the level fields near the Ganges the usual weeds of such localities are found, such as ammannia, utricularia, hygrophila and sesbania. Near the villages in this tract of country there are considerable groves of palmyra (borassus flabellifer) and date palm (phœnix sylvestris), mango orchards, and numerous more isolated examples of tamarindus, odina, sapindus and moringa. Associated with these, one frequently finds in village shrubberies glycosmis, clerodendron, solanum, jatropha, trema, streblus and similar semi-spontaneous and more or less useful species. Further from the river the country is more diversified, and sometimes a dry scrub jungle is met with, of which the principal species are glochidion and other euphorbiaceous shrubs, butea and other leguminous trees, besides various examples of ficus, schleichera, wendlandia, gmelina, wrightia, adina, and stephegyne. The grasses clothing the drier parts are generally of a coarse character, such as andropogon contortus, aciculatus, annulatus, foveolatus and pertusus, aristida adscenscionis, tragus racemosus and iseilema laxum. Other species typical of the district are various anthistriæ and penniseta, eragrostris cynosuroides, saccharum spontaneum, arundinella brasiliensis and *sabai* grass (ischœmum angustifolium). Throughout this tract the mango (mangifera indica), *pipal* (ficus religiosa) and banyan (ficus indica), are common, the other principal trees being the *bel* (ægle marmelos), *nim* (melia azadirachta), *siris* (mimosa sirissa), *sisu* (dalbergia sissoo), jack fruit tree (artocarpus integrifolia) and red cotton tree (bombax malabaricum). BOTANY.

FAUNA.

The carnivora of the district comprise leopard, hyæna, and some smaller animals, such as jackal, fox and wild cat. Wolves were formerly common; and in 1870, 229 deaths from wolfbite were reported, but they have now practically disappeared. The ungulata are represented by *nilgai* (boselaphus tragocamelus), black buck (antilope cervicapra) and wild pig.

Leopards are common in the southern hills extending south-westwards from Giriak, but confine their depredations to cattle, sheep, goats, dogs, and small ponies. Hyænas are common in the same range. The black bear (*ursus labiatus*) is also found in the Rajgir hills. He subsists mainly on jungle fruits; but he comes out into the level country at night to raid the maize and sugarcane crops, and to climb the toddy palms to drink the *tari* that is fermenting in the Pasis' pots, or in the early hot weather, when the mahua flowers are falling, to feast on the freshly fallen flowers under the trees. Wild pig abound in this neighbourhood, and also on the *chars* and *diaras* of the Son and the Ganges. *Nilgai* are common in the large *chars* and *diaras*; and in the country near the Son they are found in the mango groves and among the high crops. The *nilgai* is not greatly sought after by European sportsmen, and many Hindus have scruples regarding its slaughter. No such scruples protect the black buck (antilope cervicapra), which was formerly common, but is now only to be found, very rare and very shy, in the extreme west of the district, north of the railway line. Hares are numerous in the drier parts; jackals are common throughout the district; and porcupines and foxes are occasionally seen.

Game birds.

The game birds in the hills consist of pea-fowl, jungle fowl, grey partridge, black partridge, and bush quail. In the plains grey quail, rain quail, and buttom quail make their appearance every year. Green pigeon are common; and rock pigeons also visit the plains during harvest time. Red and yellow billed geese, red-headed pochard and white-eyed pochard, pintail and gadwall are found on the Son and Ganges, and on the larger *jhils*, by the middle of November. Besides these, the shoveller and Brahmani duck and different varieties of teal and combduck visit the district. With them come the white and the black ibis; curlew; whimbrel; jack snipe; smaller snipe of six varieties, locally known as *batara, ghotra, bagodhia, surma, sarghai, and bhurka*; golden plovers, and waders. Other cold-weather birds are the cranes known locally as *kurkura* (anthropædus virgo), and *kulung* (grus communis), and various storks, the most noteworthy among them being a gigantic stork called *lohasarang* (xenorphynohus asiaticus).

Fish. The Ganges and Son contain a great number of edible fish, such as *buari*, *tengra*, *naini*, *bachwa* and *rohu*; *hilsa* (culpea ilisha) are also found in the former and *mahsir* in the latter river. Fishing practically begins in October with the subsidence of the floods, and the busy season is from November to March, the largest hauls being made in December, January and February. Fish of all kinds and all sizes are caught, but the most valuable belong to the carp family, such as *rohu* and *katla*; *rohu* are caught up to the weight of forty pounds. *Hilsa* are caught as far up the river as Patna, as they ascend from the sea, and the hauls, though not so great as lower down the river, are occasionally very good. Crustaceous fish are common, and prawns (*jhingra*) are caught in large numbers. Porpoises abound in the Ganges, and tortoises are also numerous. Both the snub-nosed crocodile or *magar* and the fish-eating alligator called *gharial* are found in the same river.

Climate. The cold weather commences early in November and comes to an end in the middle of March. The hot weather then sets in and lasts till about the middle of June. Soon after this, the rainy season commences and continues till the end of September; but as the beginning of this season occurs when a storm from the Bay of Bengal passes over Bihar, the commencement of the monsoon may be as early as the last week of May or as late as the first or second week of July.

The climate in the cold weather is pleasant. The days are bright and warm, and the sun is not too hot: as soon as it has set, the temperature falls, and the heat of the day gives place to a sharp bracing cold. The lowest temperature known at this season of the year is 36·4° recorded in 1878. In the hot weather the temperature has been known to rise as high as 114° (recorded in 1894). The heat is greater than that of Tirhut, though not so intense as in Gaya; but, on the other hand, it is not so dry as in the latter district, and is consequently more relaxing. At this time of the year the heat is aggravated by hot parching winds and clouds of dust. In the rains the heat is moist and enervating, and the nights are oppressive.

Temperature and humidity.

Mean temperature varies from 66° in January to 88° in May, the average maximum temperature rising to 101° in April. Owing to the hot and dry westerly winds which prevail in March and April, humidity is much lower at this season than at any other times of the year and averages only fifty per cent. of saturation. With the approach of the monsoon season, the air slowly becomes more charged with moisture, and humidity remains steady at about 86 per cent. throughout July and August. In September, when periods of fine weather alternate with the cloud and rain of the monsoon, humidity is lower; and with breaks of increasing length it gradually falls to about 65 per cent. in November. There is then a slight increase, partly owing to the unsettled weather caused by the cold-season disturbances.

Winds.

From October until May the prevailing direction of wind is from the west, but a marked change takes place with the commencement of the monsoon ,which is generally caused by the first cyclonic storm which enters from the Bay of Bengal. The flow of the moist winds from the Bay is northwards over the eastern districts of Bengal proper, but afterwards they trend to the west, owing to the barrier interposed by the Himalayan range; so that after the passage of the cyclonic storms, easterly winds set in and continue with but little interruption until the middle of September, when westerly winds again become common.

Rainfall.

From November to April fine dry weather prevails with an almost entire absence of cloud and rainfall, and only a fraction of an inch of rain falls monthly. In May over an inch of rain falls on the average; and in normal years the monsoon breaks in June; but as has been already stated, the time of the commencement of the monsoon rains varies greatly. The heaviest rainfall occurs in July and August, in each of which months over twelve inches of rain may be expected. From the middle of September the monsoon current begins to fall off in strength; and if the westerly winds are stronger than usual, the storms coming inland from the Bay of Bengal recede eastwards, and rainfall is consequently deficient. The following table shows the normal rainfall, as calculated by the Meteorological Department, at the various recording stations.

The number of years over which these averages have been worked out varies with the stations; in Patna it is over seventy, for Barh, Bihar, and Dinapore over fifty, while for the smaller stations it is about forty years.

Month.	Patna.	Dinapore.	Bihar.	Barh.	Bikram.	Hilsa.	Islampur.	Asthawan.
January	0·58	0·53	0·68	0·56	0·64	0·74	0·21	0·43
February	0·67	0·59	0·79	0·73	0·72	0·88	1·15	1·07
March	0·46	0·41	0·37	0·37	0·38	0·48	0·41	0·51
April	0·31	0·27	0·39	0·23	0·29	0·37	0·51	0·41
May	1·68	1·49	1·74	1·74	1·40	1·43	0·70	1·43
June	7·83	7·50	6·73	6·39	6·92	7·35	6·08	5·94
July	11·71	11·25	11·94	11·80	11·85	11·06	8·52	8·45
August	12·73	12·41	11·36	10·91	11·66	12·71	10·69	11·42
September	7·70	7·45	6·93	7·79	7·12	7·63	7·67	6·98
October	2·68	2·78	2·16	2·10	2·31	1·96	1·20	1·61
November	0·28	0·27	0·32	0·29	0·35	0·37	0·60	0·59
December	0·11	0·14	0·14	0·11	0·07	0·07	0·18	0·33
Annual average ...	46·74	45·00	43·55	43·02	43·71	45·04	37·92	39·17

CHAPTER II.

HISTORY.

I.—THE EARLY HINDU KINGS AND THE MAURYAN EMPIRE.

THE PREHISTORIC PERIOD.

IN prehistoric times the area now contained in Patna district formed part of Magadha, which roughly corresponded with the tract, known in later days as Bihar district, which is comprised within the present districts of Patna and Gaya. By the Aryans it was regarded as a land peopled by wild tribes hardly worthy of the name of men; and as late as the sixth century B.C. it is mentioned by Baudhayana as a tract inhabited by people of mixed origin outside the pale of Aryan civilization. From the early reference to Magadha in Epic literature we may conclude that it was still in the possession of aboriginal races, who gave place to Aryan immigrants at a later period than in the country north of the Ganges, and that it continued to be the home of these tribes at a time when Tirhut and Oudh were filled with Aryan settlements. With Chedi or Bundelkhand it was under the sway of a king named Jarasandha who is a prominent figure in the great conflict between the two branches of Aryan stock recorded in the Mahabharata. The date of this monarch is too remote to be fixed with any certainty; but his name still lives in local legend, and it is known that his capital was at Rajgir, where the remains of his stronghold may still be seen in the great stone walls and causeways which skirt and climb the rocky hills.

EARLY HISTORY.

After Jarasandha a dynasty of twenty-eight kings is said to have ruled in Magadha, but nothing is known of these kings beyond their names. The first event which can claim historic reality is the rise of the Saisunaka dynasty (cir. 600 B.C.). The fifth monarch of the line, Bimbisara, was the first to extend the frontiers of Magadha by the annexation of Anga, a small kingdom corresponding with the present districts of Bhagalpur and Monghyr; and in this district he signalized his rule by building the town of Rajagriha (Old Rajgir) at the base of the hills which formed the ancient fort of Jarasandha.

The chief interest attaching to the reign of Bimbisara arises from the fact that it witnessed the foundation both of Buddhism and Jainism. Gautama Buddha came to this district at an early stage in his search after truth, and Rajgir was the first place at which he settled after leaving his father's territory. Here he attached himself as a disciple to two Brahmans, Alara and Uddaka, but failing to find enlightenment in the ecstatic meditation affected by these teachers of Brahmanical philosophy, he wandered forth in the direction of Bodh-Gaya. After the attainment of Buddhahood or supreme enlightenment, he returned to the court of Bimbisara at Rajgir, and then made his way to the deer park at Benares. Thenceforward Rajgir became a favourite resort of Buddha, and he frequently returned there, his two chief places of retreat being the Bamboo Grove and the hill called the Vulture Peak. Here for many years he preached and taught, the king himself becoming one of his disciples; here he soon succeeded in gathering a large following; and here after his death the Buddhist brotherhood assembled in the famous Sattapanni Cave and held the first Buddhist Council. **Rise of Buddhism.**

The great contemporary of Buddha, Vardhamana Mahavira, the founder of Jainism, was engaged in his ministry at the same time and in the same tract of country. Dissatisfied with the rule of the order of Parsvanatha, which did not conform with his ideal of stringency, he left the monastery at Vaisali (Basarh), and for forty-two years spent a wandering life in North and South Bihar. During this period he succeeded in gathering a large following, and about the year 490 B.C. he died at Pawapuri, a village in the Bihar subdivision. After his death, the monks of his order, who were known as the Nigranthas or men who discarded all social ties, eventually spread over the whole of India and became known as the Jainas, a name derived from the title of Jina or spiritual conqueror, which Mahavira claimed, just as Gautama claimed to be Buddha or the enlightened one. **Rise of Jainism.**

Bimbisara was succeeded (cir. 500 B.C.) by his son and murderer, Ajatasatru, who made a new capital at Rajgir to the north of the old city and next erected a fortress at the village of Patali on the southern bank of the Ganges in order to hold in check the powerful Lichchhavi clan to the north of that river. This fortified village was visited, a few months before his death, by the Lord Buddha, who prophesied its future **FOUNDATION OF PATALIPUTRA.**

greatness in the words: "Of all famous places, busy marts and centres of commerce, Pataliputra will be greatest; but three dangers will threaten it—fire, flood, and internal dissension." About half a century later (434 B.C.) Udaya, grandson of Ajatasatru, transferred hither the capital from Rajgir. Magadha had now become a great kingdom, the suzerainty of which was acknowledged as far as the Himalayas, and a central site was necessary for the capital. Such a site was found, under the shadow of Ajatasatru's fort, in Pataliputra, which stood at a point of great commercial and strategical importance, near the confluence of the great rivers of mid India.

Maurya dynasty.

The Saisunaga dynasty was extinguished about 370 B.C., and Magadha passed under the rule of the Nanda kings, who in their turn were overcome by Chandra Gupta, the founder of the Mauryan empire. Himself a native of Magadha, he headed a revolt against the Greek domination which Alexander had established in the north of India and destroyed most of the Macedonian garrisons. He then turned against the Nandas, and in 321 B.C. he captured Pataliputra. Undisputed master of Magadha and commander of a force of six hundred thousand infantry, thirty thousand cavalry, nine thousand elephants and a multitude of chariots, he proceeded to reduce to vassalage the greater part of India, until his dominions extended from the Bay of Bengal to the Arabian sea. With an ease equal to that attending his conquest, he succeeded in repelling the invasion of Seleucus Nikator, king of Syria and lord of central and western Asia, who was obliged to retire, after ceding the outlying province of Afghanistan and giving his daughter in marriage to the victorious emperor.

Megasthenes' account.

Soon after the conclusion of peace in 303 B.C., Seleucus sent Megasthenes as his envoy to the court of Chandra Gupta. Megasthenes wrote an account of what he saw, which has unfortunately been lost; but Greek historians and geographers quoted his description of Pataliputra and of the system of government of Chandra Gupta, and in this way some fragments of his work have been preserved. His account of the municipal administration of the great city of Pataliputra is quoted in chapter xvi below. Strabo has preserved for us some part of his account of Chandra Gupta's revenue administration.* It is significant that the most important duty of the revenue officers, apart from the duty of collecting the revenue,

* Strabo xv. 1.

was the control of irrigation works, inspection of the sluices by which water was let out from the main canals into the distributaries, so that all might have their fair share of it. They superintended occupations connected with the land, those of shikaris, woodcutters, carpenters, and miners; and they were also in charge of the roads, on which pillars were erected at every ten stadia (probably the short *kos* of four thousand cubits).

Spread of Jainism.

In no fragment of Megasthenes which has been preserved do we find any mention of the rise of Buddhism or Jainism. But at this period Jainism was beginning to spread over India. We learn from other sources that in the second century after Mahavira's death (about 310 B.C.), during the reign of Chandra Gupta, a very severe famine, lasting twelve years, took place in Magadha, beyond which as yet the Jain order does not appear to have spread. Under the pressure of this famine, Bhadrabahu, who was the head of the still undivided Jain community, emigrated with a portion of his people into the Canarese country in the south of India, and Sthulabhadra assumed the headship over the other portion that remained in Magadha. Towards the end of the period of famine, during the absence of Bhadrabahu, a great council assembled at Pataliputra, and collected the Jain sacred books, consisting of the twelve Angas.

Bindusara and Asoka.

It is probable that Bindusara, the son of Chandra Gupta, continued his father's career of conquest and annexation, since when his son Asoka (272-231 B.C.) succeeded to the throne the Mauryan empire extended nearly as far south as Madras, covering the whole of India north of the Pennar river except the country of Kalinga on the Bay of Bengal. Asoka conquered and annexed Kalinga, subsequently recording ine one of the Rock Edicts the feelings of profound sorrow and remorse awakened in him by the miseries caused by his campaign. It is believed that in early life Asoka was a Brahmanical Hindu specially devoted to Siva, the traditional founder of Pataliputra. He subsequently became converted to Buddhism; and he propagated his new creed with such vigour as to change it from a local sect into a world religion. After his conversion Asoka became an ardent protector of animal life; and it is possible that in the hospital for animals which he founded at Pataliputra we have the origin of the *pinjrapol* which is so commonly found in India. Towards the end of his reign he himself assumed the yellow robe, and he died at a holy hill near Rajgir. How he beautified Pataliputra, and the legends which associate particular sites in Patna with his work, are described in Chapter XVI below.

II.—THE GUPTA EMPIRE AND THE PALA KINGS.

Shortly after the death of Asoka, the Mauryan dynasty was overthrown, and the power of Magadha began to decline. Outlying provinces asserted their independence; Kharavela, king of Kalinga, claims to have led his army as far as Pataliputra, and to have there compelled the Sunga emperor to sue for peace (157 B.C.). Pataliputra continued to be the capital of the diminished kingdom of Magadha, but it does not again come into prominence until the rise of the Gupta empire in the fourth century A.D. A second Chandra Gupta, first of the Gupta line, revived the ancient glories of Magadha by extending the kingdom as far as Paryag; but Pataliputra ceased to be the royal residence after the completion of the conquests effected by his son Samudra Gupta (326-375), which necessitated the selection of a more central position for the metropolis. It still remained however the great eastern city of the empire, and we have a picture of its prosperity and of the flourishing condition of Magadha from the pen of Fa Hian (405-411). The palace of Asoka which was still standing deeply impressed the simple pilgrim, who believed it to be the work of spirits. Near a great stupa, also ascribed to Asoka, stood two great monasteries containing six or seven hundred monks which were so famous for learning that they were frequented by scholars from all parts; here Fa Hian spent three years studying Sanskrit and copying rare scriptures for which he had vainly searched in other parts of India. The country round was worthy of its capital. The towns of Magadha were the largest in mid-India, the people were rich and prosperous, they emulated each other in the practice of virtue, and justice flourished. Resthouses were provided for travellers on all the highways and charitable institutions were numerous. "The nobles and householders of the country," he says, "have founded hospitals within the city, to which the poor of all countries, the destitute, the cripples and the diseased may repair. They receive help of all kinds gratuitously; physicians treat them, and order them food and drink, medicine or decoctions—everything, in fact, that may contribute to their ease."*

*Beal's *Buddhist Records of the Western World.*

This is the last account of the splendours of Pataliputra, Hiuen Tsiang, another Chinese pilgrim who visited India, between 630 and 645, found its glory departed. "It is," he says, "an old city long deserted; now there only remain the old foundation walls. The monasteries, Hindu temples and Buddhist stupas, which lie in ruins, may be counted by hundreds, and only two or three remain entire." All that was left of the ancient city was a small town containing about a thousand houses, to the north of the old palaces and bordering on the Ganges. This devastation was probably due to the invasion of the savage Huns in the latter half of the sixth century, and later to the inroad of Sasanka, king of Central Bengal, a fanatical enemy of Buddhism, who sacked the city, broke its sacred relic, a stone marked with the footprints of Buddha, destroyed the convents and scattered the monks, and carried his ravages to the foot of the Nepal hills. The persecution of Buddhism by Sasanka had been followed by the royal patronage of Harsha Vardhana, also called Siladitya, who ruled northern India between 600 and 648. The account of Hiuen Tsiang shows that, though Pataliputra was in ruins, Magadha was the peaceful home of Buddhism, full of great shrines and splendid monasteries, chief among which was that of Nalanda, which sheltered thousands of Buddhist monks. The towns, he said, were thickly populated; the soil was rich, fertile and extensively cultivated. The people were simple, honest folk, who highly esteemed learning and profoundly respected the religion of Buddha; but there were several Hindu temples "occupied by sectaries of various persuasions, who are very numerous."

Fall of Pataliputra.

On the death of Harsha in 648, the throne was usurped by Arjuna, one of whose first acts was to attack a mission sent by the Emperor of China, kill the escort, and plunder its property. The king of Tibet sent an avenging force through Nepal, where it was joined by seven thousand Nepalese. It then swept down on the plains of Magadha, and in a battle fought on the Ganges completely defeated the Indians. The royal family was captured with twelve thousand prisoners, 580 walled cities made their submission, and Arjuna was taken in chains to Lhasa.*

Invasion of the Tibetans.

After this, the central power declined, and each small potentate carved out an independent kingdom. Early in the

The Pala kings.

---

* V. A. Smith, *Early History of India* (1908), pp. 326-27; Sarat Chandra Das, *The Ancient Kingdoms of Nepal, Puru and Magadha (from the Annals of the Thang Dynasty of China)*, Indian World, January 1907.

eighth century (cir. 740) a chieftain named Gopala became ruler of Bengal, and extended his power over Magadha. Here he made his capital at Bihar, which had taken the place of Pataliputra, and built the great Buddhist monastery of Otantapuri or Udandapura in the town. His successors were also devout Buddhists, and most of the Buddhist remains extant in the district date back to this period (800-1200). Under their rule Magadha became a great centre of missionary enterprise, sending out emissaries to teach the faith all over India and even outside its borders. Not the least notable result of this propaganda was the revival of Buddhism in Tibet, where the corrupt Lamaism prevalent was reformed in the eleventh century by Atisha, the hierarch of Magadha and abbot of the monastery of Vikramasila (the modern village of Silao).

III.—The Muhammadan conquest.

The Muhammadan conquest.

The Buddhism of Magadha was finally swept away by the Muhammadan invasion under Bakhtiyar Khilji. In 1197 the capital, Bihar, was seized by a small party of two hundred horsemen, who rushed the postern gate, and sacked the town. The slaughter of the "shaven-headed Brahmans," as the Muhammadan chronicler calls the Buddhist monks, was so complete that when the victor searched for some one capable of explaining the contents of the monastic libraries, not a living man could be found who was able to do so. "It was discovered," it was said, "that the whole fort and city was a place of study."* A similar fate befell the other Buddhist institutions, against which the combined intolerance and rapacity of the invaders were directed. The monasteries were sacked and the monks slain, many of the temples were ruthlessly destroyed or desecrated, and countless idols were broken and trodden under foot. Those monks who escaped the sword fled to Tibet, Nepal and southern India; and Buddhism as a popular religion in Bihar, its last abode in Northern India, was finally destroyed. Thenceforward Patna passed under Muhammadan rule.†

For some centuries after this, we have no separate mention of the history of the district. With the rest of South Bihar it was included in the Bengal viceroyalty under Bakhtiyar Khilji and his immediate successors, and except for a short interval when it had a separate government, it con-

*Tabakat-i-Nasiri, Elliot's *History of India*, Vol. II.

†This account of the early history of Patna has been mainly compiled from *The Early History of India*, by V. A. Smith.

tinued to be ruled by the Bengal Viceroys till 1320, when the Emperor Ghias-ud-din Tughlak again separated it. In 1397 A.D. it was annexed by the king of Jaunpur, but a century later it was again acquired by the emperors of Delhi, who continued to hold it, except for a short period during which it was subject to the kings of Gaur.

Foundation of Patna.

In the sixteenth century it again emerged from its obscurity in the time of the Emperor Babar, who in 1529 advanced as far as Maner in order to reduce the rebellious Afghan chiefs. His death in the succeeding year served as a signal to rouse the Afghans once more to assert their independence, and the struggle which ensued ended in the conquest of Northern India by Sher Shah. To his foresight must be ascribed the foundation of the city of Patna, of which the following account is given in the Tarik-i-Daudi—" Sher Shah, on his return from Bengal, in 1541, came to Patna, then a small town dependent on Bihar, which was the seat of the local government. He was standing on the bank of the Ganges, when, after much reflection, he said to those who were standing by—' If a fort were to be built in this place, the waters of the Ganges could never flow far from it, and Patna would become one of the great towns of this country. ' He ordered skilful carpenters and bricklayers to make immediately an estimate for building a fort at the place where he stood. These experienced workmen submitted an estimate of five lakhs, which on the spur of the moment was made over to trustworthy persons. The fort was completed, and was considered to be exceedingly strong. Bihar from that time was deserted, and fell to ruin; while Patna became one of the largest cities of the province. "*

The city under the protection of this fort soon became a centre of commerce, and the rapidity of its development is apparent from the account of Ralph Fitch (1586), who says :—" Patenaw is a very long and a great towne. The houses are simple, made of earth and covered with strawe; the streetes are very large. In this towne there is a trade of cotton, and cloth of cotton, much sugar, which they carry from hence to Bengala and India, very much opium and other commodities." †

*Elliot, *History of India*, Vol. IV.

†J. H. Ryley, *Ralph Fitch*, 1899. Fitch quaintly adds—"Here in Patenau I saw a dissembling prophet which sate upon an horse in the market place, and made as though he slept, and many of the people came and touched his feet with their hands, and then kissed their hands. They took him for a great man, but sure he was a lasie lubber. I left him their sleeping. The people of these countries be much given to such prating and dissembling hypocrites."

In 1620 we find Portuguese merchants at Patna; and Tavernier's account shows that a little more than a century after its foundation it was the great entrepôt of Northern India, "the largest town in Bengal and the most famous for trade." Here he met Armenian merchants from Dantzig and traders from Tippera. Musk was brought in from Tibet, and he himself purchased Rs. 26,000 worth of that commodity; caravans went to Tibet every year and Tibetans came to Patna for the coral, amber and tortoise-shell bracelets for which it was famous.

Daud Khan's rebellion.

The city was also a place of great strategical importance, and when Daud Khan was raised to the throne of Bengal by the Afghans in 1573, he made Patna and the adjoining fortress of Hajipur his headquarters. Here he successfully held out against the siege of the Mughal army under Munim Khan, and in 1574 the Emperor Akbar was forced to come in person and superintend the operations. Hajipur was taken by storm, and then, according to the Tabakat-i-Akbari, "the Emperor went out upon an elephant to reconnoitre the fort and the environs of the city, and ascended the Panj-pahari, which is opposite the fort. This Panj-pahari, or 'five domes,' is a collection of old domes (*gumbaz*), which the infidels built in old times with hard bricks placed in layers. The Afghans, who were on the walls and bastions of the fortress, saw the Emperor and his suite as he was making his survey, and in their despair and recklessness fired some guns at the Panj-pahari, but they did no injury to any one."

This was the last effort of the Afghans, for Daud Khan, learning of the loss of Hajipur by the sight of the heads of those slain in the fight, made his escape by night down the Ganges. The garrison of twenty thousand men, left without a leader, fled in all directions, and the roads were so crowded with horses, carriages, and elephants that great numbers were trampled to death. To complete their misfortunes, the bridge over the Punpun gave way; the fugitives were either drowned in the river or cut down by the swords of the Mughal cavalry, who did not desist from pursuit until they had reached Dariyapur (Mokameh).

IV.—The Rule of the Subahdars.*

The fall of Patna meant the conquest of Bengal; and henceforward the city was the headquarters of the Mughal

*For a fuller account of this period, see *Patna during the last days of the Muhammadans*, Calcutta Review, Vol. LXXVI, 1882.

Governors of Bihar. Patna now became once more a centre of political life. During this period the city witnessed the proclamation of two Mughal Emperors; it had, more than once, for its Governor a prince of the royal blood; whole armies encamped at Mithapur on the west and at Bagh Jafar Khan on the east, the latter being on several occasions the scene of desperate battles; and towards the close of their rule it was sacked by a desperate band of Afghans. In 1612 it was stormed by the pretender, Khusru, who gave up the city to plunder, and had himself proclaimed Emperor in the Governor's palace; ten years later it was seized by Shah Jahan, who held his court there for a short time during his rebellion against his father; and in 1626 prince Parwez Shah, another son of Jahangir, commemorated his rule by building the mosque now known as the Pathar Masjid or stone mosque. In 1664 Shaista Khan, an uncle of 'Aurangzeb, initiated his tenure of office by colleting a *jazia* or poll-tax from the Hindus. In 1678, in the interval between Shaista Khan's two periods of rule, Muhammad Azim, third son of 'Aurangzeb, was appointed *subahdar* ; but it was with the appointment in 1697 of 'Aurangzeb's grandson, Azim-us-Shan, that Patna attained the zenith of its splendour. This prince made his court at Patna, where he improved the fortifications, and in 1704 he named the city after himself Azimabad. Many of the nobles of Delhi came to live within its walls, and separate quarters were assigned for the retinue which gathered round the court. The noblemen had their residence in Mahalla Kaiwan Shekoh 'splendid palace,' now corrupted into Khawa Koh; Diwan Mahalla was so named, because it was assigned to the clerks of the Government offices; Mughalpura contained the quarters of the Mughals, and Lodikatra those of the Afghan Lodis. The poor and destitute were not forgotten, and alms-houses and *sarais* were built for their reception. It is said that the young prince aspired to make the city a second Delhi, but this ambition was cut short by the fratricidal war which broke out on the death of Aurangzeb, in the course of which he met his death (1712) by being swallowed up alive in a quicksand.

'At this time the Governor of Patna was Husain 'Ali Khan, one of the two Saiyids of Barhah, who played such a prominent part as king-makers in the eighteenth century. After the death of Azim-us-Shan, his son Farrukhsiyar made his way to Patna, where the Governor espoused his cause. Farrukhsiyar was welcomed with acclamation by the people, brought in great state to the fort, and enthroned as emperor in Afzal Khan's garden-house. He then set forth to Delhi, and on his establishing his throne there, many of the nobles of Azim-us-Shan's court returned to the capital. The city lost still more of these nobles soon afterwards, when the Saiyids set up Muhammad Shah (1719) as Emperor and sent Fakhr-ud-daula to Bihar; for this Governor treated the noblemen left there with great indignity, attached their *jagirs*, and drove them out of the city. They claimed redress at the court at Delhi, and after the fall of the Saiyids they succeeded in their appeal. Orders were sent dismissing Fakhr-ud-daula and annexing the *subah* of Bihar to Bengal. Bihar thus passed under the rule of the Viceroy of Bengal, and thereafter remained an appanage of that province.

European settlements.

In the meantime, the commerce of Patna had attracted the European merchant companies. The first English commercial mission set forth from Agra in 1620, two Englishmen, Hughes and Parker, being sent from Agra to Patna to purchase cloth and establish a house of business; but the great expense of land carriage, first to Agra and then to Surat, so enhanced the price of the articles that next year the trade was abandoned. A second attempt was made from Surat through Agra to establish English trade at Patna in 1632, when Peter Mundy left Agra for Patna with "eight carts laden with barrels of quicksilver and parcels of vermilion for the Honourable Company's account to be there sold, and the money to be there invested, as also to see the state of the country what hopes of benefit by trading into these parts." After staying a month at Patna, Mundy reported against the enterprise, as it was his opinion that "the sending of me to Pattana with the Company's goods may not only prove to their loss, but is also against the intent and meaning of the President and Council at Surat." When, however, the English established themselves on the seaboard of Bengal, it was possible for them to exploit the great trade of Patna with some profit; and in 1650 we find instructions given to some English pioneers sent from Balasore to Hooghly that "Patenna being on all sides concluded the best place for procuring peter, they are to make a trial how they can procure the same from thence." Shortly after this the English must have made a settlement at Patna, for in 1657 it is mentioned as a factory under the control of the head agency at Hooghly. The chief article of commerce was saltpetre, which was in great demand in Europe for the manufacture of gunpowder; but the English were not blind to the value of other trade, and a report submitted in 1661 shows how great this was. Musk was brought in from Bhutan and sent to Agra for export to Persia and Venice; drugs came from China; opium, even then the great local product,* was sold in great quantities; lac changed hands, but was very dear; the taffeties made there were better than those of Cossimbazar; and English cloth, sold by the plush yard, had made its way into the market. Under the vigorous superintendence of Job Charnock, who was chief of the factory from 1664 to 1680, the English trade developed, and fleets of Patna boats laden with saltpetre were a common sight along the Ganges. The Court of Directors were never weary of asking for saltpetre from Patna, where it could be had so good and cheap that the contract for it was discontinued on the west coast in 1668 and at Masulipatam in 1670.

The English, however, were not the only merchants in the field, for the Dutch had made a settlement there before this. In the instructions given in 1650 we find that secret enquiry was to be made how, when, and where they procured sugar; the quantity they last procured at Patna had, it was said, been well approved of, and the English were to procure some from thence by the same way or instruments they might use to procure saltpetre. Tavernier, who visited Patna with Bernier in 1666, and found it already "one of the greatest cities of India," says—"The Holland Company have a house there, by reason of their trade in saltpetre, which they refine at a great town called Choupar (Chapra). Coming to Patna, we met the Hollanders in the street returning from Choupar, who stopped our coaches to salute us. We did not part till we had emptied two bottles of Shiras wine in the open street, which is not taken notice of in that country where people meet with an entire freedom without any ceremony."

In 1680 Charnock left Patna for Cossimbazar, and the English soon become embroiled with the authorities. Next year Shaista Khan, the Viceroy of Bengal, forbade the purchase

*Captain Alexander Hamilton writes in 1727:—"Patana is the next town frequented by Europeans, where the English and Dutch have factories for saltpetre and raw silk. It produces also so much opium that it serves all the countries in India with that commodity."

of any saltpetre, threw Peacock, the new factor, into prison, and imposed a duty of 3½ per cent. on all the Company's goods. For thirty years after this we have a record of the constant difficulties which the English had to meet. In 1686 Shaista Khan sent orders to Patna to seize all the Company's property and imprison their servants; and again in 1702 all the English settled there were seized, their goods confiscated, and themselves confined for seven weeks in the common jail.

The exactions of the Viceroy nearly put an end to the trade at Patna, and for several years we find orders given by the Company now to abandon their settlement and again to retain it. In July 1704, English trade at Patna is stopped owing to the necessity of paying customs, and the Company send to recall their agent; next month they resolve after all to continue the settlement. In 1706 the Council at Calcutta seem anxious to keep the factory going, and two of its members are sent to the Patna residency with money and presents; in 1707 the Council, hearing of Aurangzeb's death and alarmed at the news that it was intended to levy contributions from all merchants, send orders to their agents to leave Patna at once with all the saltpetre they can collect. In 1709 it was again agreed after much consultation to continue the Patna factory "now the government is more settled;" but this calm did not last long. In 1712, after Farrukhsiyar advanced his claims to the throne, it was resolved to lay the city of Patna under contribution; a list of rich men was drawn up, at the head of which stood the English, and the goods of the Dutch Chief, Van Hoorn, were confiscated. A watch was set over the factory, and the English withdrew to Singia, but did not escape scot-free, as they were compelled to pay Rs. 22,000 to the Prince and Rs. 6,500 as presents to the Governor, the Barhah Saiyid Husain 'Ali. They were more fortunate than the Dutch, who were forced to hand over two lakhs of rupees. In 1715 the factory was temporarily abandoned; but experience soon showed that without a proper staff it was impossible to obtain the saltpetre and piece-goods which the Company required from Patna, and in 1718, after the embassy of John Surman to Farrukhsiyar, the Patna establishment was restored.

Maratha and Afghan raids.

In 1740 Alivardi Khan marched from Patna against the Nawab Sarfraz Khan, by whose defeat he became undisputed ruler of Bengal and Bihar. In 1741 the Governor repaired the city wall and the ditch which surrounded it, in spite of the murmurs of those who had built houses on the dilapidated fortifications, thus affording to the city some protection against the Marathas, who were beginning to overrun Bihar. In 1745, when 'Alivardi Khan's rebellious general Mustafa Khan besieged the city with his 'Afghans, the rampart and trench were carried out to Jafar Khan's garden on the east of the city. On this occasion the 'Afghans were repulsed, but in the following year they again threatened Patna, joined by Marathas from the south-west. 'Alivardi Khan came from Murshidabad by forced marches, and fought the invaders at Mahabalipur. The battle was indecisive, but the invaders withdrew. In 1748 the 'Afghans of Darbhanga came to Patna, and after they had treacherously murdered the Governor Zainuddin, they proceeded to sack the city.

The 'Afghan triumph was short-lived, as 'Alivardi Khan advanced by forced marches with a large army. Never before did a Bengal army march with the speed of this force, which had learned the tactics of rapid movement from the Marathas and was composed of soldiers eager to avenge the outrages committed on their relatives. 'Alivardi Khan met the 'Afghans at Rabi Sarai by Fatuha, and in spite of the fact that they had been joined by the Marathas, he signally defeated them, and effectually crushed the revolt.

Rebellion of Siraj-ud-daula.

'Alivardi Khan was soon forced again to come to Patna to withstand the rebellion of his favourite grandson Siraj-ud-daula, who in 1750 suddenly made his appearance there with the intention of assuming independent power. The Governor refused to deliver up the city to him; but Siraj-ud-daula proceeded to storm the walls with a small following of sixty men. He succeeded in entering the city; but as soon as the garrison came up, his handful of men was overpowered. Siraj-ud-daula fled and took refuge in a house in the suburbs; but when his grandfather arrived he was reconciled to him.

Rise of the Hasua and Tikari families.

During this troubled period two great families were establishing themselves in the south of the district. At the beginning of the eighteenth century the country from Malda, Rajgir and Amarthu to Narhat-Samai formed the zamindari of an ancient Babhan family, whose founder had, according to a tradition still current in Buchanan's time, made an end of the Ahir rule in that region. The Raja gave a lease of Malda pargana to Azmeri and Diyanath Khan, sons of Nuraon Khan, who had recently come to Patna from the Punjab. The lessees thus obtained a footing in the country, which they utilised, when the Raja made default in payment of revenue, to obtain the farm of six of his parganas. The brothers then drove the Raja to Sheor Muhammadabad; and when Farrukshiyar was at Patna they obtained from him a grant of the zamindari of the parganas which they farmed, thus permanently legalising their position. The most vigorous of the sons of Diyanath was Kamgar Khan, who lived at Hasua with his brothers Nemdar, Sardar and Waris Ali, forming the dreaded Mayi family of the middle eighteenth century. According to Buchanan, the Mayi family abetted the Marathas in their raids, and they certainly profited by the general confusion to extend their power at the expense of weaker neighbours. The zenith of the family was reached when Kamgar Khan conquered Kharakdiha, so that the Mayis ultimately occupied as zamindars an area of over four thousand square miles.

While Diyanath Khan was establishing himself in Malda and Amarthu, Bir Singh, a Bhuinhar Brahman of Sanaut pargana, was also beginning to expand his influence. The question of what was the extent of his acquisitions still affords matter for controversy in his family; but whatever may have been the limits of his zamindari, it need not be doubted that his son Sundar Singh of Tikari, who obtained from Muhammad Shah the title of Raja, increased it considerably. Kamgar Khan and Sundar Singh dominated south Bihar in 1757; and in the south-east a smaller zamindar, Bishun Singh of Siris-Kutumba, aspired to emulate them. It would have been suicidal to excite the hostility of Sundar Singh by aggression on the east; across the Son the adventurer Pahlwan Singh was almost equally dangerous, so Bishun Singh turned southwards, and seized Japla and Belaunja, the jagir of Hedayat Ali Khan.

V.—THE EARLY PERIODS OF BRITISH ASCENDANCY, 1757-1764.

During the seven years which followed the battle of Plassey, Patna was almost continuously the centre of British military operations in Hindustan. These operations in and about Patna district are of interest on account of their ultimate result, though the narrative may appear to the reader intricate and tedious; but they acquire added interest from the character of the men whose romantic exploits vivify the story: the peerless Randfurlie Knox; Shitab Rai, firm friend of Knox and Clive; or Jean Law of Lauriston, gallant champion of lost causes.

Eyre Coote's march to Patna, 1757.

Jean Law was near Rajmahal, on his way to join Siraj-ud-daula, when he heard the result of the battle of Plassey. He at once set out for Patna, with the intention of offering his services to the Governor Ramnarain, who was not expected to accept the new régime. On the 6th of July, 1757, Eyre Coote started from Murshidabad in pursuit, with 223 Europeans and five hundred sipahis. He entered Patna district on July 23rd, when he camped at Dariyapur. At Punarak, on the following day, the Europeans refused to march, discontented at the lack of their customary supply of arrack. Coote pushed on with the sipahis, and the whole body arrived at the Factory on the 26th, the Europeans having come from Punarak in boats. On that night the Europeans, being once more within reach of arrack, became drunk and disorderly, whereupon Coote flogged thirty of them after a court-martial. This severity restored discipline among the Europeans; but on the 29th the sipahis in a body laid down their arms. Coote persuaded them to return to duty, and proceeded to Maner and thence to Chapra in pursuit of Law, who had not stayed at Patna after he learned that Coote was in pursuit of him. When Coote returned to Patna, Ramnarain undertook to swear fidelity to Mir Jafar if the English would guarantee his safety, to which Coote pledged himself. In the following February Mir Jafar came to Patna, accompanied by Clive, who camped at Company Bagh at Bankipore with his army. The subahdar would have liked to bestow the government of Bihar on his brother-in-law Mir Kasim; but Clive protected Ramnarain, whose allegiance to the new régime was henceforth secured. The zamindars were summoned to a darbar at Patna, which Sundar Singh attended; but Kamgar Khan held aloof. Sundar Singh subsequently co-operated with Ramnarain in disciplinary measures against Bishun Singh of Powai; but in the following year he was prominent among the zamindars who invited the

Shahzada to invade Bihar, though he was murdered by one of his own officers at Tikari before he could take any part in the campaign.

The Shahzada's invasion, 1759.

When 'Ali Gauhar, son of Alamgir II, revolted against his father, he was invited by Kamgar Khan, Pahlwan Singh, and Sundar Singh to invade Bihar, whither he came early in 1759, accompanied by Law with two hundred Frenchmen. Kamgar Khan joined him in Bihar district, and the army proceeded to invest Patna; but the besieging army melted away, in spite of Jean Law's adjurations, on the arrival of the advanced guard of Clive's relieving force, as Macaulay has described in a graphic passage. Clive marched to the Karamnasa, clearing the country of scattered bands of plunderers; and he then returned to Bengal, leaving in Patna under Captain Cochrane two field guns, a company of European infantry, and eight companies of sipahis.

The second invasion, 1760.

When it was known that Clive was about to return to England the Shahazada, who now by his father's death could claim to be legitimately emperor, again invaded Bihar, again joined by Kamgar Khan. Early in 1760 the invading army approached Patna; and Captain Cochrane marched out with Ramnarain on the east of the city, where he entrenched himself to await the arrival of Major Caillaud's force from Bengal. Strict orders had been given that Cochrane should not engage the enemy before Caillaud's arrival; but on the 9th of February Ramnarain unwisely determined to risk an engagement, in which Captain Cochrane's force was necessarily involved. The result was complete defeat, and the only surviving European officer was Dr. Fullarton, who heroically conducted the retreat to Patna. Caillaud arrived shortly afterwards, and the emperor's army suffered defeat at Sirpur on the 22nd of February. The discomfited army withdrew to Bihar, whence the emperor marched towards Bengal, pursued by Caillaud. When the emperor and Kamgar Khan found that they could not surprise Murshidabad, they doubled back towards Patna. At Bihar they found Jean Law waiting for them; and the army proceeded to besiege Patna.

Siege of Patna and relief by Knox, 1760.

Caillaud did not immediately perceive the manœuvre of the emperor, who obtained several days' start. The defence of Patna was conducted by the Company's sipahis, amounting in all to about three hundred, and by a body of three hundred cavalry, which had been raised by Shitab Rai.* The position of the defenders was desperate, when in the early afternoon of April 28th, a body of men was seen to be approaching Hajipur. This was at first taken for the army of Kadm Husein, faujdar of Purnea, who was known to be marching to join the emperor; but it was soon discovered from the glitter of the bayonets and the colour of the uniforms that the troops were British.† Randfurlie Knox had marched three hundred miles in thirteen days to relieve Patna, with two hundred picked Europeans, a battalion of sipahis, and two guns. On the 29th of April Knox attacked Kamgar Khan's intrenchment with such vigour that that zamindar escaped with some difficulty. Kamgar Khan did not care to stay near so enterprising an enemy, and he withdrew his force to some distance. Two or three days later, the emperor's army abandoned the siege, and marched away towards Gaya.

Battle of Birpur, June 6th, 1760.

Kadm Husein, with six thousand cavalry, ten thousand infantry, and thirty guns, arrived at Hajipur at the end of the second week of June, whereupon Knox crossed the river with his little force of a thousand men, with five guns, accompanied by Shitab Rai and his three hundred. On the 16th of June, as soon as the engagement began, Knox's little band of heroes was completely surrounded ; for six hours column after column of cavalry charged down on them, steadily received with discharges of grape or at the point of the bayonet. On one occasion the English detachment was nearly overwhelmed, but a brilliant charge of the grenadiers of Knox's own battalion repulsed the enemy and saved the party. At length, tired of these fruitless attempts which had been attended with considerable loss, Kadm Husein was forced to retreat, leaving behind him four hundred dead on the field, three elephants, and eight pieces of cannon, which fell into the hands of the victors. Knox followed up the retreating army until evening closed in, capturing and blowing up a number of ammunition tumbrils. Kadm Husein had indeed

* Rao Shitab Rai, a Kayastha of exceptional character and capacity, had recently come to Patna as Imperial Diwan, and Governor of Rohtas. These were practically honorary posts under the conditions then existing; but he held large *jagirs* in Malda and Pilich parganas, which made him a wealthy man at Patna. From this period, particularly after his heroism at the battle of Birpur, his fortnnes were bound up with those of the English.

† Broome, page 298. *See also* Mr. S. C. Hill's Memoir of Knox, J. B. O. R. S. Vol. III, page 120.

been completely defeated, and he fled towards Bettiah, where he passes out of the history of Patna district.

Among the men who achieved the conquest of British India, Randfurlie Knox, loved and honoured by British and Indians alike, whose record is marred by no ignoble act, has been too little remembered, and the effect of this remarkable action at Birpur has been too little regarded. In the words of the historian of the Bengal army, from that day the English acquired a reputation for determination and invincibility that did them good stead in many a subsequent action. Shitab Rai's conduct on this occasion was admirable. Knox was lavish in praise of the courage he had displayed and the exertions he had made; and thenceforward his character was held in high esteem by all ranks of the English.* The watchers on the Patna side had never imagined that Knox had a hope of victory; and when they returned in the evening it was long before Knox and Shitab Rai could convince them that the enemy had indeed been defeated.†

Conclusion of the campaign.

No further steps were taken against the emperor during 1760; and he remained in south Bihar with Jean Law and Kamgar Khan. Carnac took command of the army at Patna on the 31st of December, and at once made preparations for disposing of the emperor's army. The armies met at Siwan on the Mahane river, nine miles from Bihar, on the 15th of January, 1761, where the emperor was defeated and Jean Law was taken prisoner. Carnac now gave the emperor no rest, until at last, wearied of the continual pursuit, he came to terms near Gaya. He then returned to Patna with the English; and the campaigns concluded with his recognition as emperor, when he was enthroned as Shah Alam in the upper room of the factory at Gulzarbagh on the 12th of March, 1761.

The Revolt of Mir Kasim.

It may well have appeared, when Clive left for England, as if the soul were departing from the body of the Government of Bengal.§ The deposition of Mir Jafar in favour of Mir Kasim soon followed, in itself an act of bad faith, involving the abandonment of Ramnarain and the Jagat Seths, and compelling even Shitab Rai to flee from Bihar. In May of 1761 Eyre Coote came to Patna as commander-in-

---

* Broome, page 302.

† *See* Sair Mutakharin II, page 353.

§ Broome, page 276.

chief, and for the time Ramnarain was safe; but in June there was an open rupture between Mir Kasim and Coote, who was recalled to Calcutta, and Ramnarain was at once removed from his post. The new Nawab set vigorously about the pacification of south Bihar; Buniad Singh and Fateh Singh of Tikari were captured and placed in confinement at Patna: Kamgar Khan took to the hills, and Bishun Singh of Powai fled to Benares. For the first time for many years revenue was realized from the southern parganas. But there were continual quarrels between Mir Kasim and the English, which were intensified when in 1762 Mr. Ellis, a personal enemy of the Nawab, was appointed Chief at Patna. Henceforth events moved rapidly towards the final rupture. From his arrival at Patna Ellis gave grounds of offence, by his indefensible arrest of an officer of the Nawab who had purchased five maunds of saltpetre, and by imprudent insistence upon search of the fort at Monghyr where two English deserters were alleged to have taken refuge. Further quarrels ensued regarding exemption of the Company's servants from internal customs duties, wherein Warren Hastings and Vansittart vainly sought to restrain the Council at Calcutta, regarding which Hastings came on a fruitless mission to Patna. The Company's Factory lies immediately outside the western wall of the city of Patna; but the main western gate of the city (*pachhim darwaza*) is nearly half a mile to the south-east down the main road. A small wicket gate stood at the entrance of the road now known as Diwan Mahalla Lane, which had been closed on a complaint from the factory that some deserters had entered the city by it; but it was found that the necessity of using the main western gate was inconvenient, and Ellis wished to have the wicket gate reopened. The Nawab refused to allow this; and there was much bickering over this small matter. The Nawab then made a stockaded entrenchment at the part of the wall which commanded the factory, which Ellis regarded as a preparation for hostilities. In May of 1763 he applied to the Council for permission to take aggressive measures, should he find the Nawab to be bent on commencing war; and this permission was unfortunately granted.

On the morning of the 25th of June Ellis, who had heard that reinforcements for the Nawab's army were approaching Patna, seized the city with the military force at his disposal, consisting of four companies of European infantry and one of artillery, with three battalions of sepoys. Such a force should have been sufficient to hold the city against all attacks; but discipline was lax; the troops scattered in search of plunder; and the Nawab's reinforcements coming from the east recaptured the city on the same afternoon. The British were now besieged in the factory by the Nawab's troops under Markar, until on the 29th of June they crossed the river, and set out for Chapra. At Manjhi they met Somru's brigade, and worn out with fatigue and hunger, they were defeated and captured.

The Nawab was now openly at war with the British, and Kamgar Khan came down from his retreat in the Chota Nagpur hills to join Mir Kasim at Bhagalpur; but instead of adding his forces to the army encamped at Udhuanala, he went on a raiding expedition into Birbhum, to divert the attention of the British forces advancing from Bengal. But the Nawab's armies were beaten wherever they met the British; the victory at Udhuanala on the 5th of September opened the way to Monghyr and Patna: and Kamgar Khan made his way home across country to Hasua, where he died shortly after.

The Patna massacre.

The victorious British army was now advancing towards Patna. Mir Kasim had already put to death Ramnarain, with Fateh Singh and Buniad Singh of Tikari; but the British prisoners remained in confinement in a house which had belonged to Haji Ahmad, brother of Alivardi Khan. When Mir Kasim heard of the fall of Monghyr he gave orders for their massacre, and the prisoners in Haji Ahmad's house were all put to death on the 5th of October. The Indian officers of the Nawab refused to carry out this work of butchery; but a willing agent was found in the Alsatian Walter Rainaud or Reinhardt, commonly known as Somru, who supervised the massacre. A number of sick and wounded prisoners in the Chahal Situn were similarly butchered on the 11th of October, the only person spared being Dr. Fullarton.

Re-capture of Patna, November 6th, 1763.

Major Adams, with Knox as his Quartermaster-General, arrived before Patna on the 28th of October. By the fifth of November breaches had been made by the north-east gate and on the eastern side of the fort, which was carried by storm on the following day. Mir Kasim Khan, who had been awaiting at Bikram the result of the siege, escaped into the territory of the Nawab of Oudh, who gave him shelter and assistance. Adams resigned the command of the army, on account of ill-health, to Knox on the 9th of December; but Knox himself was ill, and on the 28th of January 1764 he died at Bankipore, where he was buried on the east of the great house which was then building in Company Bagh.

Battle of Patna, May 3rd, 1764.

In March of 1764 Carnac took command of the army in the field, and conducted an inglorious campaign. After advancing to Buxar, he withdrew to Patna before the army of Mir Kasim and his allies Shah Alam and Shuja-ud-daula; and there he allowed himself to be invested in a manner which Knox or Adams would certainly not have suffered. The army of Carnac and Mir Jafar was encamped round the city with the right wing at Afzal Khan's garden,* where was Carnac's headquarters; while the line of the enemy stretched from Jafar Khan's garden to Bankipore. On the third of May the enemy attacked; but they were routed with great slaughter, though Carnac failed to follow up his success. On the thirtieth of May the enemy withdrew to Buxar. In August Major Hector Munro took command of the army; and on the 23rd of October he gained the decisive victory at Buxar, which made the British undisputed masters of these provinces.

The arrival in India of Lord Clive in 1765 brought to an end that intermediate period of British ascendancy in Bengal, during which the Company's civil officials had amassed wealth while the affairs of the country and the company suffered. The sordid story is relieved by the heroism of the soldiers, by the epic deeds of Knox and Shitab Rai, and the steadfastness of Adams and Munro. For Randfurlie Knox and Adams the path of duty was perhaps the road to glory; but they died, worn out with their labours, before they could see the fruit of them, while those who by following a very different path had enriched themselves lived to enjoy the wealth which they had acquired. One at least did not. William Billers, chief of Patna, had taken the usual bribes for appointments made when the fall of Mir Kasim opened opportunities to him; but he did not dare to face Lord Clive, and he committed suicide at his house in Company Bagh at Bankipore before Clive arrived.† He lies buried in the little graveyard in Company Bagh, where as Ghulam Husein Khan remarked, his tomb

* Now the compound of the Bihar School of Engineering.

† Broome, page 525; Sair Mutakharin, III, page 7.

remained to be a standing stock for the reflections of his countrymen; but it is not now distinguishable among those whose headstones have perished.

VI.—The dyarchy, 1765—1789.

In August of 1765 Clive obtained from the emperor at Allahabad the formal grant of the diwani of Bengal, Bihar and Orissa; and he made important changes in the civil and military administration. The cantonments at Bankipore, where the whole army had lately been quartered, were assigned to the third Brigade under Sir Robert Barker until three years later the Brigade was moved to the new quarters built at Dinapore. The pacification of the province of Bihar was by no means completed; but until 1857 the peace of Patna district was unbroken, except for slight disturbances in 1781, and an abortive invasion of Pindarries in 1812.

Administration of Bihar, 1765—1769. Clive appointed as Deputy Governor Dheraj Narain, brother of the murdered Ram Narain; but early in 1766 a council of three was appointed, consisting of Mr. Middleton, Chief of the Factory, Dheraj Narain, and Maharaja Shitab Rai. In the following September Thomas Rumbold was appointed Chief of Patna in Mr. Middleton's place, and Dheraj Narain was removed. Shitab Rai was now the Company's naib diwan for Bihar; and his place as agent of the emperor was taken by the Nawab Rezâ Quli Khan (Manir-ud-daula), founder of the well-known Bhikhnapahari family. Rumbold carried on the administration jointly with Shitab Rai until he went to England in 1769, when he was succeeded by James Alexander.

The famine of 1770. *Towards the end of 1769 signs of impending famine began to appear in Bihar. Earlier in the year Rumbold had given warning of danger; but in August he had reported that rain had fallen, and it was hoped that the season would be favourable. This expectation was disappointed; the premature cessation of the autumnal rains ruined the standing crops; and in January of 1770 famine had proceeded so far that Shitab Rai reported that fifty persons were dying daily of starvation in Patna. Alexander wrote at the end of January that the immediate distress was extreme, and that each day lost in deliberation added to the calamity. Nevertheless, he

*Annals of Rural Bengal, pages 19—30, 405, 415. Revenue Chief of Bihar, page 9.

stated in the same letter that he had issued orders to take for Government twenty-five seers out of each maund of grain reaped, leaving fifteen for the raiyat. Shitab Rai, taking that just and generous view of the duties of Government which we should expect from his character, boldly proposed to set aside two lakhs of rupees for relief work. But the Government of John Cartier would neither accept responsibility nor delegate it to the local officers; they agreed that something must be done; but they would not definitely approve Shitab Rai's proposal. In the following April Alexander reported that 'the depopulation in the interior part of the country is more rapid than will be imagined by any person who has not been witness to it; and such is the disposition of the people that they seem rather inclined to submit to death than extricate themselves from misery and hunger by industry and labour'. We should pronounce this estimate of the people of Patna to be unjust, if we judged its correctness by their character at the present day. In any case, the taking as revenue of five-eighths of a famine crop would be deemed nowadays a severe mode of inciting cultivators to exhibit industry and self-reliance in such circumstances. 'By this time', reports Alexander, 'the miseries of the poor increase in such a manner that no less than 150 have died in a day in Patna. In consequence of this, I disburse on the Company's account daily 380 sonat rupees, 100 of which is disbursed by the Raja. The officers at Dinapore, by a private subscription, feed a large number; and the French and Dutch give as largely as can be expected from their small factories'. The rainy season in time brought relief; but there had been considerable depopulation before that relief came, from which the country did not recover for many years.

In 1770 a change was made in the system of administration by the appointment of the Revenue Council of Patna, which consisted of James Alexander as President, with Robert Palk and George Vansittart as members, with authority over the naib-diwan in revenue matters, though Shitab Rai remained in general charge of the *nizamat* administration. The Council at once began to interfere actively in revenue affairs. On November the 5th, 1770, a large body of raiyats complained of the exactions of the renters, whereupon the council fixed the maximum rent at nine-sixteenths of the produce, compelling the farmers to undertake by their covenants not to collect at a higher rate. It is probable that in this order we

Appointment of the comptrolling council of revenue at Patna, 1770.

may find the origin of the tradition that nine-sixteenths of the produce is the normal rent in South Bihar.*

In 1772 the Directors issued their famous despatch wherein they announced their intention to 'stand forth as Diwan', ordering the removal of Shitab Rai. This order evidently caused some embarrassment to Warren Hastings and the local council, who were unwilling to put a slight upon their honoured friend; and Shitab Tai was treated with all possible consideration, though he was publicly removed from his office and sent to Calcutta for an enquiry into his administration.† He emerged from the enquiry with honour, and in the end he was reinstated; but he died shortly after his return to Patna in 1773. Thereupon his son Kallian Singh was appointed Rai-raiyan of Bihar, with an annual salary of fifty thousand rupees; and the *naibs* of Shitab Rai were reappointed, one of whom was Raja Khiali Ram, the Agarwala, whose descendants still flourish in Patna. The general revenue administration remained in the hands of the Council, of which successive presidents were Richard Barwell (1771), John Graham (1772), George Vansittart (1772), George Hurst (1773), Thomas Lane (1773), Robert Palk (1775), Isaac Sage (1776), Ewan Law (1777) and William Maxwell (1780).

The Revenue Chiefs, 1781—1786.

The administration of the revenue under the Council was unsatisfactory; and in 1781 a change was made in the system. The Council was abolished; and the farm of the whole of Bihar province was taken by the Rai-raiyan, who divided it with his *naib*, Khiali Ram.‡ The parganas made over to Khiali Ram included the wildest and least settled in Bihar; and the disturbances of the autumn of 1781 destroyed whatever chance he may have had of meeting his engagements. By the end of the year he was in confinement for arrears; and in the correspondence of the Revenue Chief we have a dreary record of endeavours to make him disgorge from his private means the balances which he had

* It is stated in the Patna Settlement Report that restrictions on collections were omitted in the *kabuliyats* of 1781, as is implied in Sir John Shore's minute of June 28th, 1789. (Harington's Analysis, Vol. III, page 451.) But in his letter of May 6th, 1788, W. A. Brooke, the Revenue Chief, distinctly asserts that the renters by their current *kabuliyats* had undertaken to leave seven-sixteenths to the raiyats, and that this was the standing rule.

† For the despatch, and the action taken on it with regard to Shitab Rai, *see* Carracioli, IV, page 251. *See* also Annals of Rural Bengal, pages 38, 39.

‡ On this experiment and its working, *see* Chapters III and V of the introduction to the *Revenue Chief of Bihar.*

failed to realise from his parganas. Kallian Singh was no more successful in the parganas which he had retained for himself. He was in arrears from his second *kist*; estate after estate was taken from him and placed under direct management, until the whole experiment was abandoned in 1783, when John Shore came to Patna and made a new settlement.

THE DISTURBANCES OF 1781.

It is significant that in Rennell's map of south Bihar the zamindaris of Narhat-Samai and Siris-Kutumba are specially shown, as if they were semi-independent states; and it was soon to be seen that each was still a potential source of disturbance. Kamgar Khan had died in 1764, but Waris 'Ali Khan, the last survivor of the brothers of Hasua, who had been expelled from Kharakdiha on the British occupation of Chota Nagpur, remained in possession of the family estates in Bihar proper, to which Iqbal 'Ali Khan,* son of Kamgar Khan, succeeded in 1778. In Siris-Kutumba Narain Singh, nephew of Bishun Singh, had succeeded to the zamindari; but he had been ousted from direct management of the estate in 1778, owing to default in payment of revenue, and he was doing what he could to obstruct the intruded farmers.

On the 22nd of August, 1781, the news came to Patna of Chait Singh's revolt, producing some alarm, which was checked by the excellent example of fortitude set by Mrs. Hastings, who was then at Bankipore, waiting for her husband's return from Benares. There was some intriguing on behalf of Chait Singh in Patna and its neighbourhood; but the only considerable zamindars who showed active sympathy with him were Narain Singh and Iqbal 'Ali Khan. Narain Singh raised a force on his estate, with which he attempted to oppose the march of Major James Crawfurd up the Grand Trunk Road from Chatra, and ultimately he joined Chait Singh's faujdar Bechu Singh. In September Iqbal 'Ali Khan, at the head of five thousand followers, began to plunder the country; but Captain Powell, with three companies from Dinapore, routed him in the Guma pass, which leads into Hazaribagh district from Rajauli. Iqbal Ali Khan fled into Kharakdiha, where he laid waste the Satganwan and Doranda estates, whence he ultimately escaped to Delhi.

---

* The name in contemporary records is ordinarily written as Akbal or Akbar Ali Khan.

Subsequent history of the Hasua estate

Iqbal 'Ali Khan's estates in Rajgir and Amarthu were granted to Ali Ibrahim Khan, who had endeavoured to prevent the Patna massacre in 1763, and had accompanied Warren Hastings on his recent journey to Benares. His brother's descendants, who are commonly known as the Nawabs of Husseinabad, still possess the property. Of the rest of the zamindari lying in the present Patna district a limited *mukarrari* grant was made to the family of Manir-ud-daula. When Iqbal Ali Khan was permitted to return to Patna at the end of 1784, the rest of his zamindari was in possession of farmers under John Shore's unexpired settlement. The farms were continued until 1788, when on the farmers' default Thomas Law completely broke up the estate, making a permanent settlement, village by village, with *maliks* and small farmers. Iqbal 'Ali Khan died in 1800, leaving no legitimate descendants.

William Augustus Brooke as Revenue Chief, 1781—1786.

William Maxwell died on August 19th, 1871, and after an interval of two months, during which James Lindsay Ross acted as Revenue Chief, he was succeeded by William Augustus Brooke. Two weary years were spent in endeavouring to realise the revenue for which Kallian Singh had engaged, until in the autumn of 1783 John Shore came to Patna, and made a re-settlement of revenue for a term of three years. Shore merely made a farming settlement, based on no accurate knowledge of assets, which was extended on its expiry from year to year until the Decennial Settlement. In addition to his responsibilities as Settlement Officer, Shore was required to deal with the scarcity created by the failure of the *Hathiya* rainfall in 1783. He did this by removing transit duties on grain, and by cancelling orders by which export of grain from Saran and Tirhut had been prohibited. One result of his recommendations was the building of the great granary, which still forms an unsightly landmark at Bankipore, of which the erection was sanctioned in January of 1784.

Formation of zila Bihar.

In July of 1787 the office of Revenue Chief was abolished; and Thomas Law became collector of the district of Bihar, conterminous with the ancient *sarkar* of that name. This district, with headquarters at Gaya, included the area now covered by the districts of Patna and Gaya, with Japla and Belaunja, and including the parganas up to the river Kiul.

Law's mukarrari settlement.

In the temporarily-settled area of the old Hasua zamindari all the farmers had defaulted by the end of 1787, and

Thomas Law conceived the scheme of making a permanent settlement with the village maliks.* There were obvious advantages to be gained by making them zamindars; their *malikana* would be added to their zamindari allowance as security for their taking pains to avoid default. Moreover, since these *maliks* possessed a prescriptive title anterior to that of the Mayi family, a permanent settlement with them would effectively keep out Iqbal Ali Khan. The aggressions of the Mayi family were comparatively recent; the memory of Kamgar Khan was still vivid, and Iqbal Ali Khan's rebellion had occurred only six years before. The local officers might well view with some concern the possibility of this family's return to power. Apart from these considerations, Thomas Law pointed out the advantages to be expected from a permanent settlement; as that the temporary farmer neglected irrigation works; whereas a permanent proprietor might be expected to take an intelligent interest in his estate. From the beginning of 1788, Law was indefatigable in urging the adoption of a permanent settlement, and although the Board of Revenue disapproved of his scheme, the Court of Directors in 1792 made his settlement permanent, complimenting him on his activity, knowledge, and humanity, in thus bringing into view the advantages of a permanent settlement. Law's settlement was undoubtedly of great importance in the development of the scheme for the permanent settlement of these provinces, because while others were hesitating, doubting, and finding difficulties in every plan proposed, Law not only bodly prepared a plan but promptly carried in into effect.

The Permanent Settlement.

The Decennial Settlement of the rest of the district began in 1789, and was completed by 1790. Parganas settled wholly or chiefly with zamindars were Baikathpur (Udwant

* These village *maliks* are found in a great part of *sarkar* Bihar; they are apparently survivals from some early revenue system. Whatever their origin may be, they appear in history as mere annuitants, never as officials with any kind of function to perform. They were entitled to a proportion of the collections of rent made by the renter or zamindar, which was often compounded for a fixed annual payment, or for certain rent-free land. It might have been supposed that rights of this kind would be insecure in the general anarchy of south Bihar during the early eighteenth century; and indeed Sundar Singh did not apparently respect their rights when he found it inconvenient to do so. But generally speaking, these rights to mere annuities, which were freely bought and sold, endured in a remarkable fashion. It is worthy of note that Chaudhri Bhelum Singh, ancestor of the Raja of Ammawan, was able successfully to resist the Mayis when they tried to dispossess him of *milkiats* which he had purchased in Malda pargana.

Singh), Masaurha (Jaswant Singh), Okri and Sanaut (Mitarjit Singh), Shahjahanpur-Bhimpur (parts of which were settled with Sheikh Fazil-ullah and other Chaudhris, ancestors of the Chaudhris of Islampur), and Tilhara (Mir Muhammad Baker Khan). Rajgir remained with Muhammad Yahya, brother of Ali Ibrahim Khan, and part of Biswak and Bhimpur with Manir-ud-daula's family. Sanda and Ballia were held by a farmer with a permanent lease. The other parganas were settled chiefly with *maliks*, as were Sanda and Ballia in June 1792, when the farmer defaulted. The Decennial Settlement was made permanent in 1793. Details of the assessment at this settlement and at the subsequent resumption of invalid revenue-free tenures, will be found in chapter XI.

VII.—PATNA DISTRICT SINCE THE PERMANENT SETTLEMENT.

With the Decennial Settlement of 1789 we enter on a new era in revenue and general administration. In 1790 the administration of the criminal law, which hitherto had rested with the Nawab-Nazim of Murshidabad, was definitely taken over by the Company; mutilation ceased to be a recognised form of punishment, unexpired sentences were scrutinised and revised, and an endeavour was made to suppress the practice of extorting confessions by torture. The first magistrate of Patna, which included only the city and Bankipore-Jaywar police circle, was the notorious Charles Francis Grand, who had to make way for Henry Douglas in 1792. Gangs of dacoits roved over Bihar district, often in league with the local Darogas. On the night of February the 1st, 1791, the camp of the 32nd N.I. at Jafar Khan's Bagh was raided and looted; and unless a boat were heavily guarded, the journey upwards from Fatuha was dangerous. The Magistrate at Gaya was too far away to be able to act effectively near Patna; and in 1798 the jurisdiction of the Magistrate at Patna was extended to cover an area of 403 square miles, from Fatuha to Maner, extending on the south to Naubatpur. As the gangs of dacoits were broken up, thaggi took the place of dacoity as the most prominent form of crime. A favourite ground of operation for the thags was the Ganges road east of Fatuha, where they were secure in the connivance of the local police, too far from the district headquarters at Gaya for effective supervision. In 1825 this led to the creation of a new district of Patna, with concurrent boundaries for revenue and police purposes, consisting of the district as it is at the present day, without the parganas of Bihar and Rajgir, which were not transferred from Bihar district to Patna until 1865.

THE MUTINY.

In 1857 the garrison at Dinapore consisted of the 10th foot* and a company of European artillery, with a company of Native artillery, and the 7th, 8th and 40th battalions of Indian infantry. Patna was then a centre of intrigue for disaffected Muhammadans; and on the 18th of June the Commissioner, William Tayler, arrested the three Maulavis who were at the head of the Patna Wahabis, and detained them as hostages for the good behaviour of their followers. On the third of July sixty or seventy Muhammadans, with drums beating and the green flag waving, suddenly rushed to attack the Roman Catholic church in the city. Rattray's Sikhs, who were in Patna, were at once ordered to the spot; but Dr. Lyell, Superintendent of the Opium Factory, thinking that his presence would overawe the rioters, rode on in advance. As he approached, several shots were fired at him and he fell mortally wounded. The moment was critical; but the Sikhs just then arrived, and quickly dispersed the crowd of fanatics. On the next day letters were found in Pir Ali's house at Patna which indicated the existence of a widespread conspiracy. The ringleaders were brought to trial; and fourteen were sentenced to death, among others the Daroga Waris Ali, who went to the gallows crying: "To the rescue, all friends of the King of Delhi."

With his garrison strengthened by two companies of the 37th foot, General Lloyd on the morning of the 25th of July removed the percussion caps which were in the magazine to the lines of the British troops, issuing orders that the caps in possession of the sepoys should be given up; but the sepoys, when called upon to obey this order, fired on their officers. The European troops were quickly on the scene; and the sepoys fled: but the general was not present, and there was nobody who would take responsibility, so that the pursuit was not continued beyond the cantonments. The main body of the mutineers made their way across the Son and joined the rebel Kuar Singh at Arrah.

An ill-fated attempt was now made to atone for the error of allowing these men to join the rebels at Arrah with their arms and accoutrements. Four hundred men of the 10th foot left in a steamer on the 29th; but the expedition was

* Now the 1st battalion of the Lincolnshire Regiment.

badly mismanaged. The troops were landed at 7 p.m., and marched in the darkness in their white summer uniforms, by the Chapra Ghât road towards Arrah. At midnight they fell into an ambuscade; and in the morning they had to retreat. Half of their numbers were left behind, and of the survivors only about fifty returned unwounded. Two hundred British soldiers and two guns were now sent to the city to overawe the disaffected, who gave no more trouble; but for the rest of the year stray bands of mutineers roamed over the district destroying thanas and looting private property; and order generally was not restored until early in 1858.*

Patna the capital of Bihar and Orissa.

Royal visits.

On December the 12th, 1911, the King-Emperor at Delhi announced the constitution of the new province of Bihar and Orissa, with Patna as its capital. From Delhi he went to Nepal; and as he passed through Patna, he went down the river by boat to see the new capital, where thousands had gathered near the Adalat Ghat to welcome him. Since that time the face of Patna has been changed by the creation of a new city to the west of the old Municipal area. In February of 1916 Lord Hardinge of Penshurst, Viceroy and Governor-General, opened the new High Court with due ceremonial. The lamented father of King George V had visited Patna in 1876, in memory of which visit stands the Bihar School of Engineering. Another Prince of Wales came to Patna in December of 1921, when he held a darbar in a pandal erected on the Bankipore maidan, and spent two days in the new capital.

ARCHAEOLOGY.

Patna is rich in remains of archæological interest, of which the Museum possesses an increasing store. There has been much activity in recent years in excavation at Rajgir, Nalanda, and Pataliputra. At these places, and at Giriak, Bihar, Tetrawan, Tilhara, Silao, Hilsa, and Maner are surviving monuments of antiquity of which an account is given in the description of each of these places in chapters XVI and XVII below.

---

* The above account has been compiled mainly from Holmes' History of the Indian Mutiny, (1891). On August the 4th, 1857, William Tayler was relieved of his post as Commissioner by the District Judge, a step of which the propriety has been much debated. It may be conceded that Sir Frederick Halliday's Minute on the Mutinies in Lower Bengal, in laying stress on the peace of the city after August, gives too little credit to the vigorous measures of Tayler, which had checked incipient rebellion before Samuells took over charge. Whether Tayler was not inclined to continue vigorous repressive measures after the necessity for them had passed is another question, to which a satisfactory answer cannot easily now be given.

CHAPTER III.

THE PEOPLE.

The earlier estimates of population.

THE first regular census was held in 1872; and no useful purpose would be served by discussing in detail the estimates of population which were made before that time. Buchanan in 1812 estimated the population of the ten police circles which roughly correspond with the present district at 1,428,820; and that of Patna City at 312,000. His figures were probably more nearly correct than any other of the early estimates: certainly more nearly correct than the guesses of William Tayler, who in 1857 estimated the population of the city at 400,000. There were defects in the machinery of the census of 1872; and the figures cannot be treated as exactly accurate; but the error was probably not very great. According to that census the population of the district was 1,559,638; and that of the city 158,900. The results of subsequent enumerations have been as follows:—

YEAR OF CENSUS.	Patna District.	Patna City.
1881	1,756,196	170,654
1891	1,773,410	165,192
1901	1,624,742	134,785
1911	1,609,631	136,153
1921	1,574,287	119,976

Regarding the result of the census of 1921, the Census Commissioner, Mr. P. C. Tallents, makes the following remarks: "There has been in the last thirty years an aggregate loss of 194,964 in the district. This is partly due to the fact that the city of Patna and other towns on the banks of the Ganges are decadent. The commerce, which supported them for so long when the river was the chief artery of communication between Bengal and upper India, has been diverted to other channels; and their occupation, and with it a good deal of their population has gone. The loss is also due even more to the ravages of epidemic disease. Since 1900 when it first broke out plague alone has caused over a quarter of a million deaths in this district. It was raging in epidemic form at the time of the census of 1901; and the decrease that is shown to have occurred in that year must be discounted to some extent on that account. It continued to deal destruction during the following decade also, but the number of deaths that it has caused since 1911 is 81,000 or 59,000 less than in the previous decade, and the last of the really bad outbreaks when the mortality rose to over 20,000 was in 1911. Violent outbreaks of cholera also are apt to occur in this district as an aftermath of the floods to which the district is liable. The high bank of the Ganges prevents the water that accumulates during the rains from flowing off rapidly and year after year a large tract of the district immediately to the south of the river becomes a sheet of water, which, while it allows wonderful *rabi* crops to be raised with the minimum of labour, does so at the cost of outbreaks of fever and cholera. Cholera has caused over 100,000 deaths since 1900, the mortality exceeding 50,000 in each decade. These two influences—the ravages of disease and the decline of the river trade—caused the decrease of the population shown by the census of 1911 and they are responsible for the further and larger decrease now shown."

Emigration.

Of late years there has been a decrease in migration both to and from the district, the decline in emigration being the more marked. But the probable result of a decrease of emigration is that more males will be found at home than would otherwise have been the case, and in the case of Patna the facts bear out this expectation; for while the loss of males in the actual population is only just over 300,

PATNA.	1921.		1911.	
	Males.	Females.	Males.	Females.
Actual population.	807,701	766,586	808,016	797,996
Immigrants ...	36,524	40,488	38,341	53,865
Emigrants ...	68,965	63,049	95,459	78,436
Natural population.	840,142	781,047	865,234	822,567

the loss in females is over 31,000. In other words here, as in a number of other districts in Bihar, the real loss of population in the last decade is masked by a decrease in emigration. Plague and influenza, so far as they differentiated in favour of either sex, have also dealt more lightly with the male sex, all of which causes have tended to increase the proportion of males in the population.

Patna has a larger cultivable area than the other districts of south Bihar, and contains altogether 740 persons to the square mile; but if its two large towns are excluded, the density is less than 700. The population is greatest in the urban and semi-urban country on the banks of the Ganges; in Dinapore thana there are 1,562, and in Phulwari 1,036 persons to the square mile. In no thana does the density fall below 500; and it is least in the agricultural thanas of Mokameh (506) and Masaurhi (581).

Density of population. The proportion of the population living in urban areas is unusually large owing to the fact that the district includes the city of Patna. At the census of 1921 the total number of persons living in urban areas was 218,895, or fourteen per cent. of the inhabitants of the district. These urban areas are the six towns of Patna, Bihar, Barh, Dinapore, Khagaul and Mokameh; but the people of Mokameh are mostly agriculturists, living in the town because the cultivated land in that neighbourhood is submerged in the rainy season. It was formerly remarked that the average number of inhabitants of a village was exceptionally small in Patna; but the explanation of this is to be found in the fact that at the Revenue survey in Patna each estate was treated as a village (mauza), and as estates had been much subdivided the number of nominal villages was large (4,952). A more reasonable unit has now been adopted; and the number of villages has been reduced to 2,596, by the inclusion of small estates within the main village in which they fall.

Village officials. The chief village officials in Patna are the *patwari*, *gumashta*, *barahil*, *gorait*, *hatwa*, and the *jeth raiyat* or *mahattwara*. The *patwari* existed originally as the servant of the state and as a check upon the revenue collector. He has since the Permanent Settlement become the servant of the zamindar. His business is to keep account of the village rent collections. A result of the subdivision of estates is that there are often several *patwaris* in one village, each keeping the accounts of his estate in that and several adjoining villages. *Patwaris* usually receive a nominal pay of about two rupees per month, but in the larger estates their pay is sometimes as much as eight or ten rupees. In addition to their pay, where pay is nominal, they receive an allowance on produce-rent collections of six-sixteenths of a seer per maund of the landlord's share. The *abwabs* known as *mangan* or *hujjatana* are frequently appropriated by the *patwari*, *gumashta*, and *barahils* in varying proportions.

The *gumashta* collects the rents, and looks after the interest of his zamindar. He frequently receives a nominal pay, with a share in *abwabs* and a commission of six-sixteenths of a seer per maund of the landlord's share in produce-rents.

The *barahils* help the *gumashta* in realising rents. Their commission on produce-rents varies: but where the *gumashta* receives six-sixteenths of a seer per maund, the *barahils* would commonly receive between them four-sixteenths. The *gorait* is the watchman of the zamindar's village office, who carries messages for the *gumashta*, and escorts to the zamindar's presence raiyats fulfilling his customary demands for *ghi*, milk, goats, or other articles which are paid for at favoured rates. He also sometimes acts as *jaribkash* in making appraisements.

The *hatwa* (weighman) is a permanent institution in villages in which a large proportion of the rent is paid in kind, where his function is to weigh the crops for division, or to make the test in disputed appraisements.

The *jeth-raiyat* or *mahatwara* is the principal cultivator of the village, who is usually appointed by the landlord on the understanding that he is to use his influence with the raiyats in the zamindar's interest. He takes advances from the zamindar when village irrigation works have to be repaired, and generally supervises the work; and if there is no *gumashta* he makes collection of rents on behalf of the landlord. He pays rent at a slightly favoured rate in return for these services.

To this list of village officials may be added the amin or *salis*, who is specially appointed by the zamindar for appraisements, the same amin not necessarily taking part in appraisements for the whole village. In estates of considerable size the amin is usually a member of the zamindar's headquarters staff, and not a resident of the village in which the appraisement is made. It will be observed that all the above officials, except the weighman, are servants of the zamindar rather than of the village.

Apart from these quasi-revenue officials there are of course the ordinary officials of the village, the barber (*hajjam*), who performs important ceremonial functions in connection with weddings and funerals in addition to the ordinary duties implied by his name: the carpenter and blacksmith, both of whom are needed for making and repairing agricultural implements, the *dhobi* or washerman, and the *chamar*, whose wife acts as midwife to the village.

Dress, houses, games and amusements.

The dress, houses, and games and amusements of the people do not differ materially from those of the people of the adjoining district of Shahabad; and they have been sufficiently described in the gazetteer of that district. It may be remarked that the young men of Patna have taken to British games with even more enthusiasm than the youth of the towns of Shahabad, particularly to football played according to the Association Code.

Food.

Rice, which is the staple food of the people in Bengal, is not the staple food of the poor in the Patna district, but rather that of the fairly well-to-do. The mass of the people live on bannocks made of flour prepared from wheat or one of the many kinds of coarse grains and pulses. These cakes are accompanied by vegetables, salt and a few simple condiments;

and the meal is varied by a porridge of the same. Maize is eaten whenever it can be procured, and also *arhar* (*cajanus indicus*) either in the form of flour or as a thick pottage. *Maruu* (*eleusine coracana*) is consumed largely in the Bihar subdivision, and besides this many kinds of millets and pulses form part of the cultivator's dietary. Among the poorer classes the morning meal usually consists of parched or boiled grains of various sorts, and the evening meal of boiled rice, with *dal* or pulse and occasionally vegetable curries.

Language. The vernacular current over the whole district is the dialect of Bihari Hindi known as Magahi or Magadhi. Magahi is properly speaking the language of the country of Magadha, which roughly corresponded to the present districts of Patna and Gaya, but the language is not confined to this area. It is also spoken over the district of Hazaribagh; on the west it extends to a portion of Palamau, and on the east to portions of the districts of Monghyr and Bhagalpur. Over the whole of this area it is one and the same dialect, with hardly any local variations. The dialect of this district is practically the same as that of Gaya but not so pure, being infected on the one hand by the Maithili spoken north of the Ganges, and on the other hand by the strong Muhammadan element of the city, from which it has borrowed several Urdu idioms.

Magahi. Magahi is condemned by speakers of other Indian languages as being as rude and uncouth as the people who use it. Like Maithili, it has a complex system of verbal conjugation, and the principal difference between the two dialects is that Maithili has been under the influence of learned Brahmans for centuries, while Magahi is the language of a people who have been dubbed boors since Vedic times. To a native of India, one of its most objectionable features is its habit of winding up every question, even when addressed to a person held in respect, with the word '*re*'. In other parts of India this word is only used in addressing an inferior, or when speaking contemptuously. Hence a man of Magah has the reputation of rudeness, and his liability to get an undeserved beating on that score has been commemorated in a popular song. Magahi has no indigenous literature, but there are many popular songs current throughout the area in which the language is spoken, and strolling bards recite various long epic peoms, such as the song of Lorik, the cow-herd hero, and the song of Gopichandra, which are known more or less over the whole of Northern India. The character in general use in writing is the Kaithi, but the Devanagari is also used by the educated classes. The number of people speaking Magahi in this district is ninety-six per cent. of the population.

Other languages. Urdu is spoken, and the Persian character used, in a more or less correct form, by the Muhammadan population of the towns, but in the interior both Musalmans and Kayasths use the Awadhi dialect of Eastern Hindi. This dialect is also used as a sort of language of politeness, especially when Europeans are addressed, by the rustics, who have picked it up from their Musalman friends and imagine it to be Hindustani of polite society. The Devanagari and the Kaithi characters are both used in writing Awadhi; and the Persian character is also used by the educated classes.

Bengali is spoken by the Bengalis settled in Patna and Bankipore; they are chiefly clerks, officials and shopkeepers. Marwari is the language of a considerable number of cloth merchants, who carry on trade in Patna city, especially in the commercial quarter of Chauk Kalan.

PRINCIPAL CASTES. Among the Muhammadans Sheikhs (56,302) and Jolahas (28,602) are most strongly represented; and the most numerous Hindu castes are Ahirs or Goalas (232,908), Kurmis (167,522), Babhans (108,263), Dusadhs (100,200), Kahars (84,531), Koiris (72,491), Rajputs (63,724), Chamars (60,472), and Telis (42,277). There are also eight castes with a strength of over 25,000, viz., Barhis, Brahmans, Dhanuks, Hajjams, Kandus, Musahars, Pasis and Kayasths.

Goalas. The Goalas or Ahirs (232,908) are the most numerous caste in the district. They are a thrifty race, selling their grain and husks, living themselves on coarse food, and cutting grass for their cattle, while their women go about selling milk, butter and *ghi*. They are generally cultivators and cattle-breeders; but many of the poorer are labourers, and a few rich zamindars are also members of the caste. They are notoriously the most quarrelsome caste in the district, constantly concerned in riots and very fond of the *lathi;* cattle trespass forms a frequent subject of dispute among them. They have the reputation of being audacious cattle stealers, and many at the bottom of the social scale are professional thieves.

On the 16th Kartik, the day after the Dewali, they observe a curious festival called Gaidarh or Sohrai. On the Dewali night rice is boiled in all the milk left in the house, and the mixture, called *khir*, is then offered to Basawan. All the cattle are left without food, and next morning their horns are painted red, and red spots are daubed on their bodies. They are then turned into a field in which is a pig with its feet tied together and are driven over the wretched animal until it has been trampled or gored to death.

Kurmis. The Kurmis (167,522) are next to Goalas the largest caste. They are almost entirely employed in cultivation, but many of the poorer are labourers. Some take service as *khidmatgars*, a few are zamindars and *thikadars*, and in the towns many are money-lenders. As cultivators, they confine themselves to the staple crops as a rule, and do not breed cattle. They are fond of petty litigation and are apt to engage in disputes about the possession of crops and land.

Their religious observances are a curious mixture. The orthodox Hanuman and Kali are favourite deities, but they also worship the Muhammadan Panch Pir, the officiating priest being a Dafali, and they propitiate a number of evil spirits and godlings, such as Goraiya. One of these, Ram Thakur, is appeased by the sacrifice of a goat, which is cooked and eaten by the family; any flesh left over is carefully buried, for if a particle is not buried and rots Ram Thakur is enraged and then his careless worshippers will suffer. In cases of illness exorcism is regularly practised, *ojhas* or wizards being called in to expel the spirits possessing a man, which are supposed to be cast out by the superior strength of the *ojha's* familiar spirit; when cast out they are imprisoned in a small bamboo tube or earthen pot, which is burnt or buried. The Churail, or disembodied spirit of a woman who has died in child-birth, is particularly feared. To pacify her, needles are driven into the ground; and when a woman dies in child-birth, her feet are pierced with needles, and sand and *urid* are thrown on her body to prevent her haunting her family. One spirit, called Bandi Mai, furnishes an exception to the general rule, in that she is regarded as benevolent ; and curiously enough, the Kurmis also worship Karta, a spirit with no image or visible representation and bearing a name which seems to show that he is intended to represent the creator of the universe.

Babhans. The Babhans (108,263) constitute the greater portion of the zamindars, agricultural *thikadars*, and well-to-do cultivators of this district. They claim to be descended from Brahmans; like Brahmans they will not hold the plough, but employ labourers for the purpose; and some have Brahmanical names, such as Pande, Misr and Tewari. According to local tradition they are descended from a number of persons collected by the Diwan of Jarasandha, king of Magadha, at a feast given by his master. Jarasandha had ordered him to secure the attendance of 100,000 Brahmans, but he could not find so many and was driven to bring in a number of men of other castes whom he invested with the sacred thread and palmed off as genuine Brahmans. This legend was probably invented to explain the claim of the Babhans to be Brahmans. They now constitute a separate caste, and their degradation probably dates back to the time when Buddhism was overthrown. It has been pointed out that Babhan is merely the Pali form of Brahman, and that the word is often found in Asoka's edicts. It has therefore been conjectured that those now known as Babhans remained Buddhists after the Brahmans around them had reverted to Hinduism, and so the Pali name continued to be applied to them; while the synonym Bhuinhar or Bhumiharaka is explained as referring to their having seized the lands attached to the old Buddhist monasteries. This theory is borne out by the Brahmanical titles which are used along with the Rajput titles of Singh, Rai and Thakur, and by the fact that in this Province they are practically confined to the area covered by the ancient kingdom of Magadha, which long remained the centre of Buddhism.

The chief deities worshipped by them are Hanuman, Sitala, Sokha, Sambhunath, Bandi and the Gram Devata. Goraiya is the form generally taken by the latter, the place of worship being a clay mound below some tree outside the village. Here offerings are made periodically on certain days in Asin, Phagun and Chait, and also on special occasions, such as at marriages or on the birth of a child; the Babhans' offerings, such as goats, sweetmeats, milk and *ghi*, are taken by Dusadhs. Evil spirits are propitiated, especially Churail and Brahm Pisach, the latter being supposed to set fire to houses.

Dusadhs. The Dusadhs (100,200) are a low caste, who work as cultivators and practically monopolize the duties of road and village watchmen, *goraits* and *chaukidars*. Those who cannot find such employment and have no land, work as general labourers, ploughmen, etc.; some of the cooks employed by Europeans are Dusadhs. They have the reputation of being inveterate thieves; but if one of them is paid a sufficient amount to act as *chaukidar*, his confrères usually abstain from plundering the houses under his charge. They are, as a rule, of a low type, and appear to have traces of aboriginal descent. The main features of their worship are the sacrifice of pigs and libations of liquor, and their ceremonies generally terminate in a drunken orgy and a feast on swine's flesh.

The gods mostly affected by them are Rahu, Salais, Sokha and Goraiya. The worship of Rahu takes place twice every year on Pus Sankranti day and on Chait Satwani day, and is held with great ceremony on the occasion of a marriage. Two bamboo posts are erected with two swords placed edge upwards across them, thus forming a small ladder. The Dusadh who officiates, and is called the Bhagat, stands on the rungs formed by the swords, chanting some incantations and holding two canes bent in the form of a bow, while some balls of flour are boiled in milk close by; these, when ready, are offered to Rahu. The next ceremony consists of three persons walking over the red-hot embers of a fire burnt in a shallow pit, viz., a Brahman, the Bhagat, and the man on whose behalf the ceremony takes place; when they have walked over the burning charcoal, sterile women snatch away small pieces of it in the belief that this will bring them children.

The Kahars (84,531) are cultivators and are also largely employed as palki-bearers and general labourers. A large number of them are personal servants, a capacity in which they are extremely useful. Like other low castes, they worship Bandi, Sokha, Ram Thakur, Panch Pir and Manust Deva. The deity last named, which is the deified spirit of a dead man, is propitiated with offerings of goats when a marriage takes place. **Kahars.**

One custom peculiar to this caste is the worship of wolves. This worship is based on a tradition that a wolf once carried off a Kahar boy, was pursued by his relatives, and induced to give him up. Since then, it is said, wolves have been worshipped by the Kahars. On the occasion of a birth or marriage, the Kahars hold a feast, and before anything is eaten, some of the food is set aside in a dish and placed in the court-yard. When the feast is over, it is thrown away, and this is regarded as an offering to the wolves. Another legend connects the Kahars, like the Babhans, with Jarasandha, and makes them the builders of the great embankment called Asurenbandh near Giriak. This legend is given in the article on Giriak; and it will suffice here to say that after the Kahars had failed in their task, Jarasandha ordered them to be brought, that he might give them their wages, for though, he said, they had been unsuccessful in winning his daughter and half his kingdom, they had nevertheless laboured hard and were deserving of some consideration. He gave each man 3½ seers of *anaj* and ever since that period 3½ seers of *anaj* have been the Kahar's legitimate wage for a day's work.

The Koiris (72,491) are industrious, peaceful and contented cultivators, in great demand among zamindars, who are always glad to settle lands with them. In addition to the staple crops, the Koiris largely cultivate potatoes and **Koiris.**

country vegetables. In cultivation, however, they are not so niggardly as the Goala; they live on better grain and give the husks to their cattle; they also do not breed cattle or sell milk, butter, etc., nor do they steal. A few of them are merchants in the town—a vocation in which their industry usually renders them successful.

Rajputs.

The Rajputs (63,724), who are the descendants of Rajput soldiers who settled at an early period in the district, are chiefly well-to-do cultivators and agricultural *thikadars;* some are zamindars and money-lenders. Their ancient village communities have in some cases survived to the present day, particularly in the Barh subdivision, where we find villages which are composed entirely of Rajputs, even down to the *chaukidar.* Many of them consider themselves superior to the Babhans, whose claims to Brahmanical origin are not always admitted. They have a reputation for bravery and honesty, and are largely employed in the police.

Chamars.

The Chamars (60,472), work as tanners and labourers, and hold a very low position, as they are continually defiled by contact with carcases, to the hides of which they have a recognised right. They are not without reason frequently suspected of poisoning cattle in order to obtain the hides. They supply the villagers with leather thongs for their whips and fastenings for their ploughs, repairing the latter when necessary. They also act as village criers and as musicians at ceremonies; their wives are the village midwives. They get grain and crops from their clients at harvest, and sometimes have small *jagirs.* Such is their reputation for stealing that the word "*chamari*" is equivalent to "*chori*", and is generally used by the villagers to mean theft. They are enabled to carry on their dishonest practices with some impunity, for fear least their wives should refuse their services at child-birth.

Telis.

The Telis (42,377), have a monopoly of making and selling oil, this being the traditional occupation of the caste. A large proportion, however, are grain merchants, and many combine money-lending with their trade. The Telis have a firm belief in evil spirits, and every Teli, whether he dies a natural or unnatural death, is believed to become a very powerful and malignant spirit called Musan; it requires, it is said, a very expert *ojha* and the strongest spells to cast out a Musan from a possessed person. Jugglers often use the skull of a Teli as a symbol of their art, and thereby invoke the aid of Musan.

The Telis were formerly a very powerful clan in Bihar, and Telarha, or as it was formerly called Tailadhaka, is said to have been a centre of their power. The great doorway at the Buddhist monastery of Nalanda was set up by one Baladitya, "chief among the wise men of the Tailadhaka clan"; it was a Teli who set up the colossal image of Buddha there, which is known as the Telia Bhandar, and another set up a great Buddhist statue at Tetrawan. Nearly the whole trade of the district is in their hands, and a popular saying is "*Turk, Teli, tar, in tinon Bihar,*" *i.e.*, Bihar is made up of Muhammadans, Telis and toddy-palms.

The Brahmans (41,265) were till quite lately averse to the study of English and thus deprived themselves of the clerical employment for which many are intellectually fitted. The most numerous divisions of Brahmans in this district are the Sakadwipi and the Kanyakubja. Among the Sakadwipi are a few landowners and cultivators, but as a class, they are the physicians and priests of the people. The Kanyakubja are mostly teachers of Sanskrit and Hindi; but many have become agriculturists and some are petty zamindars: the very poor among them become cooks, as any caste can eat food cooked by a Brahman. They have two titles, Sarwariya and Saryupari, and in general do not act as priests, as they do not receive gifts. **Brahmans.**

The Musahars, who number 40,791 are considered to be aborigines of the country and work as labourers, ploughmen, etc. They are very poor, live in wretched huts, and will eat almost any animal, even wild cats, frogs and squirrels. **Musahars.**

The Pasis (34,472) are almost entirely occupied in tapping *tar* trees and selling the *tari* liquor. Those who cannot find support in this work are labourers. Some have also a little cultivation. It is characteristic of this caste that they make offerings to the east wind in order that they may have a good toddy season. **Pasis.**

The Dhanuks (33,296) are diggers and excavators, workers on embankments, etc. Locally they are supposed **Dhanuks.**

to be descended from Kurmis who sold themselves as slaves; but the name shows that they were originally bowmen, and they are probably an offshoot from one of the non-Aryan tribes. Colonel Waddell his pointed out that the caste occupying the small wards of Patna city adjoining the old wooden walls of ancient Pataliputra consists almost exclusively of Dhanuks and he has therefore suggested that they are probably the descendants of the old soldiery who kept watch and ward over these battlements in ancient times.

Kandus. The Kandus (27,672) are the grain parchers of the district. They also sell parched grain, sweetmeats, etc., and some work as labourers. A feature of their religion is the worship of Ganinath, who has a temple at Nawada (Khusrupur) in the Barh subdivision and is worshipped elsewhere in the family *devata-ghar*. Like other low castes, they attribute illness to demoniacal possession; and the usual method of exorcism is to kill a pigeon, and pour some country spirit and a drop of the exorcist's blood on it, while the latter expels the evil spirits by means of incantations.

Hajjams. The Hajjams (27,236) are by profession barbers, being attached to certain families and paid in grain, a not unusual payment being ten seers per adult per annum; sometimes also they have small *jagirs*. They are also employed as messengers to take invitations to festivals and ceremonies, and to call *panchayats*; for this they receive payment in money or grain. At harvest time they have a recognized claim to a small quantity of grain from each cultivator among their clients, and thus always have enough to live on in good seasons, though they have no capital to fall back on in times of want. Those who attend Europeans and rich Indians are paid in cash, which they are usually able to lay by, and thus make a little money. As a rule, however, they are poor.

Barhis. The Barhis (26,828) are carpenters by profession, and as such form a recognized part of the village community. They make and repair ploughs and other agricultural implements for the villagers. They are paid partly in grain and kind, and are given about a maund of grain a year for each plough they make or mend.

Kayasths. The Kayasths, the writer caste of Bihar, number 25,276. They are largely employed in Government offices, and many as writer-constables and superior officers in the Police. They despise trade and have a good deal of class pride. Their family ceremonies are conducted with great expense, though they are usually very poor. They have a special festival, the Dawat Puja, on which they worship their pen and ink, and observe a general holiday.

Among the local social institutions the oldest established is the Bankipore Club, which has increased considerably in size in recent years. Its club house is situated on the bank of the Ganges at Bankipore, on the east of the Collectorate offices. The New Patna Club, in the new capital, owes its origin to Mr. Justice F. R. Roe, who was assisted in forming it by Sir Ali Imam, Mr. Justice P. R. Das, and Mr. Saiyid Sultan Ahmed. It has a good club building, with eighty members, European and Indian. The South Bihar Gymkhana Club also owes its origin to Mr. Justice Roe, though it has not developed as he hoped. It provides tolerable golf links and a polo ground, of which the surface is rough but not unduly hard, on the west of the new capital. The Bihar Landholders' Association, which has its headquarters at Patna, represents the interests of the landlords of the whole of Bihar. There is also a branch of the Indian National Congress, besides a branch of the Kayasth Sabha, which has been formed to further interests of the Kayasths. The Bihar Hitaishi Library is a reading club in Patna city, to which a number of educated and wealthy gentlemen belong; and another purely social institution is the Victoria Jubilee Club, which is supported by the Indian society of Bankipore and the west end of Patna. There is a Muhammadan Association, the Anjuman Islamia, which deals mainly with social questions and keeps a watchful eye on the progress of events bearing on the interests of Muhammadans, and of the Sunni sect in particular. Among other associations may be mentioned the Bihar Young Men's Institute, the Theosophical Society and the Gorakshini Sabha. The association last named, which is maintained for the protection of cattle, is chiefly supported by Marwaris and other members of the merchant class who display more fervour than most of their co-religionists towards the objects of Hindu veneration.

SOCIAL AND POLITICAL INSTITUTIONS.

With the inauguration of the new province, some ambitious attempts were made to found reputable daily

NEWSPAPERS.

newspapers in Patna, which flourished for a time, but ultimately died out. The most notable of these newspapers was the *Bihari*, which developed from the *Bihar Times*, founded in 1894. From April 1912 it was published daily. At the beginning of the war with Germany, when news was eagerly sought, it prospered; but it came to an end in 1917. The *Express*, a well-conducted paper which was financed by the Maharaja of Hathwa, appeared twice daily during the war; it afterwards became an evening newspaper, it ceased publication in May of 1922 but was again renewed in the following cold weather. Apart from the *Express*, the principal newspapers which are now published in Patna are the *Bihar Herald* and the *Searchlight*, written in English; and the *Siksha*, which is written in Hindi.

CHAPTER IV.

RELIGIONS.

THE history of religion in Patna has a special interest, as this district was the early home both of Buddhism and of Jainism. A great part of Buddha's life was spent at Rajgir, and there the first great Buddhist Council was held. Several centuries before the commencement of the Christian era, Buddhism had become the religion of the royal house, and in later days the district was a centre from which Buddhist learning radiated and Buddhist missionaries penetrated to distant parts of Asia. Patna also witnessed the rise and development of Jainism; at Pawapuri its founder Mahavira died; and it was from this district that in the fourth century B.C. the Jain order began to spread over India. Buddhism as an active form of faith has passed away, but there are still traces of its influence in a few popular superstitions; and though Jainism has an insignificant number of adherents, the sacred shrines of the land of its birth still attract pilgrims from all parts. Patna again contains the birth-place of the great Sikh leader Guru Govind Singh, one of the most sacred of all spots in the eyes of his followers; the same city was the headquarters of one of the earliest Christian Missions in Hindustan; and in later times it was the centre of the Wahabi propaganda. Throughout all these religious movements the Hinduism of the great bulk of the people has persisted, varied by many primitive superstitions and quaint observances. GENERAL ASPECTS.

1,412,233 persons, or 89 per cent. of the total population are Hindus, while 158,438, or ten per cent. are Muhammadans. The latter are therefore a comparatively small minority; but many of the leading families of the district, especially in Patna city, are Muhammadan. Christians number 3,175; and there are also a few Jains and Sikhs. Census figures (1921).

The great majority of the Hindus of Patna are uneducated men of low caste who know but little of the higher side of their religion. Reverence for Brahmans and the worship of the orthodox Hindu gods are universal, but, as a matter of HINDUISM. Popular beliefs.

every-day practice, the ordinary villager endeavours to propitiate the evil spirits and godlings, which he and his ancestors have worshipped from time immemorial. Most of these are regarded as malignant spirits, who produce illness in the family and sickness among the cattle, if not appeased. They affect the ordinary life of the peasant far more directly and vitally than the regular Hindu gods; and consequently, the great mass of the illiterate Hindus, as well as some of the most ignorant Muhammadans, are careful to make periodical offerings to them. They form no part of the orthodox Hindu pantheon, but the villagers give them a kind of brevet rank; and for practical purposes they are the gods most feared and therefore most worshipped by the majority of Hindus. There is no space here to give a full account of the various manifestations of this worship, and all that can be attempted is to mention a few instances of local deities and religious observances; some of these observances, such as the totemistic worship of wolves by Kahars, have been already referred to in the preceding chapter.

As a rule, it may be said that the spirits and godlings of this popular religion are evil and malignant; but there is one notable exception, a goddess of the Kurmis, named Bandi Mai, who, it is reported, "is believed to be very kind-hearted and does not easily lose her temper." Goats, cakes and sweetmeats are offered to her; and in some villages a gold or silver coin is placed on the mound of earth which serves as an altar. Fresh coins are added at every marriage ceremony, and when there is a large number, they are strung together and the necklace thus formed is put round the lucky bridegroom's neck. Such a genial spirit is very rare; and the majority are of a malicious nature like Naika, a newly deified spirit, who came into existence about seventy years ago. The genesis of this spirit was as follows. A villager, it is said, was possessed by an evil spirit, and on an exorcist being called in, the spirit speaking through the man's mouth declared that he was a new-comer who was desirous of worship; if this was not given, he would bring great calamities on the whole family. The man's family thereupon deified this spirit, and this worship spreading, Naika became a god of the Kandus, Tatwas and other low castes.

Another curious example of deification is that of Amasan Bibi, who is believed to have been originally a skilful lady doctor. She is now invoked by women to cure the sick, and it is common to call upon her name when administering medicine, and to place the cup, after it is empty, inverted on the ground. The custom is to take a small piece of earth, wave it thrice round the patient's head, and keep it in a small niche in the house; on recovery, sweetmeats equal in weight to this piece of earth are offered to Amasan Bibi. Goraiya is a specially popular godling in Patna. He is a male hero of Dusadh origin, who is said to have been a bandit chief. In the songs sung in his honour he is spoken of as a great warrior who came from Delhi with a few followers, and died fighting at Mehnawan near Sherpur in this district, where his chief shrine still is. He is now worshipped throughout the district by the low castes, and even by some members of the high castes, such as Babhans. The usual representation of Goraiya is a stone or mound of earth under a tree outside the village, at which offerings of goats, sweetmeats, milk and *ghi* are made, to be taken away afterwards, by the Dusadhs. A similar deified hero is Amar Singh, a Rajput who lived near Barh in a village of which all the other inhabitants were Mallahs. He was killed by them out of envy, and from that time haunted the village and tormented the Mallahs, until they promised to worship him. He is now revered throughout the district, and is propitiated by sacrifices of goats under a *pipal* tree, the head of the goat being thrown into some river. Another local deity is Ganinath, whose temple is at Nawada in the Barh subdivision.

Hindus have also adopted some religious customs from the lower class of Muhammadans. As instances of this may be mentioned the practice observed occasionally by Hindus of launching paper boats on the Ganges, after a marriage or the birth of a child, in honour of Khwaja Khizr, and the worship of Panch Pir by the Kalwars of Barh and by low castes such as Kahars, Goalas, Kandus and Kumars; it is noticeable that among the five personages who in Patna are revered as the Panch Pir are two with Hindu names, viz., Sahaja, who is identified with Mahamaya, and Ajab Hathile, who is regarded as the same as Hanuman.

Worship of Kali.

Of the more orthodox deities of the Hindu pantheon the most popular is Kali, whose chief temple is in Patna city at Kalisthan near Mangles' tank. In her various forms she is worshipped by all Hindus at all times of the year. In the form of Durga she is regarded as the tutelary goddess of the city, and there are two old shrines there dedicated to her under the name of Patan Devi, one in the Chauk and the other in 'Alamganj. Under the form of Sitala she is worshipped by all Hindus, from Brahmans down to Doms, whenever there is an epidemic of small-pox. When any one is attacked by the disease, a small piece of ground near the patient's bed is smeared with cow-dung and a fire is lit there, on which *ghi* is poured and incense burnt. A Mali is called in who sings songs in honour of Sitala, while the patient is given sweet-meats and fanned with a twig of the *nim*, which is her favourite tree.

The propitiation of Sitala is practically the only remedy resorted to on an outbreak of small-pox; and low class Hindus and Muhammadans are often afraid to have their children vaccinated lest they should incur her wrath. She is also the goddess of cholera, and whenever there is an outbreak, the people propitiate her by sprinkling in her name the entrance of their houses with *chhak* (water in which cardamom and cloves have been mixed), and the villagers subscribe to have hymns in her praise recited by the Brahmans. In the same spirit the godling Bighin Mai, who is regarded as Kali's attendant, is worshipped at cross-roads during epidemics; a pit is dug and a fire lit in it, sweetmeats are placed there and incense burnt, while the people all sing hymns in her honour.

Another peculiar form of Kali worship consists of what are known as *khappar* processions. Whenever there is an epidemic of disease, the village *ojhas* or exorcists start out carrying earthen pots in which incense is burning. Followed by the villagers, they proceed in the direction of Calcutta with deafening cries of *Kali Mai ki jai*, and leave the pots and burning incense in the next village. The inhabitants of each village in turn then take them on. The most noted temples of Sitala in the district are at Agam Kuan near the Gulzarbagh railway station and at Maghra in the Bihar sub-division, to both of which the relatives or friends of small-pox stricken patients flock to invoke Sitala to grant a cure or at least to mitigate the virulence of the disease.

It must not be supposed that demonolatry of the type described above monopolizes the religious life of the ignorant

Hindus of the district. The same village will contain a temple of Siva or Vishnu with its regular Brahman priest, as well as the little mound of earth, the tree, the block, or the stone, which marks the haunt of the evil spirit. The worship of both goes on side by side, and the same man will make his little offerings to the Gram Devata or village god whom the Brahman does not recognize, and to the orthodox gods of Brahmanical worship.

Sheo Narayanis.

In concluding this sketch of Hindu popular religion, reference may be made to the two sects known as Sheo Narayanis and Kaulas. *The Sheo Narayanis are a small sect founded about two centuries ago by a Rajput named Sheo Narayan of Ghazipur. They believe in one formless God, forbid idolatry, and venerate their original Guru, whom they regard as an incarnation of the Almighty. The sacred book of the sect is known as the Sabda-Sant or Guru Granth. It contains moral precepts and declares that salvation is to be attained only by unswerving faith in God, control over the passions, and implicit obedience to the teachings of the Guru. Their great annual festival is on the fifth night after the new moon of Magh, when they assemble in the house of one of their fraternity, and sing songs and read extracts from the Guru Granth. When a man wishes to become a Sheo Narayani, he selects one of the sect, belonging to a caste not inferior to his own, who imparts to him the *mantra* of initiation. He is then enjoined to have faith in God (Bhagwan) and the original Guru, and is given a certificate of admission. This is done in the presence of several members of the sect, whose names and addresses are noted in the certificate. The Sheo Narayanis bury their dead, and one of the great inducements to join the fraternity is said to be the knowledge that they will give a decent burial to their comrades when they die, and will not allow their bodies to be touched by sweepers. The ordinary caste restrictions are observed, save only in the case of the extremists who adopt an ascetic life. In this district Sheo Narayanis are now only found among the lowest classes, and are declining in numbers. There is one considerable colony of Chamars in Patna city; the remainder are Dusadhs and Mallahs, with a few Kurmis and Kandus. Their numbers are, however, inconsiderable.

* Bengal Census Report, 1901.

Kaulas.

The Kaulas are one of the sects professing Saktism. Starting with the premise that all things are the manifestation of one universal spirit, the sect holds as its principal tenet that nothing is common or unclean. Thus, on the one hand, the Kaulas deny the distinctions of caste, on the other, they partake of things commonly regarded as unclean. The denial of caste does not extend, however, beyond the meetings of the sect, when members of all classes eat and drink together. Even at these meetings, it is a Brahman who officiates, as in any orthodox sect; no special *tilak* is worn, only the ordinary round *sindur* mark of the Kali worshipper; and it is expressly laid down that outside the meetings of the sect each man falls into his own caste. The five essentials of worship, which always takes place at night, are fish, flesh, wine, mystical gestures with the fingers (*mudra*), and sexual intercourse. In practice, however, the fourth essential is taken to mean an edible of a round shape, such as *laddu*, *puri* or *kachauri*. They use incantations known as *kil*, *kawach* and *argala*, these being a kind of auxiliary spell prefixed to the recitation of a *mantra* either to give it efficacy or to avoid the evil which might result from some error or misquotation. *Kil* and *argala* (*i.e.*, nail and bolt) are of the former class and unlock, as it were, the efficacy of the Sastras; *kawach* is the 'armour' which protects against misuse. About 1850 a certain Pandit, named Subhankar Misr, from Benares gave a great impetus to the sect in Patna City, but the members are now on the decline. It is, however, impossible to obtain figures, as secrecy is one of the rules of the sect.

MUHAMMADANS.

The lower classes of Muhammadans in the district are deeply infected with Hindu superstitions, especially those regarding sickness and disease. As a rule, their knowledge of the faith they profess seldom extends beyond the three cardinal doctrines of the unity of God, the mission of Muhammad, and the truth of the Koran. Apart too from Hindu superstitions, there are certain practices not based on the Koran which are common even among the more educated Musalmans.

Veneration of saints.

The most common among these is the adoration of departed Pirs or saints, of whom there are several in Patna. The *dargahs* or tombs of these Pirs are places of pilgrimage to which many persons resort for the cure of disease or the exorcism of evil spirits, or to obtain the fulfilment of some cherished wish. At Bihar there are the *dargahs* of Mallik Ibrahim Bayu and Hazrat Makhdum Shah Sharif-ud-din, the tomb of the latter being held in special veneration by the Muhammadans, who assemble there at the anniversary of the death of the saint on the 5th Shawwal. At Jethuli the *dargahs* of Shihab-ud-din Jagjaut and Shah Adam Sufi are also places of pilgrimage, a fair being held there on the 21st Zikad. In Patna there are the shrines of four Pirs called Mansur, Maruf, Jafar, and Mahdi, and also the shrine of Shah Arzani, which is the site of another large gathering. At Maner again are the tombs of the famous saint Makhdum Yahia and of Shah Daulat, and here two *melas* are held every year—one on the anniversary of the saint's death and the other in commemoration of the wedding of Ghazi Mian.

Ghazi Mian's fair.

Ghazi Mian was the nephew of Mahmud of Ghazni, and the leader of one of the early invasions of Oudh. After performing prodigies of valour, he was killed in a battle with the Hindus at Bahraich in 1034 A.D. when he was only nineteen years old. He is claimed as one of the first martyrs of Islam in India, and is the type of youth and militant valour. His untimely fate has led to his veneration, and in this district the annual fair in his honour is one of the greatest gatherings in the year. It is held on the banks of the tank at Maner, and is resorted to chiefly by the lower orders of Hindus and Muhammadans. It is a bacchanalian festival or carnival like the Saturnalia, and the consumption of toddy is considerable. A mock marriage procession proceeds from the town to the tank, attended with music, and carrying earthen pitchers filled with toddy and banners called the *jhanda* of Ghazi Mian. On this occasion eunuchs assemble, and perform the ceremonies devolving on parents of the bridegroom and the bride. At a shrine on a mound east of the rest-house a strange sight is seen in the morning of the day on which the *mela* is held. Women and girls supposed to be possessed by devils prostrate themselves before the shrine in the hope of being cured. They get into an ecstatic state, and casting themselves into a trance, excite the fit to which they are liable; incense is then applied to their nostrils, and they recover. The cure of diabolical possession is attributed to the healing power of the shrine, and hysteria and catalepsy are ascribed to the malignant acts of genii.

Malliks. The Malliks of this district claim descent from Saiyid Ibrahim Bayu and his soldiers, mostly his own tribesmen and relations. It is said that he was a general of Ala-ud-din Ghori and was deputed to put down an insurrection in this part of the country. He planted garrisons in various villages and his soldiers took Hindu women as their wives and settled there. He was given the title of Mallik on account of his brilliant victories, and the name was subsequently applied to the community which he and his soldiers founded. Ibrahim Bayu's tomb is on the Pirpahari hill at Bihar, and is a famous place of pilgrimage.

Sunnis and Shiahs. The greater number of the Muhammadans are Sunnis, but there is a small minority of Shiahs. These two sects, as a rule, live amicably, and the present state of affairs is a pleasant contrast to that prevailing a century ago when the Muharram was invariably marked by disputes among the rival sects, which generally ended in rioting, bloodshed and murder.

The Wahabi movement. No account of the Patna Muhammadans would be complete without a reference to the Wahabi movement.* The Wahabis are so-called after Muhammad Wahab, who was born before the beginning of the 18th century in Nejd, a province of Central Arabia, and founded a sect of Muhammadans who rejected the glosses of the Imams and denied the authority of the Sultan, made comparatively light of the authority of Muhammad, forbade the offering of prayers to any prophet or saint, and insisted on the necessity of waging war against infidels. In the beginning of the nineteenth century the Wahabi doctrines appear to have been carried into India by pilgrims returning from Mecca, and Saiyid Ahmed Shah of Rai Bareli became the leader of the sect. In 1820 he travelled south from Delhi in order to preach reform to the people of India, and incite them to join in a *jihad*, or religious war, against the Sikhs, who had oppressed the Muhammadans of the Punjab, and forbidden them the free exercise of their religion. On his way to Bengal he arrived at Patna, accompanied by a large fleet of boats carrying upwards of five hundred enthusiastic disciples, and there enrolled a number of followers, including Wilayat Ali, Inayat Ali, Shah Muhammad Hussain, Ilahi Bakhsh, and his son Ahmed Ulla of

* For a more detailed account, see *The Wahabis in India*, by J. O'Kinealy, Calcutta Review, 1870, from which this sketch has been mainly compiled.

Sadikpur. He then departed for Calcutta; but before leaving appointed Shah Muhammad Hussain, Wilayat Ali and Inayat 'Ali as his caliphs or lieutenants at Patna, to enrol followers in his name, and gather supplies for the war against the Sikhs. In 1823 he was joined by Shah Muhammad Hussain with a large party of enthusiasts, and at a general meeting of his caliphs permanent arrangements were made to forward supplies of men and money to support the enterprise.

In accordance with this resolution, his caliphs in Bengal commenced to make strenuous efforts to support him; Patna was fixed on as the headquarters, and Shah Muhammad Hussain was acknowledged as the local chief caliph. Numerous books and pamphlets were printed for circulation, and thus fortified, this little band of fanatics went forth to urge the Muhammadans of India to unite in one body and carry on a *jihad* for the conquest of India, to gather recruits and funds for the purpose, and to insist on the claim of Saiyid Ahmed to the title of Imam Mahdi. Wilayat Ali became the apostle of the creed in Bengal, and Inayat Ali assisted him there for a short time, but his mission lay chiefly in Central India, Hyderabad and Bombay. In 1827 Saiyid 'Ahmed commenced a *jihad* against the Sikhs, liberal supplies of men and money being sent him from Bengal, and the flame of war broke out along the frontier. Peshawar was taken in 1830, and a great religious war for the conquest of the Punjab was proclaimed, for which a body of Wahabis hurried up from Patna; but in 1831 Saiyid Ahmed was killed in a battle against the Sikhs.

Wilayat Ali and Inayat Ali of Patna now became prominent leaders of the fanatical Wahabis, who after some years' fighting, for which the Patna branch furnished enthusiastic recruits, firmly established their dominion over a large extent of territory along the left bank of the Indus, stretching from Haripur to Kagan and from Sittana to Kashmir. The formation of a new Sikh power under the protection of the British Government, however, made it impossible for them to retain possession of their conquests, and in 1847 they surrendered to the British agent at Haripur. Wilayat Ali and his brother, Inayat Ali, were sent in custody to their homes at Patna, and bound down in bail of ten thousand rupees not to leave it for four years, but no steps were taken to prevent their doing so. Inayat 'Ali shortly afterwards assumed the command of the Wahabi colony at Sittana and took active measures to carry out his long cherished design of waging war against the British; but his expedition ended in complete defeat, and though Inayat Ali escaped with the main body of the Wahabis, the rear guard under Kurram Ali, a tailor of Dinapore, was cut to pieces by the British troops.

This movement was engineered from Patna, as was clearly proved by some letters seized in 1852 by the Punjab authorities. It was found that an organized conspiracy to tamper with the Native Infantry at Rawalpindi had originated at Patna, and that Wahabi leaders there, among whom was Ahmed Ulla, were collecting money and forwarding arms and supplies to the Wahabis encamped at Sittana for the purpose of the *jihad*. A search was made by the Patna Magistrate for treasonable correspondence, but the conspirators had been put on their guard and the correspondence destroyed. He reported, however, that the Wahabi sect was on the increase, and the *jihad* being preached in the houses of Wilayat Ali, Ahmed Ulla and his father Ilahi Baksh; the Wahabis were in league with the police; and Ahmed Ulla had assembled six or seven hundred men, and was prepared to resist further enquiry and raise the standard of revolt. All that appears to have been done was to order that the conspirators should be watched, though it was clearly proved that Ahmed Ulla and other residents at Patna were forwarding arms, supplies and recruits to the frontier fanatics in furtherance of their creed. The main tenets of this creed were as follows:—Firmly convinced that Saiyid Ahmed would re-appear, destroy all infidels, and subvert the British rule in India, they believed that the first duty of every true Musalman was to further the good cause to the utmost of his power, and assist in the *jihad* or holy war. He should at once join the "leader of the fighters for the faith" (*Amir-ul-mujahid-ud-din*), who was at that time Ahmed Ulla. All who died fighting for the faith would be martyrs (*shahid*); all who killed infidels would be heroes (*ghazi*); and those who shrunk from the fight and gave not their wealth in support of the crescentade were accursed (*nari*).

During the Mutiny the Wahabis rose, as related in chapter II, but the rising was quickly put down, and their power for mischief destroyed by the prompt action of Tayler in arresting Ahmed Ulla and the other Wahabi leaders. On the supersession of Tayler, Ahmed Ulla appears to have gained the confidence of his successor, who described him as "a mere bookman," and he was eventually made a Deputy Collector. The intrigues of the Patna Wahabis still went on, and in 1863 a frontier war broke out as the result of the crusade preached by them. The enquiries set on foot during and after the campaign brought to light the existence of an extensive conspiracy; eleven Wahabis were arrested, tried and found guilty. of whom five were residents of Patna; and further enquiry showing that the prime mover of the conspiracy in Bengal was Ahmed Ulla, he was arrested, tried and sentenced to transportation for life in 1865. The removal of Ahmed Ulla did not, however, put an end to the machinations of the Wahabis, for in 1868-69 it was again discovered that a *jihad* had for some time been preached, and collections in aid of the frontier fanatics made on a regularly organized system, agents being stationed all over the country. At Patna seven men were arrested and put on their trial; five were convicted and sentenced to transportation for life with forfeiture of property, including Amir Khan, a rich banker and money-lender, who was the most influential of the conspirators. An appeal to the High Court resulted in the sentence on him and one other only being confirmed; but these trials broke the power of the Wahabis.

Their modern representatives have discarded the designation of Wahabis, as it has become a term of reproach, and prefer to style themselves Ahl-i-Hadis. The latter name means people of the tradition, and the main characteristic of the sect is that they interpret for themselves the Hadis, *i.e.*, the traditional sayings of Muhammad not embodied in the Koran, and do not follow any particular Imam.

JAINISM.

Though Jainism has very few local adherents, there are some very sacred Jain shrines and places of pilgrimage which are visited every year by crowds of pilgrims. These shrines are at Patna, Rajgir, and Pawapuri. At Patna there are two temples in the quarter known as Kamaldah near the railway station. One, built on a high mound of brick ruins, bears an inscription stating that in 1848 (Sambat) the congregation dwelling at Pataliputra began the building of the temple of the illustrious Sthulabhadra. This saint was the patriarch of the early Jain church in the first part of the third century B.C., at the time when the canon of the Swetambar sect was collected by the council of Pataliputra. According to local tradition, he died at this spot, which is now a favourite place of pilgrimage amongst the Jains. In the lower temple is a shrine dedicated to Sudarsan, where the attendant priest paints every morning a fresh footprint in saffron on a block of stone, and near the door is a *pinda* or food offering to the fierce deity, Bhairab. Sudarsan is the hero of the legend given below at page 170, but according to the Hindus' account, he was father of Patali, the mythical founder of the city, the classic name of which is preserved in this inscription.

Rajgir, the ancient centre of Buddhism, is another sacred place of the Jains, who come there in great numbers to visit the shrines crowning each hill. These shrines contain numerous Jain images and generally a stone with the footprints of some Jain Tirthankar. Of all the places in the district, however, the most sacred is Pawapuri. Here a temple called Thalmandar marks the spot where Mahavira died, and another temple called Jalmandar stands in the midst of a great tank on the spot where he was burned. No living thing is killed in this sacred lake; when fish die, their bodies are carefully brought ashore and buried; and to this day the priests still chant hymns in praise of Mahavira after the lapse of 2,400 years.

SIKHS.

Patna city was the birth-place of Guru Govind Singh, the great founder of the Sikh military brotherhood, who was born in 1660 in a house near the Chauk. The spot is now marked by a temple called Har Mandir, containing his cradle and shoes and the holy book of the Sikhs, the Granth Saheb, which is said to contain the Guru's name written by himself with the point of an arrow. There is a small *sangat* or subsidiary place of worship attached to this temple; and another *sangat*, which is in the hands of the Nanakshahis, contains a sacred tree believed to have sprung up miraculously from a tooth-pick placed in the ground by Govind Singh. The temple is one of the four great sacred places of the Sikhs, who visit it on pilgrimage. The pilgrims are bound to appear before the Guru Granth Saheb on the first day of entering the town, and offer *ardas* or *kara parshad, i.e.*, sweetmeats specially prepared for the purpose. The Mahanth of this temple must be an Akali *pardeshi, i.e.*, he must belong to the puritanical sect of Akalis, and not be a native of Patna, a salutary rule preventing the funds of the temple from becoming the hereditary perquisite of any one family.

CHRISTIAN MISSIONS.

*The Jesuits had a settlement in Patna in 1620, whither they had come at the invitation of the Nawab Mukarrab Khan, who had been baptized at Goa, but did not make public profession of Christianity. This Jesuit Mission was probably short-lived; but early in the eighteenth century a permanent settlement was made as a result of the decision to establish a mission in Tibet which was entrusted to the Capuchin Fathers. In 1704 Father Joseph of Ascóli died at Patna, and in 1706 six Capuchin Fathers came there on their way to Lhasa. One was left behind at Patna, where in 1713 he erected a hospice, and Patna continued to be the basis of the Tibet Mission till 1745, when the heroic Father Horace of Penna left Lhasa and returned to Patan in Nepal, in despair at the orders that he and his companions might preach only on condition that they declared the Tibetan religion to be good and perfect. The mission hospice at Patna was destroyed on the 25th June 1763, when the English made their attack on the city, and the priests narrowly escaped being murdered by Mir Kasim Ali's soldiers during the fighting which ensued. The church was despoiled and profaned, and three fathers found praying there, one of whom was the Superior, John of Brescia, were assaulted, stripped naked, and nearly killed. The records state that the church was reopened on the 31st July 1763, and that divine service continued without interruption; the first entry is of a burial on the 14th November 1763, *i.e.*, some days after the English recaptured the city.

Father Joseph of Roveto, one of the fathers attacked by Mir Kasim's soldiers, was now appointed Prefect Apostolic of the Nepal Mission, in which Patna was then included; and owing to his exertions the present church was built on the site of the old hospice (1772-79), Signor Tiretto of Venice being the architect.

In 1845 Patna was made the headquarters of a Vicariate Apostolic; in 1886, on the establishment of the hierarchy in India, it was constituted part of the newly formed Diocese of Allahabad, but a separate bishopric of Patna has now been created. The mission has been entrusted to the Capuchin Fathers of the Province of Bologna, and the Fathers are in charge of the Catholic communities at the five stations of

* The foundation of the Jesuit mission of Patna (1620), *Catholic Herald of India*, August 22, 1906.

Patna, Khagaul, Dinapore, Bankipore and Kurji. At Bankipore there is a convent, which manages two orphanages, one for Indian girls, and the other for European and Eurasian girls, to which a boarding and day school is attached. At Kurji there is a large European boys' school maintained by the Irish Christian Brothers.

The other Christian missions in the district are of modern growth; they are the London Baptist Missionary Society, the London Baptist Zanana Mission and the Zanana Bible and Medical Mission. The London Baptist Mission has stations at Dinapore, Bankipore and Patna City, and employs a staff of four missionaries, an assistant home missionary and several evangelists. Its chief work is evangelistic, but it also keeps up a boarding school for Christians at Bankipore and several elementary schools. The London Baptist Zanana Mission, with headquarters at Bankipore, has four missionaries, who are aided in their work by several bible women. In addition to evangelistic work, it maintains a boarding school for Christian girls at Bankipore and two day schools for non-Christians. The Zanana Bible and Medical Mission possesses a well-equipped hospital, the "Duchess of Teck Hospital" in Patna city, the staff consisting of two lady doctors, two European lady superintendents and several well-trained nurses. Its work is partly evangelistic and partly medical.

CHAPTER V.

PUBLIC HEALTH.

VITAL STATISTICS.

A COMPARISON of vital statistics for any lengthy period is rendered impossible by the changes in the system of registering births and deaths which have taken place from time to time. In 1869 the duty of reporting deaths was imposed on the village *chaukidars*, and in 1876 the system was extended to births; but the returns received were so incomplete that they were soon discontinued, and, except in towns, deaths alone were registered until 1892, when the collection of statistics of births as well as of deaths was ordered, and the system now in vogue was introduced. Under this system vital occurrences are reported by the *chaukidars* to the police, and the latter submit monthly returns to the Civil Surgeon, by whom statistics for the whole district are prepared.

So far as they can be accepted—and they are sufficiently accurate for the purpose of calculating the approximate growth of the population and of showing the relative healthiness or unhealthiness of different years—the returns submitted since 1892 show that conditions were normal up to the year 1900, the recorded births exceeding the deaths by 22,762. But in January 1900 plague appeared in epidemic form, and by the close of the year the number of deaths reported as due to it was 23,022. The disease continued to rage throughout the early years of the present century, carrying off 114,000 persons during the first five years, and evidently being largely responsible for the decrease of population which appeared at the census of 1911. The following table shows the birth and death rates per 1,000 in the district, and in the principal towns, during the last ten years :—

Year.	District.		Patna City.		Bihar town.		Dinapore town.		Barh town.	
	Births.	Deaths.	Births.	Deaths.	Births.	Deaths.	Births.	Deaths.	Births.	Deaths.
1913 ...	41·18	33·04	23·24	29·33	42·67	26·34	32·97	21·01	28·56	26·59
1914 ...	40·47	34·52	19·95	34·46	37·23	27·31	35·26	28·62	30·97	30·86
1915 ...	41·79	35·84	24·63	23·07	37·58	33·14	35·52	26·62	36·44	35·78
1916 ...	40·92	33·51	23·99	24·94	39·00	33·22	36·00	33·58	37·64	35·34
1917 ...	40·96	43·43	24·98	30·86	33·62	35·50	36·53	41·57	39·72	37·31
1918 ...	37·42	63·07	24·10	32·83	31·06	37·11	31·71	31·33	34·14	38·30
1919 ...	31·76	31·17	23·26	23·84	26·03	18·38	31·65	24·50	31·73	29·76
1920 ...	35·19	34·39	27·12	26·08	26·43	22·67	36·94	28·17	29·22	29·22
1921 ...	36·34	47·54	26·60	32·27	21·21	19·83	35·29	29·78	31·05	45·85
1922 ...	37·36	23·40	31·75	22·52	18·71	18·68	33·71	22·21	42·76	28·04

The high mortality of 1918, when 101,526 deaths were registered, is to be attributed to the influenza epidemic of that year, which principally affected the rural districts. The mortality of this year was higher than in 1905 (58·74), when plague was raging in the district. In 1921 there was an epidemic of cholera which alone caused 18,745 deaths. The last decennial period is marked throughout by comparatively low death-rates in thetowns, by comparison with the earlier years of plague epidemics. During the quinquennium 1901—1905 the average death-rate in the four towns was 61 per mille.

Infant mortality.

During the ten years from 1912 to 1921 infant mortality in the district varied from 204 per thousand births in 1915 to 258 in 1918. There was a marked improvement in 1922 when the deaths fell to 170 in a thousand births. This high death-rate is attributed by the Civil Surgeon to ignorance of the ordinary rules of health, overcrowding, poverty, and the employment for labour cases of dirty and ignorant *Chamains*.

Common diseases of the district.

The Civil Surgeon has furnished the following note on the common diseases of the district :—

The diseases most prevalent in this district are 'fever', kala-azar, dysentery, cholera, plague, ankylostomiasis, trachoma and cataract. The term 'fever' includes many diseases such as malaria, pneumonia, enteric, and influenza,

Kala-azar is endemic throughout the district and it is probable that the condition formerly known as malarial cacopexia or chronic malaria was really this disease. Since the introduction of new methods of treatment ninety per cent. of cases recover, whereas formerly about ninety-five per cent. were fatal. Ankylostomiasis or hook-worm infection is exceedingly common throughout the district. It has been estimated that seventy per cent. of the village population will on examination show this infection. In the majority of cases however few, if any, symptoms are present, or they are not noticed. A very great improvement in the general health and output of work is observed when these cases are properly treated. Cases in municipal areas are fewer. The reason lies in the insanitary habits of villagers, who defæcate in the fields around the villages and infect the earth. Until this system ceases there is no possibility of eradicating this disease, because the hook-worm gains entrance to the body through the skin, especially the skin of the feet.

Plague.

Plague appears to be less virulent now and there are fewer epidemics than formerly. This disease seems to be following the usual course of epidemic diseases and it is to be hoped that in a few years it will disappear.

Water-borne diseases.

Since the introduction of a municipal water-supply the incidence of water-borne diseases has much decreased in the area of its distribution. Cholera and dysentery are however still common in the rural areas, due to contaminated water supplies.

Eye diseases.

The most common diseases of the eye are trachoma (granular lids) and cataract. The former is attributable to dust and flies combined with ignorance and poverty. The latter although common is much less so than in the upper provinces, probably owing to the fact that the longer rainy season provides more green vegetation and there is less glare.

Vaccination.

Vaccination which was in the past compulsory only in municipal areas was extended to the area under the jurisdiction of the Patna and Phulwari thanas of Patna District in 1915-16, but it is still regarded with some disfavour by certain castes and sects such as illiterate Brahmans, Rajputs and Marwaris and others. There is great opposition to the early vaccination of infants, and a strong popular prejudice against the operation being performed on children under one year of age.

In places where the Vaccination Act has not been enforced there is considerable active opposition to vaccination on account of deep-rooted faith in God as manifested in "Shakti" or energy as curing diseases. The people say that if they do not follow the dictates of the Goddess 'Jagdamba,' and if they rely on any medicine other than those prescribed by her, they will be incurring her displeasure, which they believe may lead to loss of life and property. Generally speaking vaccination is not objected to under normal conditions.

In 1921-22 the total number of persons successfully vaccinated was 62,981 (11,115 in compulsory areas and 51,866 in non-compulsory areas) representing 39·32 per mille of the population; and protection was afforded to 623 per thousand of infants under one year of age.

The annual number of successful operations in the preceding five years averaged 42·48 per mille of the population. In spite of some opposition to vaccination, Patna District has shown better results than any other district in the province.

SANITATION. The introduction of sanitary reforms in rural areas is a matter of great difficulty. Though strict in attending to their personal cleanliness, the villagers live in complete indifference to their unhealthy surroundings, and the sense of public cleanliness is wanting. The village site is generally dirty, crowded with cattle, and badly drained. The houses themselves are dark, ill-ventilated huts, built of mud dug out of some hole in the immediate vicinity, which becomes a stagnant filthy pool, the receptacle of all kinds of dirt. The wells are not properly protected, and the drainage of the houses is apt to find its way into them; while the tanks are used indiscriminately for cooking and bathing. In spite, however, of the apathy of the people and the tenacity with which they cling to customs injurious to health, many sanitary reforms have been effected by the Local Boards, which in this respect serve as models to the rest of the Province. Systematic operations have been taken in hand to keep the large villages in a sanitary condition by filling up unhealthy hollows, clearing away rank vegetation, and removing filth; and sweepers are employed in the larger villages under the control of a village headman or respectable resident. In the year 1919-20 the expenditure of the District Board on sanitation was Rs. 18,527.

In the towns the problem of sanitation is more difficult owing to the congested area which has to be dealt with. The houses are closely packed together along the main streets and in narrow side lanes; the better class of houses are built with little attempt to secure ventilation; while the majority are made of mud, built on a slightly raised floor and overcrowded with inmates. The Municipal Act gives the authorities power to deal with matters connected with the water-supply, drainage, street cleaning, sewage, etc.; and great improvements have been effected since its introduction in 1884. But the time has been too short to introduce all the reforms required, and the funds at the disposal of the municipalities are too limited to enable them to execute any large schemes which would completely remedy the insanitary conditions produced by many centuries of neglect.

MEDICAL INSTITUTIONS. The Patna General Hospital and the hospitals at Gulzarbagh, Gardanibagh, and Bikram are state institutions, while institutions supported from Local Funds are the hospitals at Patna City, Barh, Bihar, and Dinapore; and the dispensaries at Maner, Punpun, Khusrupur, Karai-Pasarai, Mokameh, Rajgir, Bharatpura, Khagaul, Masaurhi, Chandi, Islampur, Fatuha, Bakhtiarpur, Harnaut, and Paliganj. The statistics of attendance show that the popularity of the European method of treatment continues to grow. In 1895 the number of patients treated was 119,000 ; in 1905 it was 160,000 ; while by 1922 it rose to 257,000. The following table shows the number of patients treated, and the principal diseases treated, in hospitals of different classes during 1922 :—

Class of hospital.	In-patients.	Out-patients.	Cholera.	Plague.	Enteric fever.	Influenza.	Kala-azar.	Malaria.	Dysentery and diarrhœa.	Diseases of the eye.	Diseases of the ear.	Diseases of the skin.
Patna General Hospital.	3,020	41,856	45	...	132	701	1,343	5,681	1,104	3,645	3,201	5,017
Other Government hospitals.	...	42,518	5	...	34	378	63	10,183	1,746	2,411	3,373	4,952
Local Fund hospitals.	1,689	57,378	8	5	24	...	884	6,245	1,707	3,398	9,433	5,011
Dispensaries...	...	119,324	73	48	46	674	1,309	28,567	5,895	7,109	14,742	14,246

10,636 surgical operations were performed at the Patna General Hospital during the year. The number of surgical operations performed in other Government hospitals was 1,466; in hospitals supported from Local Funds 13,226; and and in dispensaries 5,657. Expenditure on the Patna General Hospital during 1922 was Rs. 1,24,200, and on other Government hospitals Rs. 13,740. The expenditure during the year on hospitals and dispensaries supported from Local Funds was Rs. 1,01,700.

CHAPTER VI.

AGRICULTURE.

GENERAL CONDITIONS.

Natural divisions.

THE district may be divided into four broadly marked tracts, of which the first three are comprised within the Bankipore, Barh and Dinapore subdivisions, while the fourth consists of the Bihar subdivision. These areas are, (1) the *diara* lands along the Ganges; (2) a long narrow strip of high land along the Ganges; (3) a broad belt of low-lying country south of the upland strip just mentioned; and (4) the Bihar subdivision. In each of these tracts agricultural conditions vary considerably, and a brief account will therefore be given of each.

Diara lands.

The *diara* lands, which are found in the bed of the Ganges, stretch along the whole of the north of the district. The manner in which they are formed and destroyed, as the main stream of the river changes its course, has been described in the account of the Ganges which is given in chapter I above. When silt has been deposited, the soil of the *diara* is extremely fertile, and grows magnificent crops ; but if its growth is arrested by the river's altering its course so that the flood-water does not cover it during the second stage of its formation, it remains sandy and barren. These *diara* lands are the most fertile in the district; they grow *bhadoi* crops before the river rises and *rabi* crops in the cold weather, both yielding excellent harvests.

The up-land tract.

The second tract is situated between the permanent bank of the Ganges and the low-lying tract to the south, and comprises all the land lying north of the East Indian Railway line throughout the breadth of the district, with the exception of a small area in the extreme north-west which is liable to inundation in the rains. In this tract *bhadoi* and *rabi* crops are chiefly grown, though rice is also cultivated in some places, especially in the neighbourhood of the Patna-Gaya Canal between Khagaul and Dinapore.

The low-land tract.

The third tract comprises the remainder of the Dinapore, Bankipore and Barh subdivisions and may be further subdivided into three separate areas. The western portion receives artificial irrigation from the canal running for about forty miles near the western border of the district, which supplies the whole of the Bikram thana and parts of the Maner, Dinapore, Phulwari, and Masaurhi thanas. Further to the west the country is intersected by the Punpun and its affluents the Morhar and Dardha. These rivers are largely used for irrigation, but when the Ganges rises, their waters are forced back and the land is flooded. The third area consists of nearly the whole of the Barh subdivision and extends from the extreme east of the district to the south of Patna city. The lands comprised in this belt of country, which are known as *tal* lands, are subject to annual inundation from the Punpun and other rivers, which meander from west to east on their way to the Ganges. To the east, however, part of the Mokameh thana is served by irrigation works of the same kind as those constructed in the Bihar subdivision. The whole of this tract produces a comparatively small crop of *bhadoi* and rice, but usually yields a good *rabi* harvest.

Bihar subdivision.

The Bihar subdivision is divided into the hills in the south and the low country to the north. The whole subdivision is intersected by streams, which in the hot and cold weather contain little or no water, but at the time of heavy rain are filled from bank to bank. The greater part is provided with a system of irrigation works intended to store and distribute the water. Reservoirs called *ahars* are built, some of which are filled with rain-water and natural drainage, while others are replenished by damming the rivers. A number of artificial channels convey the water from the rivers to the reservoirs, and other small channels conduct it to the fields of the cultivators. These irrigation works protect the greater part of the subdivision from any general failure of the crops by drought, but there are two exceptions to the general rule, *viz.*, the Islampur thana (116 square miles) in the extreme south-west, and the south-east corner of the Bihar thana. The former thana contains few efficient irrigation works, and the Phalgu river, which traverses this area, has silted up. Much of the land is high and sandy; while some of it consists of sterile soil, impregnated with carbonate of soda. The latter tract, which is comprised within the Ashthawan jurisdiction, has also lost the means of irrigation which it formerly possessed, owing to the silting up of its river channels.

Generally speaking, four classes of soils are recognized, *viz.*, (1) *kewal*, which contains about seventy per cent. of clay; (2) *doras*, which is half clay and half sand; (3) *balsundri*, in which sand preponderates over clay; and (4) *diara* land; which may be either *doras* or *balsundri* (usually the latter) but which is enriched every year by a deposit of silt. Besides these, there is in some places a white soil called *rehra*, which is rendered more or less sterile by being impregnated with carbonate of soda (*reh*); when the impregnation is so great as to render it unculturable waste, it is known as *usar*. Soils.

Kewal soil, which is a species of hard stiff clay, opening out when dry in gaping fissures, is cultivated with rice; but it is also suitable for *rabi* crops, as it retains moisture for a long period and *rabi* has to depend, to a great extent, on sub-soil moisture. One variety of *kewal* in the Barh subdivision, known as *tal* land, is too deeply submerged during the rains to grow rice, the main product of this soil elsewhere at that season, but yields splendid *rabi* crops.

Doras soil, when low-lying, produces rice and *rabi* crops; while *bhadoi* and *rabi* crops, such as maize and *arhar*, are raised on it, if it is in the uplands. The richest *doras* soil consists of what is known as the *bhith* or *dih* land, *i.e.*, the belt near the village homesteads, which is better manured and more carefully cultivated than land at a distance. Here well irrigation is largely practised, and the most valuable crops, such as spices, potatoes and vegetables, are grown extensively.

Balsundri soil is a sandy loam, which grows *bhadoi* and *rabi* crops, such as *marua* and barley; and the same crops are raised on *diara* lands, but the favourite crop in the latter is the castor-oil plant.

For the *bhadoi* and late rice harvests the distribution most favourable to agriculture—the husbandman's ideal year—is when premonitory showers, falling in May or early in June, facilitate that spade husbandry which, to secure a really good crop, must precede ploughing operations. The rain in the end of June and in July should be heavy: then should come an interval of comparatively fair weather, in which weeding operations may be successfully prosecuted. The September rains must be heavy, shading off into fine weather with Rainfall.

October showers. On the sufficiency of the September rain, more than of any other month, depends the character of the winter rice crop. Finally periodic showers from December to February inclusive are essential to a good *rabi* harvest.

Irrigation.

The subject of irrigation will be dealt with more fully in the next chapter; and it will suffice here to say that the whole district depends largely on irrigation for its crops. In the headquarters and Dinapore subdivisions the Patna-Gaya Canal, a branch of the Son canal system, supplies a considerable area. In the Bihar subdivision the landlords and cultivators maintain a large number of private irrigation works fed partly by natural drainage and partly by the rivers flowing northwards from the Gaya district. The Barh subdivision relies almost entirely upon the floods from the Ganges and other rivers to fertilize the soil for the *rabi* crops and to supply moisture for its growth; and rice is very little grown there. Well irrigation is universal in the neighbourhood of villages, where spices and vegetables are grown.

Area under cultivation.

The net cropped area is 1,073,593 acres, 81 per cent. of the whole area of the district :—a higher proportion than is found in any other district of Bihar. The area on which more than one crop is grown is 336,927 acres or 31 per cent. of the net cropped area. The proportion of *dofasli* land may not appear large, by comparison with the districts of Tirhut; but much of the land which yields more than one crop is very valuable, yielding three or four crops in the year. This is particularly so in the high land south of the Ganges near Patna, where practically the whole area is twice-cropped, with the result that the proportion of twice-cropped land to net-cropped-area is in Phulwari thana 55 per cent. and in Dinapore thana 65 per cent.

Bhadoi crops.

The *bhadoi* crops require plenty of rain with intervals of bright sunshine to bring them to maturity, and constant weeding is necessary for a good harvest. The time of sowing depends on the breaking of the monsoon; if the rainfall is early, they are sown in the beginning of June; but they can be sown as late as the middle of July without the crop being lost. Harvesting usually extends from the 15th July to the 15th October.

Maize.

The principal *bhadoi* crop is maize or Indian corn (*zea mays*), known locally as *makai* or *jancra*, which is grown on

88,880 acres or nine per cent. of the normal net cropped area. It is sown in June and July and harvested in August and September. During the latter months the lofty bamboo platform, erected by the cultivator to serve as his watch-tower while the harvest is ripening, is a striking feature of the landscape; these platforms are erected because the crop has to be carefully protected from crows and jackals. Maize is very largely the poor man's food, being consumed in the form of *sattu*, while the cobs are parched and form a favourite article of diet.

Marua.

The *bhadoi* crop most extensively grown after maize is *marua* (*eleusine coracana*), which is raised on 20,800 acres, mostly in the south of the district in the Bihar subdivision. This is a valuable millet, which is sown at the commencement of the rainy season and cut at the end of it. It is partly sown broadcast and partly transplanted to ground that afterwards gives a winter crop. The grain is largely consumed by the poorer classes in the form of *sattu*, or is converted into flour and made into a coarse bread; in bad seasons, when the rice crop fails, it supports them till the spring crops have been harvested.

Bhadoi rice.

Bhadoi rice is a comparatively unimportant crop, covering only 8,000 acres. It is usually sown broadcast in June or July, and is harvested in August or September without being transplanted.

Janera and *kodo.*

Among other *bhadoi* crops are the millets commonly known as *janera* and *kodo*. *Janera* as a *bhadoi* crop covers 5,400 acres, while as an *aghani* crop it is grown on 18,348 acres. *Kodo* (10,440 acres) is usually sown on inferior land; it is chiefly found in the west of the district in the thanas of Bikram and Maner.

AGHANI CROPS. Rice.

The most important of the *aghani* crops is rice, which is grown on 385,700 acres, a little over one-third of the net cropped area. It is sown broadcast after the commencement of the rains in June or July on land selected for seed nurseries, which has previously been ploughed three or four times. After four or six weeks, when the young plants are about a foot high, they are generally transplanted; each plant is pulled out from the land, which is soft with standing water, and planted again in rows in flooded fields in which the soil has been puddled. The rice is then left to mature, with the aid of water, till towards the end of September. The water is then drained off and the fields are allowed to dry for fifteen days, and at the end of that time they are again flooded. It is this practice, known as *nigar*, which makes the rainfall, or failing that, irrigation essential to successful harvest. These late rains (the *Hathiya*) are the most important in the year, for not only are they required to bring the winter crops to maturity, but also to provide moisture for the sowing of the *rabi* crops. Should no rain fall at this period, and if water cannot be procured from artificial sources, the plants will wither and become only fit for fodder; but if seasonable showers fall or the crops are watered from *ahars*, *pains* or canals, the rice comes to maturity in November or December, and is then reaped. The greater portion of the rice crop is transplanted, but that on inferior lands is sown broadcast. In low-lying marshy lands sowing is commenced as early as April. When the rainfall is plentiful and the land is low enough to remain constantly under water, nothing but weeding is required. On higher lands, and in case of deficient rainfall, irrigation is necessary.

A noticeable feature of rice cultivation is the way in which it is conducted according to the lunar asterisms called *nakshatras*.* The seed-beds throughout the country are, if possible, sown within a period of 15 days, called the *Adra nakshatra* which lasts from about the 20th June to the 5th July. Transplantation from the seed-beds goes on during the *Punarbas*, *Pukh* and *Asres nakshatras* (18th July—15th August). The water on the fields in which the young plant has grown up after transplantation is regularly drained off in the *Utra nakshatra* (12th—25th September), a period when, as a rule, there is little rain; and after the exposure of the soil to the air and sun, the usual heavy rain of the *Hathiya nakshatra* (26th September—7th October) is awaited. After this, it is the universal custom to keep the fields wet during the *Chitra nakshatra* (8th—20th October); and at the commencement of the *Swati nakshatra*, (21st October—3rd

* The Hindu year is divided into 27 *nakshatras*, each representing a certain portion of the moon's path in the zodiac. The agricultural year is marked out by the position of the sun in these spaces; thus, when the cultivator says that he does anything in such and such a *nakshatra*, he means that he does so when the sun is in that particular section of the zodiac. In other words, agriculture follows the solar year.

November) they are again drained, and the paddy is left to itself till the *Bisakha nakshatra* (4th—15th November) when it is cut.

Although there are sometimes slight variations in the times of sowing and transplanting from those given above, the cultivators are always careful to drain off the water from the fields in the *Utra nakshatra*. It may be said that every cultivator begins, if he possibly can, to let off the water on the first day of that *nakshatra*, and this is done, without any hesitation, in the country commanded by the canals, because the cultivator looks to them to supply him with water, whether the *Hathiya* rain fails or not. It is generally agreed that after this draining (*nigar*) rice plants cannot exist for more than from fifteen to twenty days, unless watered, without rapid deterioration; and as no cultivator will take water till the *Hathiya nakshatra* has commenced, the Canal Department is called upon to irrigate within a few days every acre under lease. If water is delayed a week after it is wanted at this stage, the crop suffers; if it is delayed three weeks, it withers beyond redemption.

Attempts have been made by the Agricultural Department with some success to encourage the extended growth of the finer qualities of paddy, particularly of the very fine varieties known as *dadkhani* and *badshah-bhog*, for which Patna has been famous for centuries. It is interesting to note that the delicious flavour of the finer qualities of Patna rice was observed by Hiuen Tsiang when he visited Magadha thirteen hundred years ago.

Sugarcane.

The only *Aghani* crop of importance which has not been mentioned is sugarcane, grown on 17,000 acres, chiefly in Bihar and Bikram thanas. This is one of the most profitable crops grown in the district in spite of the labour and expense its cultivation requires. It is a crop which not only exhausts the soil, but occupies the ground for a long period, extending over a year. It is planted during February or March, in cuttings of about a foot in length placed in rows about two feet apart. When the plant begins to sprout, it is well watered and the surrounding earth is loosened. Each plant grows into a cluster of canes, which are generally ready for cutting in January or February. The crop requires great care, and must be frequently irrigated.

RABI CROPS.

The *rabi* is the most important crop in Patna, being grown on 807,000 acres. The great *rabi* area is in Barh and Mokameh, where over ninety per cent. of the net cropped area is cultivated at this season. An interesting account of the *rabi* cultivation in the north of that area was given by the late Mr. E. J. Woodhouse, Economic Botanist to the Local Government. His description applies practically to the whole of it as far south as Sarmera, and may be quoted here:—

> "The *tal* is inundated during the rainy season, at the end of which the water drains away leaving the land dry enough for cultivation by the end of September. Cultivation can be commenced ten days after the water has left the land, and can be continued for fifteen days, after which the land cannot be worked. The land is only ploughed once and the seed sown behind the plough, after which nothing more is done. One plough was said to be able to plough thirty bighas, although I was also told that for seven hundred bighas, twelve or fourteen ploughs only were required, which means that each plough is able to work over fifty bighas of very heavy soil in fifteen days, or work at the rate of three bighas a day. A plough was expected to work one and-a-half to two bighas in a day."

Outside the *tal* area, ploughing for the *rabi* crops begins early in the rains and is continued at convenient intervals, sufficient time being given to allow the upturned soil to be exposed to the air. In the case of clay soils in unirrigated parts, more frequent ploughing is necessary for all *rabi* crops, because otherwise the soil would become so hard that, if there were no rain at the sowing time, a crop could not be sown. The time of sowing *rabi* is generally regulated by two circumstances—the heavy rains of the *Hathiya nakshatra* (26th September to 7th October), and the approaching cold season. If sown too late, the plants will not become strong enough to resist the cold; if sown too early, the heavy rain will probably drown the seed and sprouting crop, and so necessitate re-sowing. The cultivators are thus anxious to sow as soon as the heavy rains have ceased, and the general rule is that the proper time for sowing most *rabi* crops is the

Chitra nakshatra (8th to 20th October), and that it must not be delayed beyond the *Swati nakshatra* (21st October—3rd November). A sufficient supply of water is essential at this time; later on several waterings are required, and if there is no rain, the crops have to depend on well irrigation. They are finally harvested between the last week of February and the middle of April.

Gram and pulses. Gram (243,500 acres) and pulses (323,700 acres) are the most extensively cultivated of the *rabi* crops. They are grown all over the district; but they form the staple crops in the *tal* land in the east, where they are grown on over eighty per cent. of the whole cropped area. They form the most important of the grain exports of Patna district.

Barley and wheat. Barley is grown on 78,500 acres, on the sandy loam known as *balsundri*, chiefly in Masaurhi, Bikram and Islampur thanas. Wheat is grown on 56,000 acres, about five per cent. of the net cropped area. Wheat, which is regarded as the most delicate of the *rabi* crops, is sown in October and reaped in March.

Oilseeds. Oilseeds are important among the *rabi* crops. The chief are linseed and mustard, which occupied respectively 25,370 and 16,430 acres at the time of the survey (1907—9). These are crops of which the extent of cultivation varies considerably, as prices rise or fall.

Potatoes. Potatoes are grown on 10,300 acres, chiefly by Koiri cultivators, in the thanas of Patna City, Phulwari and Dinapore. Potato moth, which made its appearance in 1907, for some time caused considerable damage among the stored seed potatoes, and if protective measures had not been possible, the potato-growing industry would probably have been destroyed. As a result of experiments made by the Agricultural Department in 1909, it was discovered that potatoes placed in flat heaps of about eighteen inches high and covered with dry river sand to a depth of a few inches were protected from the moth, and would not rot. After demonstrations of the advantages of storing potatoes in this way had been made, the method was almost universally adopted by the cultivators, and the potato industry in Patna was saved. It is believed that the moth was introduced into India with Italian seed potatoes imported by Bombay merchants; it spread very rapidly over India, but in Patna district at least its ravages have now been checked, since potatoes are grown in the cold weather, when the insect is comparatively inactive, and the stored seed potatoes are protected in the manner which has been described.

Other vegetables and fruits.

Other vegetables grown are the egg-plant or *baigun* (*solanum melongena*), and groundnut (*arachis hypogœa*), while pumpkins (*lagenaria vulgaris*) and gourds (*benincasa cerifera*) may be seen climbing over the roofs of the houses in nearly every village. Onions, yams, turnips, cabbages, beans, and cucumbers are also common, and in the winter radishes, carrots and melons are cultivated. Melons are grown in considerable quantities in the fields near the bank of the Ganges; they are of two kinds, the musk melon or *kharbuza* and the water melon or *tarbuz*. Both are sown in sandy soil, generally in October, and come to maturity in March or April. There are also two kinds of cucumber, one a large variety called *kakri* and the other a smaller species called *khira*. Pumpkins and gourds are put to a variety of uses. They are eaten plain and also in curries, and the rind is used by fishermen to float their nets; while the hollow gourd is used by musicians as a sounding board for their guitars and by religious mendicants to serve as a water-bottle. Among condiments the favourite is the chilli, which is grown in large quantities near the homesteads; turmeric, coriander and ginger are also cultivated extensively.

The most popular fruit is the mango, which grows on 18,000 acres, and forms a valuable addition to the food of the people during the hot weather, though the flavour of the local fruit is inferior to that of the Malda and Bombay varieties. Of the other cultivated fruits, the commonest are the plantain, lemon, *lichi* (*nephelium litchi*), jack fruit (*artocarpus integrifolia*), custard apple (*anona squamosa*) and *bel* fruit (*ægle marmelos*). The *khajur* tree (*phœnix sylvestris*) is cultivated abundantly for the sake of its juice, which is made into liquor; and the *mahua* flower is used for the manufacture of country spirit and is also eaten by the poorer classes. Among local fruits may also be mentioned strawberries, which, though small, are of good flavour. They are grown in large quantities at Dinapore, which has as high a reputation for its strawberries as Bankipore has for its roses.

Opium.

Poppy was formerly an important crop. In 1882 the area under cultivation was 26,314 acres; but the general advance of prices of food crops made poppy a less profitable crop for the cultivator, in view of its delicacy and the large amount of attention which it needed. After the abandonment of the Patna Opium Factory in 1911, the area under poppy was only 7,700 acres; this was gradually reduced, and since 1917 there has been no poppy cultivation in the district.

In addition to the ordinary country breeds there are two local varieties of cattle, one a cross between the Hansi and the country breeds, and the other a three-quarters or half English breed known as the " Bankipore breed ". The former class are large massive animals; the bullocks do well for carts and for ploughing, but the cows are not very good milkers. The Bankipore breed is the residue of an English stock imported some fifty years ago by William Tayler, formerly Commissioner of Patna, who started a cattle farm at Lohanipur and also inaugurated an agricultural exhibition. The animals are not usually very large, but the cows are excellent milkers, giving from eight to sixteen seers daily; owing to their smaller size they cost much less to keep than the other breed. The breed has deteriorated greatly through in-breeding and want of new blood. To improve the strain the Patna District Board imported two bulls from Australia; and more recently it purchased Montgomery bulls for the improvement of the indigenous breed. CATTLE.

Cattle fairs are held at Bihta in the Dinapore subdivision twice in the year, about the 13th Phagun and the 13th Baisakh. An agricultural exhibition is held annually in connection with the former fair, towards which the District Board contributes, and which also receives grants from Imperial and Provincial Funds for prizes for cattle. A cattle fair is also held at Ainkhan Bazar in the Bikram thana of the Dinapore subdivision.

Cattle of the local breed, though hardy and suited to the climate, are generally of a very mediocre stamp; little or no care is taken in selecting bulls for breeding, immature or poor specimens being used; and the Brahmani or dedicated bulls are usually no better than their fellows, though the freedom with which they are allowed to graze keeps them in better condition. The stock has thus little chance of improvement, and besides the want of careful and systematic breeding, there is difficulty in obtaining pasturage. Grazing grounds are few, and fodder is scarce, for during the hot weather the ground retains little moisture and the grass is parched up by the burning sun. Nearly all the land available for pasturage, moreover, has been given up to cultivation; and the cattle have to be content with the scanty herbage found in the arid fields or are stall-fed on chopped straw or maize stalks.

Buffaloes are employed for the plough, especially when deep mud is being prepared for the transplantation of paddy, and are also used for slow draught work, but their chief value is for the milk which they yield in large quantities. Sheep are reared on a considerable scale in the west of the district, for the local markets at Dinapore and Patna, and for the Calcutta market. Goats are bred in almost every village, and pigs of the usual omnivorous kind are kept by the low castes. The only horses are the usual indigenous ponies; they are generally undersized and incapable of heavy work, but those used for ekkas often show remarkable endurance and fair speed. Though very hardy, they are generally broken in too early, and are sometimes starved or worked to death before they are seven or eight years old.

Veterinary assistance.

Since the publication of the first edition of the Gazetteer in 1907, the progress of veterinary work has been very considerable. At that time, there was only one veterinary hospital and a dispensary in charge of a touring veterinary assistant surgeon in the entire district; but as the advantages of controlling epidemics by scientific methods were brought under the notice of the local authorities, they realised that something more should be done to help the agricultural classes in combating the diseases which play such havoc with their live stock. There is now a touring veterinary assistant surgeon in each subdivision; and hospitals are either actually in course of construction or are sanctioned for Dinapore, Barh and Bihar, in addition to the hospital at Bankipore, which was established in 1897.

The popularity of the hospital at Bankipore can be judged from the fact that whereas in the year 1908-9 only 870 patients were treated, the number in 1921-22 was 1,669. A similar development is also noticeable in the work of the touring veterinary assistant surgeons, who treated 2,381 animals during the last year, against 105 in the year 1908-9. Until recently, Patna was more or less free from epidemics of cattle disease. Several outbreaks of rinderpest and hæmorrhagic septicæmia occurred in 1922 with the result that 1,924 cattle succumbed to attacks. The veterinary assistant surgeons protected 3,581 animals by preventive inoculation.

The district veterinary establishment consists of five veterinary assistant surgeons—one stationary and four touring. One veterinary inspector stationed at Patna supervises the work of these officers. The hospital as well as the dispensaries are under the management of the district board.

WORK OF THE AGRICULTURAL DEPARTMENT.

When the survey and settlement operations were proceeding, there was an experimental farm at Bankipore; and the results of some of the experiments made on the farm are mentioned in the Settlement Report. This farm was abandoned on the inauguration of the new capital, because it was considered that the distributary from which it was irrigated would make unhealthy the clerks' quarters which were constructed near it.

Insect pests.

The successful work of the Agricultural Department in checking the ravages of the potato moth has been mentioned above. Another serious pest in the district is the caterpillar whose scientific name is *aegrotis ypsilon*, which for the last twenty years has been damaging the *rabi* crops on the Mokameh *tal*. The insect is apparently a migrant from the hills; and the *tal* lands appear peculiarly suited to its rapid development. In some years the pest does not appear, which is probably due to the fact that the comparatively few migrating insects have perished en route; but the damage caused extends normally over about ten thousand acres. Experiments made with Andrés Maire traps indicated that the pest could be kept within bounds by catching the gravid moths immediately after their arrival at the *tal*; but the cultivators took little interest in these experiments and would not even attend to the traps, being unable to believe that the moths caught in the traps had any connection with the caterpillars that ate their crops; and the operations were abandoned in 1914-15. Demonstrations were again made in 1919-20; but the Agricultural Department has not the money or the staff to carry out the work annually, though the damage would probably be much reduced if the Andrés Maire traps were systematically used.

Groundnuts and Pusa wheat.

The Agricultural Department has now introduced the cultivation of ground-nuts, which grow well on poor sandy soils, and are much more profitable on such soils than the crops usually grown. The Department has also introduced Pusa wheat, which gives a higher yield and realises a better price than local wheat. The disadvantage of this wheat is that wild animals prefer it to local wheat because it is awnless; if only one or two men grow Pusa wheat all the nilgai and pig make a dead set at their plots, whereas if all grew it the damage would probably be no more than that now done to the local wheat.

CHAPTER VII.

IRRIGATION.

THE clay soil which is found in a large part of Patna district does not retain moisture well; and the slope from south to north is such that rain water would all run into the *tal* if measures were not taken to store it. Cultivation thus depends largely on embankments which prevent the water from running away, and on artificial stores which replenish the losses caused by evaporation. Sixty per cent. of the area under cultivation is irrigated, a large proportion than is found in any other district in Bihar. More than half of the irrigated area is under rice; and practically the whole *aghani* rice crop is irrigated. The practice of draining the fields in September, known as *nigar*, which has been described in the account of rice cultivation, renders this crop particularly dependent on an artificial supply of water to make it secure; but the systems of irrigation used in Patna, elaborate though they are, are not good enough to save the crop in a year when the *Hathiya* rain fails. The crop soon withers unless it is watered early in October, and the sudden demand for water everywhere is a severe strain on the more perfect arrangements of the Government canals. Outside the area irrigated by these canals the supply of water is not equal to so universal a demand, unless a certain amount of rain falls during the *Hathiya* asterism to assist in supplying the deficiency in the fields. Consequently a great part of the irrigated area, which is under rice, is by no means secure from danger of drought, and in years when seasonable rain fails completely or is insufficient, a great part of the rice crop is lost. On the other hand, the arrangements are usually sufficient to supply water for the sowing of *rabi* crops on the irrigated area. The growing *rabi* crop is not as a rule irrigated otherwise than by wells. Most of the *pains* are dry by January; and the beds of many of the *ahars* are cultivated in the *rabi* season. **IRRIGATED AREA.**

The sources of irrigation, with the area irrigated by each, are as follows :—

	Acres.
Government canals	153,204
Private canals	232,156
Tanks and *ahars*	261,363
Wells	73,133
Direct from rivers	52,929

The area shown as irrigated from private works includes the whole area which in the most favourable circumstances can obtain water from an irrigation work. It includes much land on the outskirts of the area irrigated by a *pain* or *ahar*, which ordinarily can receive little benefit from it.

Government canals.

The Government canals consist of the Patna-Gaya canal and its distributaries, which form a part of the Son canal system. The Patna-Gaya canal branches off from the Main Eastern Canal four miles below the anicut which crosses the Son between Barun and Dehri. It enters Patna district a little beyond Arwal, at the forty-third mile from its offtake. For some distance it runs parallel to the course of the Son; it then turns to the east, passing Bikram and Naubatpur to Khagaul, following an old bed of the Son, roughly parallel to the ancient road from Patna to Delhi. From Khagaul it flows into the Ganges at Digha, 79 miles from its head. It is connected with the river at Digha by a lock; but the course of the Ganges is here variable, and during the dry season there is often only the sandy bed of the river beneath the lock, so that through navigation may be possible only when the river is high during the monsoon. The length of the canal in Patna district is 42¼ miles, that of the parallel channels is 24 miles, and that of the distributaries is 160 miles. The Maner distributary acts as a flood bank, which protects the Dinapore cantonment from floods.

The canal, which was opened in 1877, was designed to irrigate the area between the Son and the Punpun. It commands a total area of over 400,000 acres; but the maximum area irrigated in any year was 164,338 acres in 1912-13. In 1921-22 the area under irrigation was 153,204 acres, and in the preceding five years the average area irrigated annually was 145,052 acres. The greater part of the supply of water is utilized for the irrigation of the rice crop; out of the

153,204 acres irrigated in 1921-22 no less than 137,249 acres were under rice. The water is also used largely for sugarcane, but it is not regarded as so necessary for wheat and other *rabi* crops, except after failure of the *Hathiya* rainfall. The canal is navigable; it carries a considerable trade of which the principal staples are oil-seeds, food-grains and bamboos and a bi-weekly steamer service is maintained along it; but the opening of the Grand Chord line of the East Indian Railway has had the effect of reducing the traffic. The banks of the canal have been planted with trees, of which *sisu* and *tun* thrive best.

Canal administration.

The canal system in Patna is under the control of the Superintending Engineer, Son Circle, whose headquarters are at Arrah; but the local officer in charge is the Executive Engineer, Eastern Son Division, stationed at Dehri, who is responsible for the maintenance of the canal and the conduct of irrigation operations, while a separate establishment is entertained for the collection of the revenue.

The irrigated area is divided into blocks, the lease of all the lands in each block being arranged so as to lapse in the same year; and in fixing the period of the leases efforts are made to see that leases for an equal area expire each year. Water is supplied to the cultivators on application on a prescribed form, the year being divided into three seasons, *viz.*, hot weather, *kharif* and *rabi*. A date is fixed for each season, and the lease or permit granted for that season is only in force for that particular period. Besides these season leases, there are long-term leases, or leases for a period up to ten years, which are granted at a somewhat reduced rate.

The long-term leases are only granted for compact blocks defined by well-marked boundaries of such a nature that the leased lands can be clearly distinguished from the adjoining unleased lands, and also so situated that unleased lands will not ordinarily be irrigated by water supplied for the land included in the block. These boundaries are mentioned in the application for the lease, on receipt of which a special report is submitted to the Subdivisional Officer. If the lease is likely to be approved, he issues orders for the block to be measured, and a detailed measurement of each cultivator's holding is then made. The lease is finally approved by the Divisional Canal Officer who issues the permit, but before this can be done, the majority of the cultivators (not less than 85 per cent.), who have fields within the block, must sign their names against the areas which have been measured, and which will be assessed in their names. In order to admit of a lease getting water for the season, a provisional permit is granted for the season on the area originally applied for: this permit is cancelled when the long-lease permit is finally granted. Fields which cannot be ordinarily irrigated, or for which canal water is not ordinarily required, can be excluded from the block, such fields being duly noted in the measurement paper.

In these long-term leases, water-rates are charged for the area measured and accepted by the majority of the cultivators, whether water is required or not; and the channel by which the area is irrigated must be registered as well as the name of its owner. In *rabi* and hot weather leases water is supplied on application, and water-rates are levied on the actual area irrigated, and not necessarily on that specified in the application. In order to assist the Canal Department as far as possible in regulating and distributing the water to the different cultivators named in the leases, influential men of the village, called *lambardars* or headmen, are appointed with the approval of the majority of cultivators concerned. Their duties are to assist in measurements, to report the names of the cultivators of the different holdings, and to see that water is properly distributed over the leased area. For these duties they are paid a commission of Re. 1-9-0 per cent. on all assessments of water-rates.

There are five rates charged for the water supplied, *viz.*, (1) *rabi* season leases from October 26th to March 25th at Rs. 3-8-0 an acre; (2) hot weather leases from March 26th to June 27th at Rs. 7-8-0 an acre; (3) leases during this period at Rs. 2-8-0 for each watering; (4) *kharif* season leases from June 25th to October 25th at Rs. 5-0-0 an acre; and (5) ten years' leases for block areas for any kind of crop between June 25th and March 25th at Rs. 4-8-0 an acre.

Private canals. Private canals or *pains*, though by no means unknown elsewhere, are more common in Patna than in other districts of Bihar. The rivers which come into the district from Gaya usually contain little or no water in the dry season, but are full from bank to bank in the rains. In some instances they divide into two or more streams, and thus facilitate the utilisation of their water for irrigation. More or less roughly constructed canals take off from the river banks at favourable points, and distribute the water over the country. When a flood comes down the river it fills the canals; but in September, if rain fails, dams are constructed across the streams in order to bank up the water, and turn it into the *pains*. When a *pain* is full, the dam is cut, and the stream rushes down to the next dam and fills the next *pain*. These canals are chiefly found in the Bihar subdivision : and the two largest are twelve miles south-east of Bihar. These two *pains* illustrate some of the deficiencies of this system of private irrigation, as the main stream of the Sakri river has deserted its original bed and taken to the canal, so that the water is extremely difficult to control in time of flood. Moreover, the country towards Asthawan has suffered greatly from loss of the water which used formerly to come down in the Sakri, on which the cultivators relied for irrigation of their crops. The result is due to want of engineering skill in the construction of the *pains*, and not to any deep-laid scheme for depriving the Asthawan area of its water ; but whatever the cause may be, the prosperity of the cultivators in this area has been destroyed, without benefit elsewhere which is really equivalent to the injury.

Ahars.

An *ahar* is an U-shaped or rectangular tank, which is supplied with water by a *pain*, or by an artificial catchment basin placed across the line of drainage. Embankments are built on three sides of the rectangle, the highest bank being at the end where the water would ordinarily emerge, while one side is left open to allow the water to enter. If a small *ahar* is built across a drainage channel, a narrow cut is made at the deepest end to let out surplus water; if the *ahar* is a large one a weir is made for this purpose, so that the water may escape and fill other *ahars* lower down. The water flows through a weir from the *ahar* to the channels leading to the field; when the water is low it is taken from the *ahar* by means of the lifting arrangements described below.

Wells.

Wells are commonly used for irrigation in the high land to the north, and for *rabi* crops in the *tal* land. They are also used for irrigating the land in the neighbourhood of the village sites. Garden produce is almost always irrigated from wells, with an intricate series of water channels leading from the well to the plots to be irrigated. Though the area irrigated from wells is only 73,133 acres, they are almost as important a source of irrigation as *pains* or *ahars*, owing to the remarkable industry of the cultivators who utilise this means of watering their crops, and to the value of the crop thus watered.

Embankments.

Genrabandi is the name for the series of embankments which prevent the water from escaping from the fields. The *gherwa* or outer embankment is about four feet high; within is a series of smaller embankments (*genra*), and last of all are the ordinary *ails* round individual fields. The maintenance of these embankments is as important as that of the *pain* or *ahar*, and is usually controlled, with the rest of the arrangements for irrigation, by the landlord.

Lifting arrangements.* Latha.

The *latha* is a long beam working on an upright forked post which serves as a fulcrum. The beam is weighted at one end with a log or a stone, and a cone-shaped bucket (*kunri*) is attached by a rope to the other end. The cultivator pulls down the rope till the bucket is immersed, the weight attached to the lever then lifts it, and the bucket is emptied into the water channel.

Bullock-runs.

Bullock runs are most commonly used for irrigating from wells in the west of the district. A large leather bucket is fastened to a rope which passes over a pulley supported by a forked post, and is attached at the other end to the yoke of a pair of bullocks. An inclined plane is dug on the far side of the well, down which the bullocks run when the bucket is filled, and so bring it to the surface. The bucket is emptied into the water channel; the bullocks, now free of weight, climb up the inclined plane, the bucket is again lowered into the well, and the process described is repeated.

Karin.

The *karin* is a water scoop shaped like a "dug-out" canoe cut in half. It is usually made of a single piece of wood, but iron *karins* are by no means uncommon. The broad open end rests on the water channel which is to irrigate the fields, and the pointed end is dipped into the reservoir. The water is raised by a lever overhead with a weight at the end of it.

---

* NOTE.—Pictures illustrating these devices are given in Dr. Grierson's 'Bihar Peasant Life'; *latha* at page 206, bullock runs at page 208, and *karin* and *chanr* at page 210. Reference to these pictures will make the descriptions plain.

The *karin* is used for raising water from *ahars* or from a lower channel to a higher, where water is plentiful, and has not to be lifted to a considerable height.

Chanr. The *Chanr* is a bamboo basket with raised edges. It has cords attached on both sides which are held by two men. These men swing the basket backwards and then bring it sharply down into the water, carrying the swing on till the basket reaches the level of the water channel by which the field is to be irrigated.

Water cannot be raised to a very great height by the *karin* or *chanr*, and when the level of the reservoir is low, a succession of such appliances is often necessary to lift it to the height required. Irrigation is not easy work in Patna. Even when the means of irrigation are supplied, the utmost industry is required from the raiyats who make use of them to raise the water to the level of their fields.

Control of private irrigation works. The systems of irrigation from *pains* and *ahars* are ordinarily controlled by the landlords; and the arrangement by which different villages obtain water on different days is so complicated that it could perhaps hardly be managed by the raiyats themselves. The question of how much water each village is to take naturally gives rise to many disputes; and it is frequently a cause of riots when water is scarce. The landlord's agent can act with authority in a large estate, such as that of the Raja of Ammawan; but many estates have been so subdivided that the landlords are no more than small peasant proprietors: in such estates the cultivators have practically to settle among themselves the order of taking water. This they do with much bickering, but with some respect for precedent. What is remarkable is not that riots occur, but that they do not occur more frequently.

Cost. The cost of these rough and ready irrigation works is not very great. It was found in the survey and settlement proceedings in this district that the cost varied from four to twelve annas an acre. When the Tikari estate was under the Court of Wards, it was calculated that seven per cent. of the rental in irrigated villages must be spent on maintenance and repair of irrigation works. The cuttings leading to raiyats' own holdings, the lifting arrangements for filling them, and the dam in the *pain* by which they are flooded, are ordinarily provided by the raiyats themselves. In some highly subdivided estates, where each landlord has to contribute eight or ten annas a year for this work, it could apparently be done as well by the cultivators; but even where the fields are obviously suffering from neglect of the main work, which the cultivators could repair with little labour, raiyats are slow to do work for which landlords are responsible.

Produce-rents and irrigation.

The fear has been often expressed that, if produce-rents were commuted to cash, landlords would no longer trouble to maintain irrigation works, because they would no longer have a direct interest in the outturn. The view that produce-rents prevail in Patna and Gaya districts because so large an area is irrigated, is without historical foundation ; but it does not follow that landlords would prefer cash rents on irrigated lands now because they preferred them a hundred years ago. The cash rents which landlords now receive in Patna are high; but they have no longer the imperative necessity for prompt realisation which they then felt, when revenue was proportionately high, and failure to realise rent would involve default in revenue. This is not the place for a detailed discussion of a question of this nature; but it is one which cannot be ignored when produce-rents are being commuted to cash.

CHAPTER VIII.

NATURAL CALAMITIES.

"GENERALLY, the Soubah of Behar," wrote James Grant in 1787, "derives its superiority over most of the other provinces of the Mogul Empire from the great natural advantages of a temperate climate; high and fertile soil, well watered, productive of the drier grains, and all the luxuries required by the more active, warlike inhabitants of the north; with a centrical situation, having easy communication internally, and serving as an emporium, or by means of the river Ganges, a thoroughfare to facilitate the commercial intercourse between Bengal, as well as foreign maritime countries, and the more interior provinces of Hindostan. Agriculture, manufactures and commerce have always highly flourished in this favoured province.*" These remarks applied, and still apply, to the Patna district, a fertile tract of alluvial soil intersected by numerous rivers, which has been developed by some of the most industrious, adroit and capable husbandmen in India; but it suffered severely from famine in 1770, as has been described in chapter II above. When the failure of the autumn rains of 1783 again caused temporary scarcity in Patna, John Shore, after taking what measures he could for relief of the local shortage of grain, procured sanction for the building of the great granary at Bankipore for the perpetual prevention of famine. It was intended that grain should be poured in at the top of this granary and taken out through the small doors at the bottom; but owing to a mistake of the builders the doors were made to open inwards. It has never been filled in anticipation of scarcity; and indeed the loss from damp, rats and insects would render such a scheme of storing grain wasteful and impracticable. FAMINES.

Conditions in Patna now are very different from those of 1770. The district is unusually well supplied with communications, with the main line of the East Indian Railway traversing it from east to west, while the Patna-Gaya Railway and the

* The Fifth Report of the Select Committee on the Affairs of the East India Company (1812).

light railways which run to Rajgir and Islampur pass through it from north to south. The Ganges, with its large traffic in boats and steamers, flows along its whole northern length, and the Son forms its western boundary, while the city of Patna itself is one of the largest grain marts in the Province. The interior is well provided with means of communication and is fertilized by numerous streams and rivers. Add to this the fact that the people are not dependent on any single crop or the crops of any single season, as the area under cultivation is divided among *aghani* (31 per cent.), *rabi* (57) and *bhadoi* (9) crops; and the result is that the district is practically immune from any general famine. Even if the local rainfall fails, the cultivators are able to obtain a store of water for their crops from the rivers flowing from the south and from the canal system in the west; while grain can be imported by rail, road, canal and river, and distributed by carts or pack-bullocks to all parts of the interior. No district in the Patna Division offers so many facilities for private trade or is so well protected against exhaustion of its food supply. Since the great famine of 1770 it has never suffered from any widespread scarcity, and even in 1897, when other districts suffered from one of the greatest famines on record, it was very slightly affected.

Famine of 1866.

When the famine of 1866 burst upon Bihar, there was a definite theory of famine relief, recognizing the responsibility of Government; and the East Indian Railway had been extended (1862) through the district and the means of internal communications increased and improved. Consequently, though high prices prevailed, distress was neither general nor severe. It began to be felt to a certain extent among the poorer classes in October 1865; and it was most intense in the south near the Gaya district and in a portion of the Bihar subdivision, owing to the partial failure of the rice crop, which was almost the sole cultivation in that part of the district. In June 1866 work was offered to the distressed on the repair of roads and excavation of tanks within the tracts where the pressure was greatest; but less than 1,000 persons attended the works. Gratuitous relief was also afforded at 7 centres, but this relief was almost entirely confined to paupers, mendicants and persons coming from other districts: the daily average number of persons supported in this way, and at the charge of the local funds, from the end of June till the end of November 1866, was only 2,147. The number of deaths reported by the police, as having occurred from starvation or from disease induced by want of proper food, was 907.

The high prices ruling during this famine were due not so much to the failure of the local produce, as to previous excessive exportation and the demand from the surrounding districts. Owing to the general high level of prices in Lower Bengal, the importations of rice were much below the average of previous years; but large imports of other kinds of grain commenced about June and continued till the abundant autumn harvest caused a fall in prices.

Famine of 1874.

Again in 1874 the district was far less affected than other parts of Bihar, and though there was scarcity, it never culminated in famine. The first marked event which contributed to the scarcity was an inundation in July 1873, which seriously affected the prospects of the standing crops. While only a moderate amount of rain is required for the Indian-corn and *marua*, which form the staple food of the lower classes, and to mature the rice seedlings, no less than 13·4 inches fell in that month, followed by heavy showers in August, amounting to 11·78 inches more. In the headquarters subdivision, the country lying to the south and south-west of Bankipore was almost entirely submerged; but this state of things was not entirely out of the ordinary course, and in September 1873 the zamindars complained more of the want of rain than of the damage done by the inundation. The Barh subdivision, which is chiefly a *rabi* and *bhadoi* country, suffered most by the floods; but the Bihar subdivision was not affected. On the whole, the rice crop gave hopes of a moderate outturn, if there was a good fall of rain in September and October. But only ·93 of an inch of rain fell at Bankipore in the first half of September, while in Barh, Bihar and Dinapore the rainfall amounted to 1·30, 1·71 and ·75 inches respectively. In the latter half of the month, there was ·1 inch at Bankipore, ·34 in Barh, ·21 in Bihar, but there was no rain at all in the Dinapore subdivision. In the months of October and November there was not a drop of rain anywhere, except ·12 inch in Barh and ·15 inch in Dinapore; and in December there was only ·13 inch in the headquarters subdivision and no rain in all the other subdivisions. The result was a very scanty harvest of the rice crop. In the Bihar subdivision, indeed, there was about one-third of the usual outturn; but in the rest of the district there was, as compared with ordinary years, only from one-eighth to one-sixteenth of a fair harvest.

As to the effects of the scarcity and consequent rise in the prices of food grains on the people, though the lower classes were hard pressed, there was nothing like a famine. Grain was poured in by private traders in very large quantities; and works were opened in every part of the district where there was the slightest demand for labour. Not a seer of grain was spent in this district in charitable relief; for where there was any demand for this kind of relief, in order to meet the needs of beggars and other destitute people, private charity, stimulated by the of September, and by the end of October the deficiency amounted to 10·53 inches or 25 per cent. of the average.

Famine of 1897. The district again escaped the stress of famine in 1897, though other districts of the Division suffered and the rainfall of 1896 was both unseasonable and deficient. The rains broke late, at the end of June, and were heavy, the rainfall in that month being 7·19 inches. More rain followed in the first half of July, and some little damage was done by floods. A prolonged drought succeeded, which lasted till the middle of August, during which month 10·05 inches fell. This fall saved the *bhadoi* and enabled the raiyats to transplant the rice seedlings, though the operation was later than usual and was not completed till well into September. A third downpour occurred in the middle of September, but it was only about half the average, and up to this time the deficiency from the 1st April was 7·28 inches. Not a drop fell after the 18th of September, and by the end of October the deficiency amounted to 10·53 inches or 25 per cent. of the average.

No parts of this district were, however, seriously in danger : the rainfall was not so deficient as elsewhere, and all available water from the Son Canal was utilized : the result was that the *bhadoi* turned out a 10-anna crop, the *aghani* rice was 10½ annas, and the *rabi*, owing to the frequent showers throughout the cold weather, amounted to 12 annas. Fears were at first entertained for the Islampur thana, but these soon passed away, and the only cause of inconvenience was the high range of prices, which from October 1896 undoubtedly pressed hardly on the large urban population and on the many who live on small fixed incomes. Practically, no relief had to be afforded except to starved wanderers and travellers passing along the highway between the United Provinces and Bengal, who required assistance at kitchens and poor houses.

Tracts liable to famine. It will thus be seen that Patna escaped almost unscathed from the great famines of the 19th century; and an immunity from general famine may fairly be claimed for it. There are, however, two parts of the district liable to suffer from temporary scarcity—the south-east corner of the Bihar thana and the south of Islampur thana. The reason in each case is the same, *viz.*, that these areas have, owing to the silting up of certain channels, lost the means of irrigation which they formerly possessed.

FLOODS. In the north of the district floods are occasionally caused by the Ganges and Son overflowing their banks; but such inundations rarely do any serious damage. The cultivators have their flimsy huts washed down, but these are easily and quickly replaced, and they are recompensed by the fact that the soil is fertilized by a rich deposit of silt.

In the south also local floods are sometimes caused by the rivers breaching their banks owing to abnormally heavy rains in the hills, and occasionally also by a river leaving its old course and appropriating the channel of a *pain* or artificial irrigation channel. These floods however are of very short duration and cause comparatively little distress.

Flood of 1901. Of late years the most serious inundations have been those of 1901, 1913 and 1923. The flood of September 1901 was the result of a simultaneous rise of the Son and the Ganges, when the Son, being unable to discharge its water into the Ganges, forced its way over its eastern bank and poured over the low-lying land towards Maner. The Ganges itself inundated the country along its banks throughout the length of the district, while at Digha it rushed down the Patna-Gaya canal and breached its western bank two miles from its mouth. Two hundred and fifty-seven villages were flooded, but the damage caused was comparatively slight. Only one person was drawned, a man who was caught with his buffalo in a whirlpool near Maner. One remarkable escape is recorded. A man and his daughter living on a *diara* opposite the city were carried away on their cowshed on the night of the 4th of September. On the afternoon of the 6th the woman was discovered opposite Barh on half the roof and was rescued, while the man was carried down as far as Mokameh and was then brought to land. Over a thousand houses were destroyed; and the *bhadai* crops were ruined on the *diara* lands;

but this loss was to some extent counterbalanced by the silt left by the receding water, which was of great value for the *rabi* and winter rice crops. The flood subsided within twenty-four hours: and to this fact must be attributed the comparative slightness of the damage done.

The flood of 1913. The flood of 1913 was more serious in its consequences. Heavy and continuous rain fell between the 7th and the 11th of August in Patna, which was already saturated. At the same time there was heavy rain in Hazaribagh and Gaya, where twenty-two inches fell during this period; and all this water sought an exit to the Ganges through Patna district. The result was heavy flooding of the sadr, Barh, and Bihar subdivisions. The consequences were most serious in the Barh subdivision, where forty human beings and 547 cattle were drowned, 23,360 houses were completely destroyed, and over 87,000 maunds of standing grain were lost. In Bihar the loss of human life was less; but six persons were drowned, and 228 head of cattle were lost, while the damage to houses was estimated by the Collector at sixty thousand rupees. In the sadr subdivision two human lives were lost in the flood; while 7,385 houses were destroyed. The sum of over thirteen thousand rupees was promptly distributed in gratuitous relief, and over 1½ lakhs of rupees were advanced to the sufferers in the form of *takkavi* loans.

The flood of 1923. In August of 1923 a sudden rise of the Son which occurred when the Ganges was already in flood submerged a large part of the Dinapore subdivision and all the *diara* areas, and seriously threatened part of the new capital at Patna. On the 19th of August the level of the Son at the Dehri weir was 343·90 feet, 1¼ feet higher than the highest level hitherto recorded. The level of the Ganges was already 1½ feet higher than had ever been known before; and the result was that the bank of the Patna-Gaya canal was breached, and the western and northern portions of the Dinapore subdivision were flooded. The subdivisional magistrate of Dinapore promptly chartered steamers from Digha to bring off the people from the submerged *diara* areas; and only four human lives and 150 head of cattle were lost, less than might have been expected from the suddenness and violence of the flood. 130 square miles of the Dinapore subdivision were affected by the flood; and here 10,000 houses were damaged or destroyed, and three-fourths of the *bhadai* crops were lost. Gratuitous relief was promptly given from Government grants and private charity, and agricultural loans were issued to distressed raiyats. The Collector reports that Co-operative Credit Societies rendered valuable assistance by advancing loans from their funds. The embankment along the Bankipore-Digha road was overtopped or breached in many places, with the result that villages between the river and the New Capital were inundated; but the flood subsided before the Capital was damaged. It is proposed to improve the protective works which cover Dinapore and Patna by providing for the future against even higher floods than this.

CHAPTER XI.

RENTS, WAGES AND PRICES.

THE chief distinctive features of rents in Patna are, first, the high incidence of cash-rents; and secondly, the prevalence of produce rents. Over 40 per cent. of the whole cultivated area, or 414,000 acres, are held on produce-rent. Buchanan estimated in 1812 that the percentage of land held on produce rent was 56½, remarking that commutation of produce-rents was proceeding rapidly. At that time cash rent was paid only for the best land, and at comparatively high rates. During the resumption settlements *bhaoli* land was always treated as inferior to that for which cash rent was paid; and it was valued lower for assessment of revenue. In 1851, when the Court of Directors called for a report on the produce rent system in Patna, the Commissioner reported that cash rent was paid for irrigated land, while produce rent was ordinarily paid for high land. Zamindars at that time disliked produce rents, and would have preferred cash rent; but raiyats were not anxious for cash rents; they disliked the *danabandi* system, but they would prefer *batai* to a cash system.

The theory which has been so often put forward, that produce rents are necessarily bound up with the irrigation systems of Patna, is thus apparently inconsistent with the agrarian history of the district; but the inconsistency is more apparent than real. So long as the revenue which zamindars had to pay punctually represented a large proportion of the total value of the crops, it was to the interest of the zamindars to obtain cash rents rather than grain, if the cash rent was fixed at sufficiently high rates; and it was to their interest to maintain irrigation works such as would make it possible for the raiyats to pay these rents, since if the raiyat did not pay his rent the zamindar would default in payment of revenue. As the relative value of silver fell, the zamindars had no longer this pressing anxiety recurring as each instalment of revenue fell due; and ultimately the rise in the price of grain made produce rents as valuable as high cash rents. From 1859 the enhancement of existing cash rents was not so easily done as hitherto; and since 1885 it has been comparatively difficult. Since the Bengal Tenancy Act became law, zamindars generally have been endeavouring to obtain produce rent for as much land as possible. There is no necessity here for the institution of suits for enhancement on the ground of rise in prices; produce rents automatically are enhanced in value as prices rise, and to the full extent of the rise. It is to be feared that the interdependence of irrigation and produce rents does not produce so happy a result as the apologists of the system suggest. It is true that where rent is paid in kind the landlord who neglects his liabilities in respect of irrigation works will at once feel the result in his pocket, and that these high rents do give him a direct inducement to do his duty; but the raiyats generally detest the appraisement system which prevails so largely in the district.

SYSTEMS OF PRODUCE RENT.

The principal systems of produce rent found in the district are those in which the rent varies with the outturn, the proportion of the crop payable as rent being fixed; these are *danabandi* or appraisement, and *batai* or division of crops. There are also systems less commonly found, under which a fixed amount of grain is annually payable as rent, known as *mankhap* or *chauraha*.

Zabti crops.

When sugarcane is grown on land which is held under the *danabandi* or *batai* system, cash rent is always paid for it, at certain customary rates which vary in different villages. Cash rent was always paid when poppy was cultivated; but this crop is not now grown in Patna. Among these special crops we nearly always find potatoes; and in some cases rice is the only crop which is appraised or divided, all other crops being paid for at the cash rates. Baden Powell in his Land Systems of British India speaks of these as *zabti* crops, interpreting the word as meaning sequestered or set aside. They are commonly known in Patna as *hastobudi* crops; but it is probable that the term *zabti* used in this connection had originally its ordinary meaning, and that these crops, which were never divided, were originally treated as attached until the raiyat furnished security for payment of the rent. This is evidently the meaning of the term *zabti danabandi* which survives as a description of the appraisement system in Patna. Under this system the raiyat is now legally entitled to remove his crop after appraisement; but in the eighteenth century he was not allowed to do this unless he furnished security for payment of the rent assessed.*

* *See* the letter of the Revenue Chief of Bihar of October 30th, 1786, (No. 92 in Selections from the correspondence of the Revenue Chief).

BATAI.

The system which is most common in the district is that of *batai*, by which the crops are divided on the threshing-floor. The watchman, the reapers, and the weighman are paid from the whole crop, and the balance is divided in the appointed shares between landlord and tenant. Straw and husks, as under the appraisement system, are the property of the tenant. Raiyats prefer this to the appraisement system, partly because it affords opportunities for pilfering before division of the crop, but chiefly because they are less harassed under it than under the other system.

DANABANDI.

The appraisement system (*danabandi*) is nearly as common a *batai*. Appraisement is made by an amin or *salis* in presence of the raiyat, the *gumashta* and the *patwari* ; there may be present also a *jaribkash* (usually the *gorait*), the *barahil* and the *jeth* raiyat or *mahatwara*. The appraisement is made by the amin, whose estimate is discussed by the assembled company. If the raiyat cannot be persuaded to accept the appraisement, the crop must be tested by cutting two *dhurs* (less often two kattas), one selected by the raiyat and the other by the landlord's party.

Mafi or *minhai.*

After appraisement, before the calculation of shares is made, a deduction of two seers or more in the maund is allowed to the raiyat. In the west of the district this deduction is rarely less than five and is most commonly seven seers. Buchanan mentions the allowance as covering the expense of harvest; it is possible that it was originally intended to cover the cost of cultivation, and that the allowance of two seers common in the east of the district has been whittled down from an amount which was originally larger.

Cost of reaping, etc.

There is much variation in practice regarding payment of the cost of reaping and watching the crops. Sometimes the watchman is paid by both parties, sometimes by the landlord alone. The remuneration of the reaper is ordinarily one bundle out of every twenty-one; this is sometimes borne by both parties, sometimes by the raiyat alone.

THE LANDLORD'S SHARE.

Under the farming system which prevailed throughout the eighteenth century, though the raiyat's share after the customary deductions was nominally half, the farmers exacted *abwabs*, until as Ghulam Husain Khan said, the raiyats did not receive even a fourth of the crop.* In 1770 a large body of raiyats complained to the Patna Council, with the result that on November the 5th of that year, it was determined that a clause should be inserted in the renters' covenants, by which they undertook, when collecting rent in kind, to leave $17\frac{1}{2}$ seers in the maund to the raiyat.† This condition was retained in the covenants until 1788;‡ and we have here the evident origin of the tradition that nine-sixteenths of the crop is the normal rent in Patna. This tradition is so strong that it is curious to observe that during the survey and settlement proceedings it rarely happened that the zamindars' papers showed that nine-sixteenths represented the landlord's share. These papers almost invariably showed the true rent as twenty seers in the maund out of what was left after deduction of *mafi*. In addition to this there were frequently a number of *abwabs*, of which the first in the list was most commonly an *abwab* of $2\frac{1}{2}$ seers, described in the east of the district as *dahiyak*, and in the west as *kharcha*. But *dahiyak* is not always $2\frac{1}{2}$ seers, and it very rarely stands alone as an *abwab*, so that the matter cannot be simply dismissed with the explanation that this is the normal rent of nine-sixteenths, split up for convenience of arithmetical calculation. And in this connection it should be remembered that the covenants of 1770 did not establish a standard rent, but merely stated a maximum which must not be exceeded.

Other *abwabs* commonly found with produce rents in the survey and settlement proceedings were *nocha* (what is snatched away); *mangan* (that which is asked for), "a kind of forced benevolence;" *hujatana*, ordinarily a perquisite of the patwari. These *abwabs* vary from four chittacks to a seer in the maund There were also *abwabs* with arithmetical names, *panseri*, *manseri*, *derseri*, *doseri*, and even *chaut* of five seers in the maund, by which the nominal demand was raised to twenty-five, twenty-six, or twenty-eight seers in the maund.

***Mankhap* and *chauraha*.**

Mankhap and *chauraha* are fixed rents, not in the sense that raiyats paying rent under these systems are raiyats at fixed rates, but in the sense that the amount of rent payable is known beforehand, and does not vary with the outturn. When the rent is fixed in cleaned rice it is known as *chauraha*.

* *See* Sir John Shore's Minute of April 2nd, 1788, Appendix XVII. Harington's Analysis, Vol. III.

† Harington's Analysis, Vol. II, page 246.

‡ Selections from the correspondence of the Revenue Chief, pages 11 and 161.

These rents are commonly found on landlords' privileged lands. They are occasionally also exacted for land which formed raiyats' holdings bought at auction by the zamindar, or falling into his hands by failure of heirs. Such rents are ordinarily high; they vary from four to eight maunds of rice per bigha, with a certain amount of *khesari* in addition. Six maunds of rice and one maund of *khesari* per bigha is a common rate, which represents a very high rent. Indeed the *chauraha* rent sometimes stands for the whole crop. The explanation ordinarily given is that the landlord is entitled to free labour (*begari*) from his raiyat on the *zirat* land, and that instead of giving this, it is less troublesome to the raiyat to cultivate the *zirat* land himself, and give the crop to the landlord, taking in return only the straw. The market value of the straw is often from seven to ten rupees per acre, so that even where the landlord takes the whole of the grain, the tenant does receive some slight return for his labour. The theory otherwise would leave the tenant of the *chauraha* holding as the unfortunate scapegoat for the *begari* labour of the whole community. In a good year he may have a little rice left over, but he will rarely have very much thus left. The cultivators apparently are contented that a small area should be held under this system. The old *nankar* and *malikana* lands, which were formerly the proprietors' private lands, have now in almost every village become merged in a mass of so-called *khudkasht* land, which includes every raiyati holding that has ever fallen in or been bought by the landlord. The attempt to assess all these lands at *chauraha* rents is occasionally made, but it is strongly resented in the village. It was found during the survey and settlement proceedings that general anarchy had been produced in consequence of such attempts by the landlords in certain villages in the Barh and Bihar subdivisions. The margin left to the cultivators, in the best of years, is so small under these rents, that they are quite impossible if applied to a considerable area.

Commutation of produce rents.

Dr. Buchanan remarked in 1812 that the most noticeable change that was then taking place was that cash rents were taking the place of produce rents. This process was to some extent reversed after the Bengal Tenancy Act became law; and it has been the settled policy in many estates to obtain produce rent for as much land as possible. A considerable amount of commutation was done by the revenue officers who were engaged in the survey and settlement operations; and much has been done by the Collectorate staff since those operations were completed. The following table shows the result of these cases during the survey and settlement operations (1907—12) :—

Subdivision.	Area affected.	Average rent per acre.
	Acres.	Rs. a.
Sadr	3,968	7 3
Dinapore	756	7 0
Barh	7,670	7 8
Bihar	7,231	9 9

The area held by settled and occupancy raiyats on cash rent is 521,000 acres, at an average rent of Rs. 7-8-0 an acre. The highest rents are found in Hilsa (nine rupees), Islampur (ten rupees) and Dinapore (Rs. 10-5-0). The lowest rents are in Maner (Rs. 6-2-0), which is probably to be attributed partly to the fact that this pargana had close relations with Shahabad at the end of the eighteenth century, when the guzashtadars of that district were fighting for their rights. The tradition of a fixed pargana rate has not completely died out in Maner ; and though raiyats at fixed rates are rare, there has apparently here been more resistance to enhancement of rent than elsewhere. According to the statistics the lowest rents are paid in the east of the Barh subdivision (Mokameh, Rs. 4-12-0 and Barh, Rs. 6-6-0); but these figures are misleading There is here a large area which is assessed to rent under the *hastobudi* system described below; and the figures given in the statistics of the survey and settlement proceedings are those of the minimum rent payable. **CASH RENTS.**

Hastobudi is a term which is used to describe many kinds of rent in Patna district. It is ordinarily used for the *zabti* crops which have already been mentioned. It is also used to describe systems known elsewhere as *halhasili* or *jaidadi*. Under the *halhasili* system a proportionate remission from the standard rent is made if the crop is poor; under the *jaidadi* system rent is remitted only if the crop fails. The most common form of *hastobudi* rent is found in the flooded tracts in the east of the district. The rent of the land is assumed to be payable for the *rabi* crop, and an additional rent in cash or kind is assessed when *aghani* or *bhadoi* rice is grown. If the rent for rice is assessed in cash, it is subject to remission according to the outturn. It will be sufficiently illustrated by describing the system in village Panagar in Mokameh. The rent of the land is Rs. 3-6-0 per bigha. **Hastobudi.**

This is payable in any case, and is assumed to be the rent for the *rabi* crop. If paddy is grown the rent is from Rs. 6-13-0 to Rs. 8-13-0, subject to remission if the crop is poor. Nothing beyond the normal rent of Rs. 3-6-0 is paid if the crop fails entirely. A variation of this system is that by which rent of three or four rupees is paid for the *rabi* crop: while if paddy is grown the crop is divided with the landlord. In Karara, in the same thana, the effect of this system, by which the landlord formerly divided the rice, was to put an end to the cultivation of rice altogether, since the landlord did nothing to maintain embankments and the raiyats had found it unprofitable to pay half the rice crop to the landlord when it survived, whereas they lost it all in an ordinary year. The rice crop is very precarious in this flooded area, and its safety depends upon whether the enbankments can keep out the water in time of flood. When embankments are maintained by the landlords, raiyats generally acquiesce in this system. It is an application of the principle commonly recognised in this district, that rent, whether paid in cash or in kind, represents a definite share of the whole crop, to which the landlord has a traditional right.

Abwab.

In the course of the survey and settlement proceedings it appeared that the levying of *abwabs* was as common in the case of cash rents as in that of produce rents. The commonest of these cesses was *batta company*, which originally represented the loss in exchange of *sicca* rupees for standard rupees. It was usually levied at half an anna in the rupee. Similar in amount was *batta inamuli*, originally imposed for the cost of exchanging copper coins in which rent was paid for the silver required for the payment of revenue. Other *abwabs* were *pkehi* (nominally for the amin who measures *bhaoli* land, and so an unfair exaction from cash-paying raiyats), at two annas per bigha or thereabouts, *sidha* (a sumptuary allowance to the landlord), at six annas per tenant; *nispast*, a fee for measurement of the holding; *hujatana* at one anna in the rupee, and *kharcha* at half an anna, nominally for village officials of the landlord. *Mangan* at varying rates was common, as were *abwabs* with arithmetical names as *doanni* and *charanni*, at two and four annas per bigha held by the raiyats.

Land measures, etc.

The standard bigha of Patna district is measured with a rod of 5½ cubits (*haths*), which is equivalent to 8¼ feet. Twenty rods measure one side of a bigha, which thus varies with the size of the rod. The standard bigha contains 3,025 square yards, while the larger bigha, measured with a pole of six cubits, contains 3,600 square yards. Fractions of an anna in zamindari accounts are still shown in *dams*, one *dam* representing one-twentieth of an anna. These fractions, for purposes of payment of rent, are ordinarily applied to the unminted copper coins known as Gorakhpuri pice, of which the standard rate of exchange is eighty to the rupee.

Occupancy rights, etc.

There are 3,359 tenancies of raiyats at fixed rates in the district, covering 6,370 acres, or a little over one-half per cent of the occupied area. The bulk of the land is cultivated by settled or occupancy raiyats, by whom 904,864 acres are held in 522,089 parcels. These raiyats thus hold eighty-four per cent. of the occupied area.

WAGES.

There has been a great advance in the wages of labour since the first edition of this Gazetteer was published in 1907. At that time wages in Patna were far below those prevailing in Bengal; but a great change has been produced by the demand for labour in building the new capital. In 1871 the rates were reported to be four times what they were formerly, but even so they were low enough. Coolies or labourers were paid at the rate of two annas per diem, and agricultural day labourers earned one anna for a day's work, but were usually paid in grain, at the rate of three seers of paddy or *khesari*, representing a money wage of an anna or a little more. Smiths got from one to four annas and carpenters from 2½ to three annas daily. In 1907 the rates were, in the case of unskilled labour, 3½ annas per diem for a male adult cooly, three annas for a woman and 2½ annas for a boy; and in the case of skilled labour, five to six annas for a carpenter or mason, according to their skill, and six to eight annas for a blacksmith. At the present day the rates in urban areas are for unskilled labour six to eight annas a day, ten to twelve annas for carpenters and masons, and twelve annas to a rupee for blacksmiths. These rates are subject to variation according to the local demand; and large building operations, particularly if the contractors are known to be pressed for time, bring about considerable temporary advances in rates.

Outside urban areas remuneration for labour is largely given in kind; carpenters and masons earn little less than in the towns, and most of the agricultural labour is still performed by *kamiyas* who are maintained by their employers. For cutting, threshing and carrying crops labourers are paid by a certain proportion of the grain with which they deal, as has been described above, the rate for harvesting being commonly one bundle in fifteen. In the Mokameh Tal, where a great deal of labour is imported from Monghyr district for agricultural operations, ploughmen are paid a rupee a day, while sowers receive twelve annas.

PRICES.

The rise in prices which was noticed by Mr. O'Malley as in progress when the first edition of this Gazetteer was published has been accelerated in recent years. The following table shows the average prices of staple food crops in Patna, published by authority of the Local Government under section 39 of the Bengal Tenancy Act, for the last twenty-two years :—

Year.	Sadr.		Barh.		Dinapore.		Bihar.		
	Makai.	Rice.	Makai.	Rice.	Barley.	Rice.	Wheat.	Marua.	Rice.
	S. ch.	S. ch.	S. ch.	S. ch.	S. ch.	S. ch.	S. ch.	S. ch.	S. ch.
1901	19 15	13 0½	17 14	12 0	18 2⅞	11 14½	10 7⅛	... ...	10 5⅛
1902	23 3	12 15	22 3⅛	12 6	20 6⅜	12 14¾	12 2	... ...	11 7⅝
1903	25 9⅛	14 12	23 12	13 11⅛	26 1⅞	14 7⅞	14 4¾	... ...	13 8⅞
1904	27 6⅛	15 15⅛	25 5⅛	13 13⅝	25 14⅞	14 14⅛	16 14⅝	... ...	14 2⅛
1905	19 11⅞	13 8⅛	18 2	12 15⅞	20 4⅞	12 8⅛	13 2¾	... ...	12 6⅞
1906	12 9	10 2	12 0	9 9⅛	15 4⅞	9 10⅞	10 7⅞	... ...	10 1⅞
1907	13 8⅛	8 10	11 10⅛	7 11⅞	13 15⅞	8 3⅞	8 14⅞	... ...	8 11
1908	10 11⅞	7 13⅞	10 9	7 5	12 2⅛	7 10	10 7	... ...	7 1⅛
1909	15 15	10 0	15 4	8 13	16 9	9 5	... ...	14 0	8 10
1910	18 14	12 12	18 6	12 14	20 14	12 7	... ...	20 12	13 0
1911	19 15	13 3	19 0	12 15	20 14	12 13	... ...	21 13	13 8
1912	17 12	11 8	17 8	11 2	16 10	10 15	... ...	18 14	11 5
1913	14 10	8 7	14 2	8 8	15 8	8 5	... ...	12 9	8 1
1914	11 4	8 4	11 12	8 7	12 0	7 13	... ...	13 5	8 4
1915	12 7	7 15	11 15	7 13	12 2	7 14	... ...	11 9	7 9
1916	14 12	8 13	14 3	8 10	13 1	8 0	... ...	12 10	9 4
1917	17 14	11 0	17 6	11 5	14 6	11 1	... ...	15 7	11 0
1918	13 3	9 2	13 4	9 2	14 2	9 3	... ...	11 0	10 0
1919	7 8	5 11	7 3	5 7	8 7	5 10	... ...	7 3	5 6
1920	8 4	6 9	9 4	6 6	7 14	5 15	... ...	7 11	6 11
1921	9 3	6 9	9 11	6 10	9 5	6 10	... ...	8 10	6 6
1922	10 11	6 12	10 0	5 14	9 11	6 6	... ...	8 14	6 7

It is of some interest to compare the present prices of food-grains with those obtaining in former periods of scarcity. In 1866, the year of the Orissa famine, when Patna was slightly affected, the maximum price of common rice was 11 seers 8 chitaks per rupee, of wheat 7 seers 4 chitaks, and of maize 12 seers 4 chitaks per rupee. In May 1874, at the height of the famine, rice sold at 12 seers per rupee, wheat at 15 seers 10 chitaks, and maize at 18 seers 8 chitaks per rupee. In the famine of 1897 the highest price of common rice was 7 seers 12 chitaks in July 1897. Famine prices.

The abnormal rise in prices has told heavily on landlords whose rents are fixed in cash, and generally on all persons with fixed cash incomes. It has made landlords less willing than ever to commute produce rents to cash, in spite of the inconveniences which attend the produce-rent systems. Cultivators in the district generally have gained little from the rise in the prices of food-grains, since the prices of other necessaries have risen also, and they have never enjoyed much surplus income for expenditure on luxuries; but the prosperous cultivators who flourish in the neighbourhood of Patna and Dinapore have certainly profited by the general rise in prices of all classes of produce, as have the larger raiyats elsewhere. MATERIAL CONDITION OF THE PEOPLE.

In the villages, the artisans who form an essential part of the village community are partly paid for their work in kind, and are thus indirectly supported by agriculture. In the towns there is a great demand for labour, particularly in Patna; and cases of acute poverty are rarely met with among the labouring classes. The increased local demand has reduced the number of labourers who annually migrate in the cold season, but many thousands of the adult males are found spread over other parts of India in quasi-permanent employ, and all these persons make remittances to their homes; while those who migrate for a time bring back with them the balance of their savings. In this way, large sums of money are sent or brought into the district every year, and are expended in the support of the labourers' families. Labouring classes.

Hitherto in most villages agricultural labour has been performed by *kamiyas*, whose position is that of serfs. The *kamiya* undertakes, in consideration of an advance or loan, to work for his master until the loan is repaid. The agreements *Kamiyas.*

were such that they could not legally be enforced; but *kamiyas* did not know this, and they practically only differed from slaves in the fact that if they could obtain the amount of money advanced under the bond they could redeem themselves. The Kamiauti Agreements Act (VIII of 1920), makes such contracts void if the term for which labour is to be rendered exceeds one year, if the debt is not to be extinguished with the term, or if fair remuneration is not to be provided for the labour. The Act does not apply to agreements entered into by "skilled workmen," so that the old *kamiauti* conditions may still apply to labour rendered by such persons as Chamars.

Co-operative credit.

The co-operative credit movement has made great progress in Patna district. There are central Banks at Barh, Bihar and Masaurhi with a working capital of Rs. 8,49,000, and thirteen guarantee unions supervising the working of their affiliated societies. There are 322 societies in the district, with a working capital of Rs. 8,81,000. It is reported that those who have joined the movement have largely improved their material condition. The general interest which the society has in the solvency of each of its members tends to check extravagance; and in many villages the members settle their own disputes without going to the courts.

CHAPTER X.

OCCUPATIONS, MANUFACTURES AND TRADE.

Occupations. As in other parts of the Province, the majority of the people are dependent on agriculture for their livelihood, 72 per cent. of the population being engaged in agricultural pursuits. Of the total number dependent on agriculture 45 per cent. are actual workers, including 374,000 rent-payers, 174,000 field labourers and 10,500 rent-receivers. The Kurmis and Koiris are the principal agricultural castes; but the large castes of Ahirs and Babhans are also mainly cultivators; though the former are also usually herdsmen, and the latter petty landlords. Besides those supported by agriculture, there are 4,200 persons, with 3,800 dependents, classed as vegetable providers, the market gardeners of the district, who make large profits by growing vegetables on the rich land in the vicinity of village homesteads. The agricultural labouring class is chiefly composed of the lower castes, such as Dusadhs, Chamars and Musahars.

Industries support a little under ten per cent. of the population. Of the industrial population in this district fifty per cent. are actual workers, among whom are 5,000 cow keepers, 6,000 oil-pressers and sellers, 4,000 toddy drawers, 2,000 masons, 6,000 cotton weavers, 3,000 tailors, 3,000 goldsmiths, 4,000 carpenters, and 2,000 shoe-makers, as well as numerous grain and pulse dealers, grain parchers, tobacco sellers, thatchers, and basket and mat-makers.

Next in importance come the classes supported by trade and commerce who account for six per cent. of the population; 48 per cent. of these are actual workers. The professional classes account for 2·8 per cent. of the population; 44 per cent. of these are classed as actual workers, including 5,000 priests.

Manufactures.

When the District Gazetteer was published in 1907, the manufacture of opium, for which Patna had been famous for centuries, was the most important industry in the district, next to which in importance came the distillation of spirits. Neither of these industries has now any place in the district. The manufacture of opium at Patna was abandoned in 1911; and spirit for local consumption is no longer distilled locally. The most important industry is found in the oil and flour mills of Patna and its vicinity. Oil mills are fairly common in the towns; but as a rule they are on a very small scale.

Factories.

The official list of factories includes the Government Drawing Office and Press, and the Workshops of the Bihar School of Engineering, of the East Indian Railway at Khagaul. of the Bengal and North-Western Railway at Mokameh, and of the India General and Rivers Steam Navigation Company at Digha. It includes also four private printing presses at Bankipore, and the following factories, *viz.* :—

Sri Bihariji oil and flour mills, Patna City.
Aryan oil and flour mills and foundry, Dinapore.
Vishwakarma oil and flour mills and foundry, Digha.
Patna oil mill, Begampur.
Mokameh oil mill, Mokameh.
Patna iron foundry, Begampur.
Bankipore iron works, Mithapur.
Patna ice factory, Gulzarbagh.

Iron foundries.

In the Vishwakarma and Aryan mills there are cupolas and the machinery necessary for small and medium-sized castings; the work done is ordinarily in connection with the maintenance of the mills, but orders from other establishments are undertaken. Of foundries proper there are the Patna Iron Foundry and the Bankipur Iron Works. Both do a general factory business, but specialise on sugarcane crushing machinery of small size. The Patna Iron Foundry also makes a speciality of cast iron railings.

Mines.

There are no mines at work in the district. Formerly a small gold-mine was worked at Kalianpur, three miles from Rajgir, but the work done was merely of a prospecting nature, a few tons of quartz being taken out of different pits and tested, and there were no real mining operations resulting in a definite output. The mine was abandoned, after a very short existence, in 1892.

Hand industries. Nowhere is the decline of Patna as a manufacturing centre more noticeable than in the matter of hand industries. Practically every kind of industry is carried on, but none of them are of special importance or extent; and with the exception of the linen, furniture and cabinetware of Dinapore, few of the local products are exported. Carpets, brocades, embroidery, pottery, brasswork, toys, fireworks, lac ornaments, gold and silver wire and leaf, glass-ware, boots and shoes and cabinets are made in Patna city, carpets in Sultanganj, Pirbahor and Chauk, and embroidery and brocade work in the Chauk and Khwaja Kalan thanas. Durable furniture and cabinets are made at Dinapore. The manufactures of the Barh subdivision consist of jessamine oil (*chameli*), coarse cloth, and brass and bell-metal utensils, and those of the Bihar subdivision are soap, silk fabrics, tubes for hookahs, muslin, cotton cloth and brass and iron ware. The more important and interesting of these industries are described below.

Weaving. Weaving was formerly the great industry of the district, but it is now declining owing to the competition of comparatively cheap machine-made piece-goods. Cotton weaving is still, however, carried on to a small extent in nearly every village, and on a larger scale in the city of Patna and in the towns of Bihar and Dinapore. The chief article manufactured is a coarse cotton cloth called *motia* or *gazi*, which is chiefly used by the poorer classes in the cold weather. It is warm and durable, and is used for making *dhotis*, jackets, wrappers and quilts for men, and for *saris* and bodices for women. The cloth is popular among the poorer classes, who cannot afford to purchase woollen fabrics for the winter. Blanket weaving is also carried on to a limited extent by Gareris, especially in the Masaurhi thana. Towels, bed-sheets, table cloths and napkins of a superior kind are manufactured at Dinapore; at Bihar good muslin is produced; and *newar* tape is made in Patna city.

Carpet making is practically confined to the latter place, which is described in the Monograph on Carpet-weaving in Bengal (1907) as "the great seat of *dari* manufacture in Bihar". Here a large number of the cotton floor cloths called *daris* and *satranjis* are woven in Sultanganj, Alamganj and Pirbahor;

and cotton *dulichas* and woollen *asans* in the two thanas first named. A small quantity of the coarse carpets called *kalins* are sold to wholesale dealers and exported to Calcutta: and woollen carpets of a better kind are made on a small scale in Sultanganj, Pirbahor and Chauk.

Silk weaving is now almost confined to the Bihar subdivision. The weavers produce tusser silk fabrics, which obtain a local sale and are also exported to Calcutta, but they mostly turn out cotton cloth, called *bafta*, composed of a mixture of cotton and silk. In Fatuha thana in the Barh subdivision there were till comparatively recent times over 1,000 looms engaged in cotton and silk weaving, but the industry has declined and the number of weavers has largely decreased; the only place where silk is now woven to any extent is Raipura (Fatuha).

Glassware. Patna city is almost the only place in the Lower Provinces where glass is made. A large number of bottles for holding scent, lamps and bangles are made out of Son sand mixed with soda (*khari*). The glass produced is, as a rule, green and impure, but some pure white glass vessels are made from broken railway lamp glass; ordinary English glass assumes, it is said, a milky colour when remelted. Vases of European design in coloured glass are also made, the workmen colouring the glass with sulphate of copper, indigo blue and other ingredients, while blue glass is made by adding an oxide of tin. The process of melting is very simple. A furnace with a blast is prepared, and over this is the annealing chamber; the broken glass is fixed on a blow pipe or metal rod; and having been melted or softened, is blown or pressed into the desired shape. The Lodi Katra quarter is the centre of the industry.

Cabinet ware. Patna and Dinapore are celebrated for their skilled carpenters, whose dexterity is attested by the handsome carved balconies found in these towns. A large quantity of European furniture and other cabinet work of good quality is made at Dinapore and Patna and exported to other places. Dog-carts and *palkis* are also made in the same two towns.

Embroidery. Gold and silver embroidery and brocade work are carried on in the Chauk and Khwaja Kalan thanas in Patna city, where there are about 1,000 men employed in this industry, and also to a limited extent in Bihar town. The embroidery, which is of two kinds, known as *kamdani* and *zardozi*, is chiefly applied to caps and to the trappings of horses and elephants; it has not the reputation of Lucknow or Benares work. The gold and silver wire and leaf used are made locally, but most of the gold thread comes from Benares and the United Provinces.

Stone-carving. Stone-cutting is carried on in Marufganj in Patna city. The stone used is chiefly sandstone (locally known as Mirzapuri stone), which is brought down by river in rough-hewn slabs from Bindhachal and Chunar, in the Mirzapur district. Granite is also imported from Sasaram and Monghyr, but in smaller quantities; this stone is harder and the *sils* (*i.e.*, slabs for grinding curry) and *jantas* (hand-mills) made of it are sold at higher prices. The articles principally made are figures of Hindu gods, very roughly shaped ; curry-stones (*sils*), hand-grinding stones (*janta*), pestles (*lorha*), potter's wheels (*chakki*), and stone plates and cups. There is a constant demand for these articles from all parts of Patna, and they are also supplied to other districts.

There is very little lapidary's work carried on in the city of Patna or in its vicinity, with the exception of carving small pieces of crystal or pebbles (imported principally from the hills of Monghyr and Bhagalpur) and polishing them into small stones, called *naginas*, for setting in rings, necklaces, or amulets. Some business is also done in carving phylacteries of hexagonal shape, with appropriate verses from the Koran inscribed on them, to serve as charms against disease. These are principally used by Musalmans and low caste Hindus, who prize them as preventives against attacks of disease, the " evil eye " and other similar influences. In Patna the *hakkaks* or lapidaries are all Musalmans, who have followed the trade for generations past. There are also a few families of lapidaries in Bihar and its vicinity; but in every case these men have some other trade to supplement their work in stone, as alone it is not sufficiently remunerative to support them.

Wood-carving. Regarding the wood-carving industry, the following remarks may be quoted from " A Monograph on Wood-Carving in Bengal " by Chevalier O. Ghilardi :—" The existence of wood-carving at the present day is practically nominal. Judging, however, from the remains of the older wood-carvings in the line of houses extending from Bankipore to Patna, it is clear that much better work was produced in the past, when this industry appears to have enjoyed a period of happy florid forms, with which the work done at present cannot bear comparison. It would appear that all the old carving visible along the road was cast more or less from the same mould, so little is the variety in form and design; still we can observe a special characteristic in each group of carvings, which distinguishes it from those of the other villages. The carving to which I allude is that in connection with the buildings, such as the pillars, architraves and brackets supporting their verandahs and roofs. Unfortunately, nowadays, the taste of the inhabitants has changed. When a house is near to fall in pieces, and it is rebuilt, no more carved pillars are used; bricks are the only substitute. Originally, most of those pillars were first worked by the turner, even those with large diameters, and afterwards carved by clever artisans. The wood used here is teak-wood in general, but sometimes sisoo and paisor. When the present proprietor of a house changes the old pillars, the work of the turner is dispensed with, and the pillars, although fairly well carved, remain of a quadrangular form. This is easily gathered from the fact that all the quadrangular carved pillars are invariably the new ones. The friezes also are good, and a few of the panels, too; but in general this carving, although effective, is of very rough execution, and cannot stand comparison with that by the artisans of Lahore, Delhi and Agra. There are few wood-carvers at present at Patna, and the decay in this profession has proceeded so far that none of the new buildings on the long road between Bankipore and Patna have any wood-carving at all."

Gold and silver work.

Patna, with Cuttack, Murshidabad and Monghyr, forms one of the principal centres of the gold and silversmith's art in this Province. Gold and silver ornaments are principally made in the city of Patna, but there are also gold and silversmiths in the mufassal towns and every large village. Gold ornaments form the most costly portion of the dowry given to a girl, and are also worn by certain classes of men, *e.g.*, Rajputs and Babhans wear a gold necklace and armlets, while a well-to-do Goala or Dhobi wears, as a token of his affluence, gold earrings, a gold necklace, armlet or bracelet. Silver ornaments are used by those who cannot afford to wear gold ornaments, and a set of silver vessels, consisting of a *pan*-box, *attar* tray, flower-vase, and rose-water bottle with a tray, is usually presented as a dowry by members of the middle class; the more wealthy add to these a horse and an elephant, with trappings and ornaments for both, a silver *tanjan* or sedan, silver sceptres, maces, wands and spears. These articles are borrowed on occasions of weddings or display; and silver chairs, sceptres, maces and wands are kept by Rajas and Nawabs, and are lent by them on ceremonial occasions.

Other industries. The other industries are insignificant and merely meet local demands. There is a small business in harness and shoe-making in Patna city; and the same place contains a considerable number of braziers, whose yearly outturn has been valued at Rs. 50,000 ; the brass vessels they produce are strictly utilitarian, and there is little or no attempt at ornamentation. The value of the iron work manufactured annually has been estimated as over Rs. 50,000, iron bird-cages being a speciality of the Patna blacksmiths. The manufacture of *naichas* or tubes for hookahs is a speciality of the Bihar subdivision.

TRADE. The principal imports are coal, kerosene oil, iron and steel, salt, wheat and flour, rice, gunny-bags, and cotton piece-goods. The principal exports are gram and pulses, fruit and vegetables, linseed, oil-cake, sugar, and wheat. One-fourth of the piece-goods, gunny-bags and salt, and one-eighth of the kerosene oil is imported by river; otherwise the imports by river are small. Little is exported by river except gram and pulses and wheat. This decline in the importance of the traffic by river from the days when the Ganges was the principal line of communication between Upper India and Bengal largely accounts for the decay of Patna and Barh as centres of trade. Moreover, the railway companies charge a freight between intermediate stations out of proportion to the through freight to Calcutta. It is cheaper to book goods direct to Calcutta than (as formerly) to rail them to Patna, and thence to send them down by river; and consequently the smaller merchants, who used to bring their goods and grain to Patna, now find it more advantageous to send them direct to Calcutta. Other important markets are Dinapore, Bihar, Barh, Mokameh, Islampur, Fatuha and Hilsa. The principal trading castes are Telis, Agarwalas, and the various mercantile castes collectively called Baniyas. The transport by river is mostly in the hands of Musalmans, Tiyars and Mallahs, and that by road in the hands of Goalas and Kurmis.

Fairs.

The marginal statement shows the largest fairs held in the district. None, however, are of any great importance, except that held at Rajgir, which takes place every three years. There is only one cattle-fair, *viz.*, that held at Bihta, which attracts about 5,000 persons. As a rule, the people obtain their cattle and horses from the fairs held at Sonpur in the Saran district and at Barahpur in Shahabad.

NAME.		PLACE.
Rajgir fair	...	Rajgir.
Chath	...	Aungari.
Maghi Purnamashi		Barh Umanath.
Gaya Pind	...	Punpun.
Satwani	...	Barh Umanath.
Chiragha	...	Bihar.
Shivratri	...	Atama.
id.	...	Bihta.
id.	...	Baikathpur.
Chaiti Chhath	...	Bargaon.
Katki Chhath	...	Bargaon.

Weights and measures.

The standard seer of 80 *tolas*, known as the *pakka* seer, is in use in the chief centres of trade, the weights being made of metal and stamped. Outside Patna and Dinapore, however, most of the weighing is done by what is known as the *kachcha* seer, which is supposed to consist of a multiple of so many *gandis* (a *gandi* being equivalent to 4 *tolas*), and varies from 44 to 84 *tolas*. The weight used is often a mere lump of stone unstamped and of no definite weight, and the facility afforded for cheating is obvious. The *paseri*, which is supposed to be equal to 5 seers, similarly varies from 5 to 7 seers. Among jewellers and apothecaries the following scale of weights is observed :—8 *ratis* = 1 *masha*, 12 *mashas* = 1 rupee.

For measures of length both the English yard of 36 inches, called the *nambari gaz*, and a local yard of 39 inches, called the *bara gaz*, are commonly employed; the latter is sometimes also 40½ or 41½ inches. For domestic purposes the *hath* or cubit averaging 18 inches and the *balisht* or span of 9 inches are generally used. The principal measures of capacity are all based on the seer, and there are very few cases where standard measures, such as gallons, are used. When sold in large quantities, liquids are often weighed against regular weights; and when sold retail, the commonest measures are vessels made of tin, clay or bamboo. Earthen pots and bamboo *chungas* are in wide use for liquids of all kinds and also bottles of uncertain capacity, which are supposed to hold the equivalent of a seer or part of a seer.

CHAPTER XI.

MEANS OF COMMUNICATION.

Development of communications.

THE account of the roads given by Buchanan at the beginning of the nineteenth century presents a vivid picture of the deficiency of communications at that time. " During the rainy season," he says, " all internal commerce is at a complete standstill, as the roads are then so bad, as not to admit of even cattle travelling with back loads. I have seen no country, that could be called at all civilized, where so little attention has been paid to this important subject, and even in the vicinity of the jails, where many convicts sentenced to labour are confined, very little has been done. The cross roads from market to market are those which are chiefly wanted, and no one who has not seen the condition of these could believe that a country so extremely populous and rich, and having such occasion for land conveyance, could be so ill provided. The object in such roads is not to enable gentlemen to drive their curricles, but to enable cattle carrying back loads to pass at all seasons from one market to another, and in the fair season to enable carts to do the same."

This is not a very high standard, but even so the roads of Patna fell below it, and internal communication was almost entirely confined to pack-bullocks. The Ganges was the great highway between the district and other parts of India, and it continued to form practically the only route to Bengal until 1862, when the main line of the East Indian Railway was extended through the district. In 1877 the Patna-Gaya Canal was opened, and thus provided another means of traffic; in 1879 the Patna-Gaya State Railway was started; in 1903 the Bakhtiyarpur-Bihar light railway was opened for traffic; and recently this line has been extended to Rajgir; and another light railway has been opened from Fatuha to Islampur.

The district is now well provided with communications. The East Indian Railway runs through its northern thanas from end to end; the Patna-Gaya Line and the two light railways intersect the district from north to south; the Patna-Gaya canal skirts the whole of its western border; and the Ganges, with a large boat traffic, bounds it on the north. Besides these main routes, it is well provided with roads connecting the more important bazars and marts; and though it is still somewhat badly off as regards cross roads, practically every village can be reached by pack-bullocks, which are numerous and largely used.

ROADS.

The District Board maintains 157 miles of metalled and 455 miles of unmetalled roads, while 24 miles of metalled road are under the charge of the Public Works Department. This shows a great improvement on the state of affairs prevailing fifty years ago when the total length of all the provincial and district roads was only 469 miles. In addition to these main roads, there are a number of village roads, with a length of 756 miles, maintained by the Local Boards. The roads of fifty years ago included a first-class road which ran from Patna to Gaya, which unfortunately has now disappeared. This road was taken for the Patna-Gaya railway, and the track which now runs by the railway line is usually impassable for wheeled traffic, so that in order to travel by road to Gaya it is necessary to go by way of Bihar and Nawada.

The two great historic roads of the district are the roads which run by the Ganges and Son. The first runs from Koilwar Ghat through Maner, Dinapore, Patna, Barh and Dariapur, whence it runs to Monghyr and Bhagalpur on the east. This is the ancient route from Bihar by Sakrigali to Bengal. It is metalled from Maner to Fatuha, and is a fine broad well-shaded road throughout. The second ancient road runs through Phulwari, Naubatpur, and Bikram to Kanpa, whence it runs parallel with the Son into Gaya district. This is the old road from Patna to Delhi. The best *mufassal* roads are those from Patna to Hilsa through Fatuha; and from Patna to Bikram, through Maner and Bihta.

The west of the district is well provided with good roads; but in the centre and east much of the internal traffic is carried on by means of pack-bullocks, owing to the obstruction of rivers, streams and irrigation channels to carts which attempt to leave the main routes. It is not until the end of the cold weather that the interior of this part of the district is opened to them. The carts in use are similar to those used in other parts of Bihar.

RAILWAYS. The main line of the East Indian Railway traverses the north of the district for 86 miles from east to west, entering it at Burhee station and leaving it a short distance to the west of Bihta, where a fine lattice-girder bridge has been built across the Son. This great work was commenced for a single line of rails in 1855, and after many interruptions during the Mutiny, was completed in 1862; the second line was begun in 1868 and finished in 1870. The total length of the bridge from back to back of the abutments is 4,199 feet, divided among 28 spans of 150 feet each. Underneath each line of rail is a sub-way for foot-passengers and beasts of burden, for which tolls are levied by the railway company. A branch line from Mokameh Junction to Mokameh Ghat connects with the Bengal and North-Western Railway, and another short branch line runs from Bankipore to Digha Ghat, in connection with a ferry steamer of the same railway. Bankipore is also the junction for the Patna-Gaya Railway, which runs south through the Bankipore subdivision, leaving it near Nadaul station 23 miles from Bankipore. Further to the east are the light railways, from Fatuha to Islampur (27 miles), and from Bakhtiyarpur to Bihar and Rajgir ($32\frac{3}{4}$ miles), whereby the interior of the Barh and Bihar subdivisions is linked up with the East Indian Railway system.

WATER COMMUNICATIONS. The Ganges is the chief waterway of the district; but owing to the diversion of its upper waters for irrigation purposes, it can only be navigated above Digha by small steamers of light draught. The Indian Navigation and Railway Company, jointly with the Rivers Steam Navigation Company, maintain regular steamer services along it. Large stern-wheel steamers ply between Goalundo and Digha, which contains the local head office of the Company. Passengers and goods are transhipped at Digha, whence smaller steamers ply to Buxar on the Ganges and to Barhaj on the Gogra. Steamer stations in Patna district are at Hardi Chhapra, Marufganj, Fatuha, Baikantpur, Barh and Mokameh.

Navigation on the Son is intermittent and of little commercial importance. In the dry season the small depth of water prevents boats of more than twenty maunds burden proceeding up-stream, while the violent floods in the rains equally deter large boats, though boats of five or six hundred maunds occasionally sail up it. The other rivers are not navigable, for with one or two exceptions they are almost dry throughout the hot and cold weather ; in the rains they fill very quickly, but as rapidly subside. When they are in flood, they soon become unfordable, and, as a rule, no boats are obtainable, except at the ferries, which are few and far between. The country people, however, provide a ready substitute in the shape of rafts made of a light framework of bamboos supported on inverted earthenware pots. The Patna-Gaya Canal, which traverses the Dinapore and Bankipore subdivisions, is navigable, and a large number of bamboos are brought down by it to Digha. There is a bi-weekly steamer service on it between Khagaul and Mahabalipur in the south of the headquarters subdivision..

Ferries. Outside Patna and Bankipore, the principal ferries are those on the Ganges at Hardi Chhapra, Sherpur and Daudpur in the Dinapore subdivision, all situated along the Dinapore-Maner road, and at Bakhtiyarpur, Barh, Athmal Gola and Mokameh in the Barh subdivision. These are first-class ferries managed by the District Board of Patna. The *ghats* in Bankipore and Patna are at Digha, Mahendru, Ranighat, Pathrighat, Adrak, Marufganj, Damriahi and Jethuli. They are let in one lot with the *ghats* of the opposite bank by the Magistrate of Patna, who distributes the rent between the District Boards of Saran and Muzaffarpur and the Patna Municipality.

Boats. The boats used in the district are all country made, the principal centres of the industry being Patna city, Banka Ghat and Fatuha. They are, in general, broad in the beam, and can therefore be used in comparatively shallow water. The larger boats have a roof-like deck to protect the goods inside from the weather. There is one mast, on which a cloth sail full of rents and patches is hoisted when the wind is favourable. When going down stream, they are propelled from the stern by means of long bamboo punt-poles, and are steered by a huge rudder of the rudest construction. On the return journey, which is generally made when the river is at its lowest, the boats are tracked up against the stream by means of ropes fastened to the top of the mast, but should there be any wind, the tow ropes are coiled up and the sail is hoisted. For crossing the Ganges or the Son, smaller boats are used. Some are decked with bamboos or boards, on which a little straw is sometimes put for conveying horses or bullock-carts; passengers are generally taken across in undecked boats. These boats are propelled by bamboo punt-poles, and sometimes also with a pair of oars. The rowers sit near the prow, all on the same seat; and the oars, which are formed of a bit of board tied with rope to a short bamboo handle, work against pegs to which they are loosely fastened with rope.

A long narrow dug-out, cut from the trunk of a tree, is often used for crossing rivers. Sometimes two of these dug-outs are lashed together to support a bamboo raft. During the rains the villagers use the small rafts which have been described above. Seated astride of one of these primitive but effective rafts, they manage to cross flooded rivers or streams too deep to ford.

POSTAL COMMUNICATIONS.

There are altogether 522 miles of postal communication in the district and 77 post offices. The number of postal articles delivered in 1922-23 was 6,278,625, including letters, postcards, packets and newspapers; the value of money orders issued was Rs. 49,06,527 and of those paid Rs. 61,72,590, and there were 17,830 accounts in the Savings Bank, the total amount of the deposits being Rs. 10,78,831. There are also 23 telegraph offices and the number of messages sent and received by them was 74,149 and 92,940, respectively.

CHAPTER XII.

LAND REVENUE ADMINISTRATION.

IN the second chapter of this Gazetteer some account has been given of experiments in Revenue Administration which were made between 1765 and 1789. These early experiments were all based on the farming system which had been developed from the beginning of the eighteenth century; but they failed because while the nominal assessment increased, the effect of turning loose a horde of greedy adventurers on the raiyats had been to discourage cultivation, and to reduce the real assets of estates. The Permanent Settlement, by giving security of property, encouraged the increase of cultivation; and in districts which were largely uncultivated in 1789 zamindars could, by bringing in raiyats from Oudh, avail themselves of the advantages which the Permanent Settlement was intended to confer. But the Settlement of 1789 was based on the inflated nominal demand which had been created by the competitive bids of farmers who almost invariably failed to meet their engagements; and in an area like the present Patna district, where there was comparatively little cultivable waste, we need not be surprised to find that during the first ten years of the Settlement, it failed to fulfil the hopes of Lord Cornwallis and Thomas Law. The rise in the money value of the produce of the soil ultimately made the assessment tolerable, but only after many of those who had taken settlement in 1789 had lost their estates. Moreover, the pressure of the heavy revenue demand compelled landlords to exact high rents from the raiyats, and to collect them with severity, with the approval of the Collectors, who were principally concerned with realising the whole revenue demand. The effect of the pressure of these early years is to be seen in the high rents which are common in the district at the present day.

The assessment of 1766.

The revenue assessment of Akbar had been enhanced in the twenty-seventh year of Aurangzeb's reign. Alivardi Khan revised the assessment in 1750; and Muhammad Reza Khan, taking this as his standard, made a new assessment in

1766. Akbar's assessment of Sarkar Bihar was 20·79 lakhs of rupees, which was enhanced in 1685 to 36·49 lakhs, and in 1750 to 38·48 lakhs. Muhammad Reza Khan took this as the basis of his assessment in 1766, and his gross valuation of Bihar district, including Ramgarh, was Rs. 38,48,800. He resumed *jagirs* of the annual value of three lakhs of rupees; there remained *jagirs* of the value of Rs. 3,60,365, *malikana* and *nankar* of Rs. 9,64,975, and zamindari allowances of Rs. 3,08,648. The net revenue of Bihar district was thus Rs. 22,14,812.

These statistics are taken from Grant's account of the finance of Bihar in the *Fifth Report*, from which the following figures are extracted for parganas lying partly or wholly in the present Patna district.* It will be observed that there are considerable differences between Grant's net revenue and the subsequent assessments of John Shore and Thomas Law. Grant's *asl* includes alienated revenue, the nominal annual value of *jagirs* and *nankar* land, as well as zamindari allowances.

Pargana.	Area in square miles.	Assessment of 1766, according to Grant.		Shore's assessment (1783).	Permanent settlement assessment, 1788-1790.	Assessment after resumption proceedings.
		Asl.	Net.			
		Rs.	Rs.	Rs.	Rs.	Rs.
Bihar	209	2,00,000	31,528	† 1,08,000	86,125	1,46,119
Azimabad ...	139·7	1,65,585	32,000	54,501	59,570	1,11,720
Arwal	223	1,74,878	1,47,583	82,000	51,747	‡ 1,05,723
Masaurha ...	173·3				42,138	58,066
Maner	199·7	1,17,967	48,804	49,001	69,745	1,15,668
Malda	93·6	2,60,861	1,15,890	13,001	28,058	‡ 41,326
Pilich	140·3			(SeeBiha·)	89,333	1,15,486
Sanda	12·4	2,54,834	20,061	51,000	47,818	74,914
Balia	102·4				61,920	1,30,314
Shajahanpur ...	61·4	1,25,737	*Nil*	2,900	2,537	65,930
Bhimpur	69·3					67,031
Gayaspur... ...	431·4	2,72,653	85,257	67,190	86,145	1,67,345
Tilbara	159·2	1,87,466	1,22,392	75,001	81,250	1,79,050
Bai katpur ...	2 7	13,912	574	2,801	3,255	3,288
Phulwari ...	72·38	72,931	*Nil*	35,001	42,174	66,256
Biswak*	156	...	...	28,001	73,955	1,|5,545
Rajgir*	37	...	...	26,002	26,002	25,355

* Assessments of parganas (except Malda and Pilich) which were included in the Hasua zamindari are not given separately by Grant. Ragjir was permanently settled in 1781. For Narhat, Okri, Samai and Sanaut, *see* Chapter XVII. Only small portions of these parganas are in Patna district.

† John Shore made a consolidated assessment for Bihar and Pilich.

‡ Arwal is now in Gaya district. Of the area of Malda 1·40 square miles lie in Patna, with revenue of Rs. 567. The rest of the pargana now belongs to Monghyr.

Law's mukarrari settlement.

An account has been given in chapter II of how John Shore's farming settlement was unsatisfactory in its results, and how Thomas Law, despairing of the farming system, made his *mukarrari* settlement with village *maliks* in 1788. The Board of Revenue disapproved of this settlement; but Thomas Law persistently pressed the advantages of a permanent settlement: and he persuaded Lord Cornwallis and the Board of Directors to confirm his *mukarraridars*. In the scheme of the Permanent Settlement, and the wording of the Bihar Regulations, the effect of Thomas Law's writings is largely to be seen; but the term "proprietor of the soil" admits of more than one interpretation: and Thomas Law, in making the Decennial Settlement for the rest of the district, did not settle with village *maliks* when there was a zamindar prepared to take settlement. The settlement with *maliks* was not a success; and in Bihar pargana, the scene of the first experiment, or in Gayaspur where *maliks* generally obtained settlement in 1789, few of the new *mukarraridars* survived to the end of the eighteenth century. One of Law's main principles was that settlement should be made village by village, a principle which he tried unsuccessfully to impose in Bengal after he had become a member of the Board of Revenue. His 'village' unfortunately was not a definite geographical unit, but the charge of a single patwari. So long as the kanungos were retained, and the kanungos' register was kept up, there was probably no trouble; but since the abolition of the kanungos these 'Collectorate villages', known often only by the name of the *malik* who took settlement, have been the source of much confusion in Patna district.

The Permanent Settlement.

The average incidence of land-revenue after the Decennial Settlement was Re. 1-3-0 per acre of revenue-paying land. This was a high rate; and until the end of the eighteenth century there was considerable difficulty in realisation of revenue, particularly from the village *maliks* who had obtained settlement in Bihar and Gayaspur. Act VII of 1799 gave increased powers of distraint to landlords; its provisions were undoubtedly hard on the raiyats, but something of the kind was necessary in Patna if the Permanent Settlement was to be preserved. It was not until the early years of the nineteenth century, as the relative value of silver fell, that the burden became more moderate, and what was at first a very heavy revenue assessment became ultimately light.

Revenue-free tenures, 1789

At the Permanent Settlement nearly forty per cent. of the area of the district escaped assessment, while Government postponed enquiry into the occupiers' claims to hold it revenue free; but this fact afforded no relief to zamindars who did not happen also to hold such revenue-free estates, though great jagirdars like Kallian Singh became very wealthy. In Bihar district 106,000 acres were claimed as *altamgha* grants, (permanent grants by the Mughal Emperor under the great seal). 132,800 acres were claimed as *kharij jama* grants, to be distinguished from *altamgha* grants as having been made by provincial governors. Land claimed under grants for religious purposes included, *aima* grants (115,000 acres), *khairat* (72,300 acres), *Bishunpirit* and *Sivotar* (14,000 acres), and *Brahmotar* (3,700 acres). Land claimed as special *jagirs* included 84,000 acres; 38,000 acres were claimed as *madad ma'ash*, while 17,000 acres were claimed as *sarsikhan* land, given to descendants of zamindars killed in battle. The only other tenures under which large areas were cltimed were simply described as *mafi* (10,000 acres); while *jagir English*, settlements of retired sepoys, accounted for 15,000 acres.

The resumption settlements.

The enquiry into the validity of these various claims was postponed from time to time; a little was done in 1819, but it was not until 1835 that special resumption and settlement officers were appointed. Resumed grants were settled under Regulation VII of 1822. The person preferred for settlement was the holder of the revenue-free grant (*ahlima'ash*), failing whom, settlement was made where possible with the *malik*—that is to say, the village *malik*, not the zamindar. Under the rules in accordance with which the bulk of the resumed grants were settled, settlement was made at half assets if the new estate was to be held by the *malik*, and at half assets increased by half the *malikana* where *malikana* had to be paid. Government thus, in such estates, bore half of the *malikana* charge; and the *malik* henceforth drew his *malikana* from the treasury. This arrangement was however not universally made ; and many estates are burdened with a liability to pay *malikana* to descendants of the ancient *maliks*.

***Zaid-fihrist* lands.**

Three thousand, two hundred and sixteen acres, in small parcels, escaped the notice of the resumption officers, so that they were neither resumed nor confirmed as revenue-free.

These little estates were detected at the Revenue Survey in 1840-41; they were entered in a special register as *zaid-fihrist* lands; but they were never resumed: and since 1914 they have been treated as confirmed revenue-free estates.

The present assessment. The effect of the resumption proceedings was to raise the revenue demand in the present Patna district by Rs. 4,94,000. The present demand is Rs. 15,39,600, of which the assessment on permanently settled estates is Rs. 13,96,196, while the balance is assessed on temporarily-settled and Government estates. Against the land revenue is to be set the Government liability for *malikana*, amounting to Rs. 30,841, payable in respect of 1,405 estates.

Cesses. According to the revaluation under the Cess Act which was completed in 1916, the gross rental of the district is Rs. 1,04,62,859; and the current demand for cess is Rs. 6,04,693, distributed as follows :—

	Rs.
Revenue-paying estates	5,66,628
Revenue-free estates	27,924
Rent-free lands	10,141

PROPRIETORS. A century ago the greatest landowner in the district was the Maharaja Kallian Singh, son of Shitab Rai, and premier nobleman of Bihar. The resumption of the great *jagirs* which Kallian Singh had inherited with the office of naib-diwan reduced the family's importance; and it gradually decayed until the death of Kunwar Rup Narain Singh, the last survivor of the male line, early in the present century. Second in rank only to Shitab Rai's family was that of Manir-ud-daula. Reza Quli Khan, Manir-ud-daula, died in 1774, but the title of Nawab Manir ud-daula and the bulk of his *jagirs* were extended to his son. With each generation *jagirs* were resumed and estates were alienated, until little is now left, though the descendants of the Nawab, living in his garden house, whence they are commonly known as the Bhikhnapahari family, enjoy high social standing in Patna. The powerful Hasua family ended with Iqbal Ali Khan, who had lost his great possessions by his rebellion in 1781. A descendant of Muhammad Baqir Khan lives at Tilhara; but the zamindari of that pargana is now shared among a number of comparatively petty landlords.

Of the historical families of the district, only those of Tikari, Masaurha, Rajgir and Islampur survive as considerable zamindars. The property of the Tikari zamindars lies chiefly in the separated portion of *zila* Bihar, as does that of the zamindars of Rajgir (the Hosseinabad family, descended from the brother of Ibrahim Ali Khan with whom Rajgir was settled in 1782). The Masaurha family, descended from collateral branches of that of Raja Jaswant Singh, dominate the pargana as a clan, though there has been much subdivision of proprietary rights. They are commonly known as the Babus of Sehra, Bharatpura and Dharhara; and an account of them is given in chapter xvii. The Chaudhris of Islampur, a family of smaller local importance, retain much of their ancestors' zamindari in Shahjahanpur and Bhimpur parganas.

Ammawan. The most powerful zamindar of Patna district is now Raja Harihar Prashad Sinha Bahadur of Ammawan who is descended from Basdeo Rai, a Bhumihar Brahman, who acquired *milkiat* property in Malda pargana in or about the year 1670 A.D. which his grandson Chaudhri Bhelam Singh considerably extended by purchase. Among the family archives is a record of how their ancestors successfully resisted the attempt of the formidable Mayis to oust them from their *milkiat*. The ancestors of the present Raja did not convert their *milkiats* into zamindari in 1788, at Thomas Law's permanent settlement of Malda, so that they retained only their *malikana* rights, of which an interesting survival is to be seen in the annual gifts which the shopkeepers of Barbigha make to the Raja. In the middle of the nineteenth century Babu Karam Chand Singh acquired a considerable zamindari about Ammawan and Harganwan, which was extended by the father of the present proprietor. The Raja has married the proprietress of the seven-anna Tikari estate.

The Guzri family. The most prominent residents of Patna, including the leaders of the professional classes, hold comparatively little landed property in the district, owing chiefly to the fact that the excessive subdivision of proprietary rights makes it difficult to acquire a compact estate. The most considerable zamindars among the residents of this urban area are the members of the Guzri family, including the descendants of Nawab Vilayat Ali Khan, and the great-grandson of Nawab Lutf Ali Khan, Khan Bahadur Saiyid Muhammad Ismail, formerly chairman of the Patna City Municipality. The family originally came from Medina to Meshed in Khorasan, whence in the middle of the eighteenth century they came to India, settling first in Oudh, and moving to Patna at the beginning of the nineteenth century. Their progenitor who came to Patna became Mir Munshi of the Company's Factory, and acquired much property in land in Bihar. In the middle of the nineteenth century the family was represented by the Nawabs Vilayat Ali Khan and Lutf 'Ali Khan, each of whom came into prominence in 1857. Lutf Ali Khan, who became a Companion of the Order of the Indian Empire, contributed largely to the foundation of the Bihar School of Engineering; and his son, Nawab Haji Saiyid Badshah Nawab Razvi, made over a considerable portion of his estates in Patna for the support of female education in Bihar.

TENURE-HOLDERS.

Apart from the tenures of the *maliks*, the tenures known as *dastur mukaddami* and *dastur kanungoi* are probably the most ancient. There are in the district many settlements of invalided sepoys (*jagir English*), made under Regulations of February 18th, 1789, XLIII of 1793, I of 1804 and II of 1808. The settlements, which were known as thanas, lay chiefly on the main lines of communication, so that Dr. Buchanan, as he went up and down the roads of the district, was always coming upon them. Much of the land which was brought under cultivation by the original invalids has been alienated by their descendants; but the homestead land, which was separately specified in the *patta*, and the common grazing land and parade ground of the thana are still frequently held by the descendants of the original holders, known locally as *khana muafi sakunat* and *ghulam gardish*.

Relations of landlord and tenant.

The prevalence of the systems by which the rent payable varies with the produce gives at each harvest occasion for friction between landlords and tenants; but in the larger estates these systems are generally worked with moderation. They undeniably give opportunities to speculative purchasers to annul for practical purposes all the protection which agrarian legislation has afforded to occupancy raiyats, of which advantage has sometimes been taken. On the other hand raiyats have frequently combined to buy shares in estates, so that they have acquired proprietary rights in their own holdings, and the number of peasant proprietors in this district is thus exceptionally large. In this connection it is interesting to notice the extent to which subdivision of proprietary rights has gone in Patna district. In 1789, though even then many of the estates were petty *milkiats*, there were only 1,156 estates in the district. By 1876 the number had increased to 5,930. There are now 15,107 revenue-paying and 1,411 revenue-free estates. Moreover, the estates themselves are held by a multitude of co-sharers, so that the average area held by a single sharer is now less than ten acres. This kind of peasant-proprietor flourishes particularly in Barh and Bikram thanas; in the latter thana typical instances quoted in the Settlement Report are found in Bawan, with 231 sharers in 238 acres, and in Sihora, where 44 sharers hold 58 acres.

CHAPTER XIII.

GENERAL ADMINISTRATION.

THE LEGISLATIVE COUNCIL.

PATNA district returns five members to the Legislative Council :—three by the Non-Muhammadan and two by the Muhammadan electorate, apart from the share which the landholders and the urban population take in returning their members for the Patna Division. A member is also returned by the Patna University.

DISTRICT ADMINISTRATION.

Bankipore is the headquarters of the Commissioner of the Patna division and of the Magistrate and Collector of the district, which for administrative purposes is divided into the subdivisions of Bankipore, Patna City, Barh, Bihar and Dinapore. The Magistrate-Collector is ordinarily assisted by an additional District Magistrate, who is stationed in the city, and holds charge of the Patna City subdivision. The headquarters staff consists at present of seven deputy collectors and three sub-deputy collectors, while the subdivisional magistrates are each assisted by a deputy or sub-deputy magistrate. Dinapore Cantonment is ordinarily in charge of a military cantonment magistrate. In addition to the general staff there are special officers in charge of the departments of excise and income-tax.

REVENUE.

The main heads of revenue in the district are land revenue, excise, stamps and income-tax. Land revenue has been discussed above in chapter xii.

Excise.

In the decade ending with 1900-1 the excise revenue rose from Rs. 6,50,800 to Rs. 7,70,500. In 1905-6 when the first edition of this Gazetteer was published the revenue from this source was Rs. 8,64,435. The excise revenue during the last five years has been as follows, *viz.* :—

YEAR.	Rs.
1917-18	10,92,769
1918-19	12,00,063
1919-20	12,48,844
1920-21	12,92,200
1921-22	14,61,350

The greater portion of the excise revenue is derived from the sale of the country spirit prepared by distillation from molasses and the flower of the mahua tree (*bassia latifolia*). The receipts from this source amounted in 1921-22 to Rs. 9,08,265. There are 118 shops in the district licensed for the sale of country spirit. For sale of the fermented liquor known as *tari* 939 shops are licensed; and the revenue from this source in 1921-22 was Rs. 2,12,139. Receipts from hemp drugs and opium account for practically all the remainder of the excise revenue. The greater part is derived from the duty and license fees on *ganja* (Rs. 2,25,000 in 1921-22). The receipts from opium in the same year were Rs. 99,643.

Stamps.

The revenue from stamps during the last five years has been as follows, viz. :—

	Court-fee stamps.	Non-judicial stamps.
	Rs.	Rs.
1917-18	6,43,610	1,50,688
1918-19	6,09,313	1,49,390
1919-20	6,97,846	1,96,287
1920-21	6,79,855	1,83,126
1921-22	8,03,193	2,17,406

The revenue from judicial stamps in 1905-6 was Rs. 3,04,907; but the position of Patna district with regard to this source of revenue has been completely changed by the institution of the High Court.

Income-tax.

The revenue from income-tax has risen from Rs. 79,152 in 1905-6 to Rs. 1,40,485 in 1922.

Registration.

There are nine officers for the registration of assurances under Act III of 1877. In 1905, 15,168 documents were registered in the district; receipts were Rs. 40,613 and expenditure Rs. 13,829. The marginal statement shows the number of documents registered, and receipts and expenditure at each office in the district in 1922.

Office.	Documents registered.	Receipts.	Expenditure.
		Rs.	Rs.
Bankipore ...	5,184	45,023	11,618
Jhauganj ...	2,992	12,754	4,754
Barh ...	3,679	11,664	2,870
Bihar	3,464	13,426	3,821
Dinapore ...	3,257	10,025	2,417
Hilsa	2,265	7,682	2,249
Masaurhi ...	1,608	5,374	2,349
Mokameh ...	1,374	5,820	2,757
Bikram	2,245	5,983	3,158
Total ...	26,068	1,17,751	35,993

ADMINISTRATION OF JUSTICE.

The civil courts are those of the district judge, three subordinate judges, and three munsifs at Bankipore, munsifs at Barh and Bihar, and a small cause court judge at Dinapore, who is the subdivisional magistrate. Civil work is on the whole similar to that of other Bihar districts; but the chief distinguishing feature in the rent-suit work is the large number of claims for arrears of produce-rent which is the result of the prevalence of that system, particularly in the Bihar subdivision.

Criminal justice.

Criminal justice is administered by the district and sessions judge, the district magistrate, the additional district magistrate, and the stipendiary and honorary magistrates at headquarters and subdivisional stations. The sanctioned staff at Bankipore consists of four deputy magistrates exercising first class powers, and two exercising second or third class powers, with two sub-deputy collectors. The additional district magistrate at Patna City is assisted by a deputy magistrate exercising first class powers; and the subdivisional magistrate of Bihar is assisted by two sub-deputy magistrates. Each of the other subdivisional magistrates is assisted by a sub-deputy collector. There are benches of honorary magistrates at Bankipore, Jhauganj, Barh, Bihar, Dinapore, Khagaul and Sadikpur.

Public Works Department.

Patna is the headquarters of the Superintending Engineer of the Eastern Circle and of the Executive Engineers who are respectively in charge of the new capital (special works division) and the Patna division; while the headquarters of the Eastern Son irrigation division are at Dehri.

Police.

For police purposes the district is divided into thirty-two thanas or police circles with thirty-one outposts. In the survey and settlement proceedings the thanas then existing were adopted for revenue divisions in place of the old parganas; but many of the stations which then formed outposts are now independent police-stations, so that for police purposes all the old thanas have been subdivided except Fatuha and Islampur. The general control is with the Superintendent of Police, who ordinarily has under him an assistant superintendent, two deputy superintendents, twelve inspectors, 73 sub-inspectors, 150 head-constables and 1,323 constables. The rural force for the watch and ward of villages consists of 287 dafadars and three thousand chaukidars.

There is a District Jail at Bankipore and a subsidiary jail at each of the outlying subdivisional stations of Barh and Bihar, besides a lock-up at Dinapore for under-trial prisoners. The jail at Bankipore has accommodation for 411 prisoners distributed as follows :—barracks are provided for 294 male convicts, 28 female convicts, 27 juvenile convicts, 44 under-trial prisoners, and 10 civil prisoners ; and there are separate cells for six male and two female convicts. The hospital has accommodation for 25 prisoners. The principal industries are the manufacture of carpets and mustard oil. The sub-jail at Barh has accommodation for 24 male and 4 female prisoners, and that at Bihar for 31 male and 4 female prisoners. Jails.

CHAPTER XIV.

LOCAL SELF-GOVERNMENT.

DISTRICT AND LOCAL BOARDS.

OUTSIDE municipal areas, local affairs are managed by the District Board which has jurisdiction over the whole district, and by the Local Boards which have been constituted for each subdivision. The District Board until recently consisted of six official and eighteen non-official members, of whom twelve were elected, with an elected non-official chairman; but it now consists of forty members, of whom thirty are elected. In the Local Boards two-thirds of the members consist of members elected to the District Board by the electorate of the area over which the Local Board has authority, while the remaining members are nominated by the District Board. The District Board is responsible for the maintenance of roads, bridges and roadside rest-houses, and has the general superintendence of primary and middle schools. It is also entrusted with the management of pounds and public ferries, the control over local dispensaries, the provision of a proper water-supply, and village sanitation. The work which is being done under these various heads is described in chapters V, VI, XI and XV of this Gazetteer; and it is unnecessary to describe it again here. To the Local Boards, which work in subordination to the District Board, are delegated the administration of the sums allotted for the construction and repair of village roads, the supervision of local sanitation, and of local cattle pounds and dispensaries.

Income.

In Patna, as in other districts, cesses levied under the Cess Act form the principal source of income of the District Board; and the incidence of taxation is slightly over six annas per head of the population. The gross rental of the district, according to the revaluation which was completed for cess purposes between 1913 and 1916, is Rs. 1,04,62,859. The following table shows the income of the Board, with the principal sources, for the five years ending with 1921-22.

	1917-18.	1918-19.	1919-20.	1920-21.	1921-22.
	Rs.	Rs.	Rs.	Rs.	Rs.
Total receipts	8,22,086	7,96,237	7,78,546	7,51,646	7,73,222
Principal heads—					
Local rates	6,26,821	6,15,434	5,91,442	6,27,455	6,03,600
Cattle-pounds	10,386	10,088	11,252	9,068	8,384
School fees	5,156	2,732	3,271	3,061	3,087
Railways	5,582	...	4,900	...	59,319
Ferry tolls	12,043	10,365	11,303	8,134	12,846
Contributions from Government.	1,35,980	1,07,521	1,26,048	68,641	55,641

The following table shows expenditure during the same period :—

	1917-18.	1918-19.	1919-20.	1920-21.	1921-22.
	Rs.	Rs.	Rs.	Rs.	Rs.
Total expenditure ...	7,21,689	6,51.136	7,67,695	7,70,790	7,64,934
Principal heads—					
Administration ...	16,441	17,570	24,022	41,883	57,600
Cattle-pounds	4,197	1,750	2,806	1,812	1,507
Education	93,675	1,00,647	1,23,281	1,27,793	1,41,981
Medical charges	60,767	73,365	81,250	72,322	1,00,562
Veterinary, etc.	7,076	5,392	15,074	6,644	10,827
Pensions	3,061	3,046	4,110	7,659	6,211
Civil works, (roads, etc.).	5,30,157	4,44,434	5,04,425	5,02,014	4.43.588

MUNICIPALITIES.

There are five municipalities in Patna district, at Patna, Barh, Bihar, Dinapore and Khagaul, to which may be added the Patna Administration Committee, which is charged with the municipal administration of the area included in the new capital.

Patna City.

The most important of the municipalities is that of Patna City, established in 1864. The area within municipal limits includes Patna City proper, and its suburbs up to and including Bankipore. There are 27,600 ratepayers; and the municipality consists of 40 members, of whom 32 are elected. The principal source of income is a tax of 9½ per cent. on the annual value of holdings, with a latrine fee of 6¼ per cent. An efficient water-supply has now been provided for the western portion of the municipal area; but the municipality, though it enjoys a comparatively large income, serves a proportionately large area: and here as elsewhere schemes for the proper drainage and water-supply of the whole municipal area are hampered by lack of funds. The following table shows the income and expenditure of the municipality for the five years ending with 1921-22:—

INCOME.

	1917-18.	1918-19.	1919-20.	1920-21.	1921-22.
	Rs.	Rs.	Rs.	Rs.	Rs.
Total income	3,70,900	3,24,874	7,56,712	4,40,415	3,78,726
Sales of securities ...	2,26,209	3,00,371	23,935	...	...
Loans and advances ...	58,346	37,381	1,63,228	32,911	17,586
Total receipts	6,55,455	6,62,626	9,43,875	4,73,326	3,96,312
Principal heads—					
Rates and taxes ...	2,38,260	2,55,820	2,78,327	2,78,623	2,89,068
Cattle-pounds	688	564	1,041	405	790
Hackney carriages ...	3,362	3,300	3,164	3,436	3,673
Markets	829	767	1,000	760	805
Grants from Govt. ...	90,432	51,280	4,30,504	1,35,486	63,852
Grants from Local Funds.	12,500	2,500	11,000	4,000	4,000

EXPENDITURE.

	1917-18.	1918-19.	1919-20.	1920-21.	1921-22.
	Rs.	Rs.	Rs.	Rs.	Rs.
Expenditure	7,06,820	7,01,048	6,77,110	4,53,894	3,63,630
Repayment of loans, etc.	56,280	48,673	61,891	1,69,335	73,187
Total disbursements ...	7,63,100	7,49,721	7,39,001	6,23,229	4,36,817
Principal heads—					
Administration ...	18,567	19,893	23,820	20,911	28,821
Lighting	19,977	24,977	28,791	29,071	30,715
Water-supply— capital	2,70,363	3,17,625	2,16,092	1,04,292	33,020
Water-supply — establishment.	2,846	3,002	3,310	4,732	3,343
Drainage—capital ...	5,124	20,513	14,107	5,171	2,512
Drainage — establishment.	9,680	13,161	15,392	18,676	23,919
Conservancy	2,02,184	1,84,414	1,42,578	1,39,357	1,37,442
Hospitals, etc. ...	77,713	11,122	9,307	9,852	10,897
Roads	55,305	49,123	55,855	65,194	35,853
Education	13,564	14,342	12,362	12,548	13,122

Barh was constituted a municipality in 1870 and has a municipal board consisting of 10 members, of whom 8 are elected. The area within municipal limits is 2·87 square miles, and the number of ratepayers is 1,940. The following table shows the income and expenditure of the municipality for the five years ending with 1921-22:— **Barh.**

INCOME.

	1917-18.	1918-19.	1919-20.	1920-21.	1921-22.
	Rs.	Rs.	Rs.	Rs.	Rs.
Income	21,607	17,799	19,399	21,342	23,777
Loans and advances ...	2,984	1,749	2,000	2,000	1,588
Total receipts	24,591	19,548	21,399	23,342	25,365
Principal heads—					
Rates and taxes ...	12,195	11,820	11,363	14,599	15,015
Cattle-pounds	1,138	592	544	796	723
Grants from Govt. ...	3,109	2,518	3,460	1,574	4,237
Grants from Local Funds.	4,000	2,000	2,803	2,900	3,161
Markets and slaughter-houses.	...	...	...	92	69

EXPENDITURE.

	1917-18.	1918-19.	1919-20.	1920-21.	1921-22.
	Rs.	Rs.	Rs.	Rs.	Rs.
Expenditure	21,218	17,534	20,112	23,794	21,614
Repayment of advances	1,500	4,697	2,150	2,175	1,849
Total disbursements ...	22,718	22,231	22,262	25,969	23,463
Principal heads—					
Administration ...	1,455	1,483	1,690	2,356	1,729
Lighting	998	1,268	1,039	1,624	1,801
Conservancy	3,596	3,676	4,397	6,107	5,479
Hospitals, etc. ...	8,861	4,630	5,563	7,523	6,819
Markets and slaughter-houses.	1,110	421	182	3	5
Roads	2,343	2,277	2,015	2,333	520
Education	770	1,505	2,910	1,529	2,078

Bihar was constituted a municipality in 1869 and has a municipal board consisting of 20 commissioners, of whom 16 **Bihar.**

are elected. The area within municipal limits is 8 square miles, and the number of ratepayers is 7,600. A statement of income and expenditure for the five years ending with 1921-22 is annexed :—

INCOME.

	1917-18.	1918-19.	1919-20.	1920-21.	1921-22.
	Rs.	Rs.	Rs.	Rs.	Rs.
Income	41,867	44,637	40,960	40,170	40,658
Loans and advances ...	...	2,627	3,710	4,375	3,240
Total receipts	41,867	47,264	44,670	44,545	43,898
Principal heads—					
Rates and taxes ...	32,212	30,560	28,957	28,787	29,214
Cattle-pounds	637	685	535	590	404
Markets, etc.	488	590	653	459	541
Grants from Govt. ...	4,230	8,588	4,871	5,733	2,104
Grants from Local Funds.	3,000	2,350	5,103	3,000	7,023

EXPENDITURE.

	1917-18.	1918-19.	1919-20.	1920-21.	1921-22.
	Rs.	Rs.	Rs.	Rs.	Rs.
Expenditure	43,175	45,687	38,004	44,098	40,333
Repayment of advances	100	354	5,102	3,600	3,463
Total disbursements ...	43,275	46,041	43,106	47,698	43,796
Principal heads—					
Administration ...	2,782	2,826	4,088	2,770	3,570
Lighting	1,317	1,069	1,775	1,606	1,638
Drainage	2,146	2,245	2,247	3,518	1,112
Conservancy	13,226	15,236	11,785	12,263	14,114
Hospitals	9,619	8,895	7,969	8,973	10,747
Roads	6,322	5,737	2,881	5,579	290
Education	2,687	2,652	2,801	3,321	3,875

Dinapore. The municipality of Dinapore Nizamat was constituted in 1869, and has a municipal board consisting of 20 commissioners, of whom 16 are elected. The area within municipal limits is 5 square miles, and there are 4,878 ratepayers. Income and expenditure during the 5 years ending with 1921-22 was as follows :—

INCOME.

	1917-18.	1918-19.	1919-20.	1920-21.	1921-22.
	Rs.	Rs.	Rs.	Rs.	Rs.
Income	31,613	33,868	33,906	38,324	31,176
Sale of securities ...	11,988	...	...	13,800	...
Loans and advances ...	4,105	4,797	3,369	3,960	5,199
Total receipts	47,706	38,665	37,275	56,084	36,375
Principal heads—					
Rates and taxes ...	24,737	22,787	21,167	21,373	21,518
Cattle-pounds	202	88	152	135	200
Grants from Govt. ...	3,362	3,290	2,439	7,441	2,021
Grants from Local Funds.	1,700	4,500	6,626	6,097	5,844

EXPENDITURE.

	1917-18.	1918-19.	1919-20.	1920-21.	1921-22.
	Rs.	Rs.	Rs.	Rs.	Rs.
Expenditure	30,647	35,590	31,994	32,294	36,612
Investments	13,000	...	800	13,000	200
Repayment of advances	4,596	5,971	7,191	7,976	1,560
Total disbursements ...	48,243	41,561	39,985	53,270	38,372
Principal heads—					
Administration ...	2,550	3,026	3,087	3,336	3,280
Lighting	2,126	1,649	2,531	1,993	2,564
Conservancy	9,498	9,924	12,696	13,009	14,363
Hospitals, etc. ...	4,671	7,787	6,997	6,929	11,181
Markets, etc.	3,261	550	...	...	...
Roads	2,835	2,482	2,574	2,684	1,154
Education	4,786	6,671	3,048	2,921	2,835

The town of Khagaul was constituted a municipality on the 1st of July, 1907. There are 1,338 ratepayers, and the municipal board consists of 11 commissioners, of whom 9 are **Khagaul.**

elected. Income and expenditure during the 5 years ending with 1921-22 has been as follows:—

INCOME.

	1917-18.	1918-19.	1919-20.	1920-21.	1921-22.
	Rs.	Rs.	Rs.	Rs.	Rs.
Total income	14,189	13,609	13,461	17,193	14,693
Principal heads—					
Rates and taxes ...	12,372	12,245	12,147	12,566	12,560
Cattle-pounds	282	282	280	120	120
Grants from Govt. ...	340	340	340	3,914	1,586

EXPENDITURE.

	1917-18.	1918-19.	1919-20.	1920-21.	1921-22.
	Rs.	Rs.	Rs.	Rs.	Rs.
Total disbursements ...	15,534	13,634	15,849	14,823	14,775
Principal heads—					
Administration ...	2,649	2,299	2,554	2,738	3,092
Lighting	2,444	2,365	2,232	2,584	2,599
Conservancy	5,826	5,451	5,975	5,394	5,208
Roads	1,715	364	737	181	448
Education	834	794	813	832	768

Patna Administration Committee.

The Patna Administration Committee consists of 9 members, nominated under Act I of 1915, for the administration of the area contained within the new capital, in respect of lighting, drainage, conservancy, and the municipal market, and in the application of the building regulations. There are 720 ratepayers, and the income from rates and taxes in 1921-22 was Rs. 68,231; but hitherto the main source of income has been the grant from Government, since the Committee is dealing with a city still in course of completion. In 1921-22 the Committee spent Rs. 6,772 on administration, Rs. 5,810 on lighting, Rs. 31,928 on conservancy, and Rs. 5,400 on other sanitary requirements.

CHAPTER XV.

EDUCATION.

Progress of education.

THE state of education in the district at the beginning of the nineteenth century may be gathered from the following account written in 1812 by Dr. Buchanan :—" There are no public schools, and there is no *guru* or teacher who is not a servant to some wealthy man. The *gurus*, however, are generally allowed to instruct the children of the neighbours, and a hut is built for a school-house without the village, lest the *guru* should have too frequent opportunities of seeing the women. These school-houses are called *pindas*, a name applicable to several things considered sacred. In parts of the country where sugarcane grows, the boiling-house usually serves for a school." Persian was the language used in the courts, and many Hindus were taught to read and write the Persian character before they began Hindi ; but the greater part of them proceeded little further than learning to understand and write a revenue account, and were not able to understand or to indite a letter properly. Such an accomplishment entitled a man to be called a munshi. There were some half dozen maulavis who instructed a few young men in Persian literature and Arabic science, and there were thirty-eight *pandits* teaching the higher sciences of the Hindus, grammar, law and metaphysics; but by far the greater part of the landholders consisted of mere peasants, half of whom could not read, though the head of each family generally acquired the art of being able to make a mark resembling the characters which composed his name. The total number of persons fit to act as writers was estimated at nearly twenty thousand or 1·2 per cent. of the population.

During the first half of the nineteenth century the State left the care of education to private enterprise; the only schools in the district were the *maktabs* and *pindas*, as the schools teaching Persian and Hindi were called ; and nothing was done to supplement this indigenous system of education. In 1845 the famous educational despatch was issued, in which the Court of Directors laid down that Government should afford assistance to "the more extended and systematic promotion of general education in India," and sketched a complete scheme of public education controlled and aided, and in part directly managed, by the State. In accordance with these orders, Government began to establish schools, and in 1860-61 there were nine vernacular schools maintained by it, the number of pupils under instruction being 399. In 1862 the Patna College was opened, and in 1870-71 there were, in addition to this institution, 23 Government and aided schools attended by 1,530 scholars. In 1880-81, besides the Patna College, there were three aided and four unaided high schools with a total attendance of 781 boys; sixteen middle vernacular, 46 lower vernacular and 1,633 primary schools teaching 927, 2,095 and 23,154 pupils respectively; and in addition to these aided schools, there were 464 unaided institutions with 6,955 pupils. The Government survey school and the Patna normal school had 29 and 101 pupils respectively; the Temple Medical School, established in 1874, had 146 pupils; and there was a law school attached to the Patna College with 41 law students. At the end of the decade there were 1,373 public and 612 private institutions containing 31,918 and 4,559 pupils respectively, making a total of 1,985 schools with 36,477 pupils; and in 1900-01 there were 1,626 schools with 38,162 pupils. The figures for later years are shown in the table below:—

Class of Institutions.	1910-11.		1921-22.	
	Institutions.	Pupils.	Institutions.	Pupils.
I.—Public Institutions.				
For Males.				
Colleges	4	545	6	1,282
High schools	13	3,148	17	3,080
Middle English schools	6	381	10	770
Middle vernacular schools	6	414	8	649
Upper primary schools	47	2,017	85	4,523
Lower primary schools	1,173	30,574	1,194	31,217
Special schools	25	787	29	1,410
Total	1,274	37,866	1,349	42,931

CLASS OF INSTITUTIONS.	1910-11.		1921-22.	
	Institutions.	Pupils.	Institutions.	Pupils.
I.—PUBLIC INSTITUTIONS—concld.				
FOR FEMALES.				
High schools	1	72	1	111
Middle English schools	1	49	2	185
Upper primary schools	...	...	6	223
Lower primary schools	145	1,950	226	3,963
Special schools	18	351	3	54
TOTAL	165	2,422	238	4,536
Total of public institutions ...	1,439	40,288	1,587	47,467
II.—PRIVATE INSTITUTIONS.				
For males	397	4,810	199	3,967
For females	2	21	5	55
TOTAL	399	4,831	204	4,022
Grand Total of all institutions ...	1,838	45,119	1,791	51,489

It will be seen that the number of public schools and of pupils in them continues to rise, while private institutions are gradually becoming merged into the departmental system.

Literate population.

The census statistics reproduced in the margin show the percentage of persons returned as literate, *i.e.*, as able to read and write. In 1901 the total number of such persons was 109,648, representing 6·8 per cent. of the population, and of these 7,981 could read and write English. In 1921 the figure had risen to 137,038, representing 8·7 per cent. of the population, of whom 16,267 could read and write English. Patna has a higher percentage of literacy than any other district of the province as regards both sexes, the preeminence being marked in the case of the female sex.

Year.	Males.	Females.
1881 ...	6·7	0·9
1891 ...	9·9	0·4
1901 ...	12·3	0·6
1911 ...	12·6	0·9
1921 ...	15·6	1·4

European education.

The oldest European school in the district is *St. Joseph's School* at Bankipore, which was opened in 1853. This is a Roman Catholic boarding and day school for girls, managed by the nuns of the Institute of the Blessed Virgin Mary; it has 171 borders and 24 day scholars, half of the latter being boys. *St. Michael's High School,* which is situated at Kurji, midway between Bankipore and Dinapore, owing its existence to Monsignor Zuber, Vicar Apostolic of Patna, who in 1854 purchased the grounds in which it stands, with the object of forming a community of Indian Christians. The Mutiny, however, wrecked the scheme, for the converts were dispersed, and the place was left without inmates. When order was restored, Dr. Hartmann, then Vicar Apostolic of Patna, opened in the building an orphanage for children left parentless by the Mutiny; and this was the beginning of the present establishment. More buildings were added, and the institution gradually grew, till it became in course of time a large boarding house and orphanage combined. In 1894 it was handed over to the Irish Christian Brothers, under whose management it has become a very successful school. The number of boys in the school is 194, including a large number of orphans, and the staff consists of nine brothers, five secular teachers, a nurse and a matron. The only other school in the district for Europeans is that at Khagaul, which is maintained by the East Indian Railway. There are 33 boys and 34 girls on the roll, all day scholars.

Indian education.

Patna is now the home of a University, which was established on October 1st, 1917. The scheme for a university was drawn up by a committee appointed in the year 1913 under the chairmanship of the late Sir Robert Nathan, K.C.S.I. It was contemplated that there should be a teaching and residential university at Patna, to be located on a site immediately to the west of the New Capital, and that in addition the university should exercise control over the other colleges in the province in much the same way as such control had previously been exercised by the university of Calcutta. Unfortunately, financial considerations have prevented the materialisation of the scheme for a central university; and the university has at present no buildings of its own except its office at Bankipore. Land has indeed been acquired as suggested by the committee of 1913, but both on financial and on general grounds the desirability of transplanting the whole university has been questioned. Meanwhile the teaching activities of the university are performed by its constituent colleges, the work of which has benefited by the share which their teachers now have in controlling the policy of the university. The number of candidates registered for examination in 1920 was 4,298 at the matriculation, 1,059 at the intermediate, 502 at the degree, and 29 at the higher degree stage, while 34 candidates appeared in education and 390 in law.

The six colleges in the district are two first-grade Arts Colleges, *viz.* Patna College and the Bihar National College, two second-grade Arts Colleges, *viz.* New College and the Nalanda College at Bihar, and a Training College for teachers and a Law College, both at Patna.

Patna College

Patna College was first opened as a Government school in 1860 under the local Committee of Public Instruction. In 1862 it was made a collegiate school, and in 1863 it was raised to the status of a college. A law department was added in 1864, but in the year 1909 this section of the college developed into a separate institution. Informal higher degree classes in history and economics were opened in 1911, but with the formation of the new university it was recognised that this branch of the work needed to be expanded and placed on a surer footing. Uncertainty regarding the location of the proposed central university made the erection of new buildings impossible, but room was found by removing the intermediate classes in Arts to the collegiate school, a change which is referred to later. The necessary space having thus been obtained, arrangements were made in 1919 to teach up to M. A. Standard in English, mathematics and Sanskrit, the old classes in history and economics being at the same time reorganised and provided with an adequate staff. In the following year work was started up to the M. A. standard in Persian and to the M. Sc. standard in physics and chemistry. The staff consists of 36 members, of whom twelve are in the Indian Educational Service, sixteen in the Bihar and Orissa Educational Service, and eight in the Subordinate Educational Service. The number of students on the roll is 355, including 86 in the higher degree classes. The hostel accommodation is sufficient for 136 boarders, and the direct cost of the college in 1921-22 was Rs. 2,42,000.

Bihar National College. The Bihar National College was founded in 1883 as a high school by Babu Biseswar Singh, a pleader practising at Patna. In 1889 it was raised to the status of a second-grade college and in 1892 it was raised to the B. A. standard. It was first aided by Government in the year 1907, and now receives a grant of Rs. 2,950 a month. It teaches up to the degree standard in arts and science in the pass course only. The staff consists of 23 teachers and the number of students on 31st March 1922 was 390. The direct cost of the college in 1921-22 was Rs. 67,157. There is hostel accommodation for about eighty boarders.

New College. New College at Patna was formed in the year 1911 by transferring the intermediate classes in Arts back from Patna College to the Patna Collegiate School, the institution from which they had developed nearly sixty years before. The four lower classes of the Collegiate School were closed at the same time in order to set free the necessary space. There are now 178 pupils in the college classes and the total direct expenditure on those classes in 1921-22 was Rs. 39,080. The establishment of this college, combining as it does the intermediate classes with the higher classes of a school, anticipated one of the most important recommendations of the Calcutta University Commission; and its career is being watched with interest. The staff has recently been revised on the basis that every teacher, except certain specialists, should be capable of teaching school and college classes alike, and the total number of teachers employed is now 22.

Nalanda College. The Nalanda College at Bihar was established in July 1920 on lines similar to those of New College. It owes its existence to an endowment made by the late Rai Bahadur Edal Singh, which yields an income of Rs. 8,000 a year and thus practically meets the cost of the college classes, which last year was Rs. 8,972; while the number of pupils on the roll was 31.

The Patna Training College. The Patna Training College was opened in the year 1908 as an institution designed to train twelve students for the diploma of Licentiate in Teaching. From 1915 it has trained candidates for the degree of Bachelor of Education and the number of annual admissions was then raised to forty. The course, both in the B. Ed. and in the L. T. classes, covers one session; and the number of students admitted to each class is twenty. Until 1921 the college was practically reserved for persons who had already obtained employment, and particularly employment under Government. Since then, however, half of the places have been reserved for candidates for employment. Persons already employed receive full pay while under training, while other students receive subsistence allowances of Rs. 35 if graduates and Rs. 25 if holders of the intermediate certificate (persons with lower qualifications are not eligible for admission). The staff consists of two officers in the Indian Educational Service and three in the Bihar and Orissa Educational Service; and there is excellent hostel accommodation for all the students.

Patna Law College

The Patna Law College developed out of the law classes at Patna College. It is housed in a residential building recently acquired at Chauhatta. Students are prepared for the degree of Bachelor of Law and for the pleadership certificate, either course being for three years, though only graduates may be admitted to the former. There are 272 students in the B.L. classes and 18 in the pleadership classes. The staff consists of a whole-time principal and six part-time lecturers for the B. L. classes, and one part-time lecturer for the pleadership work.

High schools.

Of the seventeen high schools for boys (including the school sections of New College and the Nalanda College), three are maintained by Government and nine receive grants-in-aid, the remainder being unaided institutions. The schools maintained by Government are New College (school section), the Patna City School and the Patna High School in the New Capital, and those aided by it are the schools at Bihar, Barh, Mokameh Ghat, Bharatpura, Dinapore and Khagaul, the Ram Mohan Roy Seminary and Pataliputra High School in Bankipore, and the Muhammadan Anglo-Arabic School in Patna City. Of the unaided high schools one, the Gruning Soghra Waqf School, is at Bihar; one, the Aryan high school, is at Dinapore; and three are within the municipal limits of Patna, *viz.*, the Bihar National Collegiate School, T. K. Ghosh's Academy, and the Anglo-Sanskrit School There is also a high school for girls at Bankipore.

Middle schools.

The middle English schools for boys, with one exception, are all aided by Government. The school which serves as the practising school of the Patna Training School is under the direct management of Government. The middle vernacular schools are all under the direct control of the District Board. The middle English schools for girls are mentioned later.

Primary schools.

Of the 1,279 primary schools for boys, 208 receive no support from public funds. Of the remainder, the practising schools attached to the *guru* training schools are directly managed by Government, while the District Board also directly maintains a small number of schools. The great majority, however, are of the class known as stipendiary; that is to say, the establishment of the school and its location depend upon the teacher himself, and the District Board gives a small stipend to supplement the teacher's income from fees. The stipends paid have always been small, and financial reasons have prevented any increase in them commensurate with the increase in the cost of living.

Special schools.

The 29 institutions shown as special schools for males are the Bihar School of Engineering, the Bihar Weaving School, the Temple Medical School, nine training schools, two commercial schools, a madrasa, and fourteen Sanskrit *tols*.

The Bihar School of Engineering.

The Bihar School of Engineering owes its origin to a fund raised by the residents of Bihar to commemorate the visit of the Prince of Wales to Patna in the year 1876. It was opened as a school of engineering twenty years later, preference in admission being given to Biharis. The management of the school was transferred from the Education Department to the Department of Industries on 1st September 1921, and a strong Governing Body has been appointed to control the examinations and other matters connected with the school. There are at present upper subordinate and lower subordinate classes in which overseers and sub-overseers respectively are trained, and also classes for artisans. The overseer course is for three years and is followed by practical training for another year, while the sub-overseer course is of two years only; the standard for admission to either of these classes is the matriculation certificate or a pass at an equivalent examination held at the school. The roll number is now 153 and the students who pass out readily obtain employment, for of 193 such students during the past five years 184 have obtained posts. The school has a fine building on the banks of the Ganges; and there are also two well-fitted workshops, and hostel accommodation for all the students other than the artisans. The question of adding college classes is now under consideration.

The Bihar Weaving School.

The Bihar Weaving School was started during the year 1910. The teaching staff consist of an instructor and a *mistri* ; and of two batches of the students each are admitted annually for a course of training which lasts for one year. During their training they receive a monthly stipend of six rupees each and, when they leave the school, each is presented with a fly-shuttle sley. The cost of the school last year was Rs. 3,132 to Government and Rs. 862 to the District Board.

The Temple Medical School.

The Temple Medical School was started in 1874 in order to afford medical education in the vernacular to Biharis and to relieve the Medical College at Calcutta of its military sub-assistant surgeon class. It was moved to its present site on the banks of the Ganges in 1875; and since then the accommodation has been greatly improved, among the additions being hostels for students of both sexes and an anatomical theatre. Further large developments are in contemplation in connection with the scheme to develop the school into a college. The Patna General Hospital, which immediately adjoins the school, provides the necessary clinical material. The number of students is now 267 and the staff consists of the Civil Surgeon of Patna as Superintendent, eight assistant surgeons and five sub-assistant surgeons. At the conclusion of their course, which lasts for four years, the successful students are given the diploma of Licensed Medical Practitioner. There is also a class for compounders, to which thirty admissions may be made annually. The number of female students is very small, for since 1892, when the admission of such students was sanctioned, only nine have successfully completed the course.

Training schools.

The training schools include a first-grade training school at Patna and eight elementary training schools. The former was until recently designed to give a three years' course to students with middle qualifications, but this arrangement has recently been altered and a two years' course is now given to matriculates or, if such students are not available, to students who have failed at the matriculation. The students receive stipends during their training, and on its successful completion obtain posts as vernacular teachers in secondary schools. The number of admissions is 25 every year. The elementary training schools are designed to train vernacular teachers for primary schools. Each school can hold seventeen teachers, the course being one year for students with middle qualifications and two years for others. At all the training schools hostel accommodation is provided for all the pupils.

Madrasas.

The only other special school of importance is the Madrasa Islamia Shamsul Huda, which was founded by Mr. Saiyid Nurul Huda, C.I.E., and taken under Government management during the year 1919-20. This institution is still in its infancy, but spacious new buildings are under construction; and it is hoped that in due course it will develop into an important centre of Islamic learning. It has now 141 pupils..

The education of girls.

The development of female education in Patna is comparatively recent. The returns for 1880-81 shew only one school for girls with 65 pupils, and only 28 girls attending boys' school. In 1890-91 the number of girls' schools had increased to 80, and the attendance to 1,257 girls, besides 317 girls reading in boys' schools, making a total of 1,574; and in 1901 there were 65 girls' schools with 939 pupils, in addition to 173 girls attending boys' schools. In 1910-11 the number of girls in girls' schools was 2,443, and in boys' schools 787. In 1920-21 the figures were 4,591 and 62 ; and in 1921-22, 4,566 and 92.

Secondary schools for girls.

The high school for girls is that at Bankipore which was founded in 1867 by the Bengali community. Formerly an aided school, it was taken under Government management in 1914. It has now 111 pupils and is housed in a building known as the Bari Nepali Kothi close to the Gola. The Chhoti Nepali Kothi, which adjoins it, has recently been given to the school for use as a hostel. The two middle English schools for girls are one maintained by the Baptist Mission at Bankipore and one maintained by Government as the practising school of the Badshah Nawab Razvi Training College, which is mentioned later.

Primary schools for girls.

The remarks already made regarding primary schools for boys apply also to primary schools for girls. A special difficulty which these schools have to face is that of obtaining qualified women to work as teachers. In the *mufassal* most of the teachers are men, but in Patna itself there are eighteen women teachers called *atus* working among the Muhammadans. A lady Superintendent has been appointed to supervise their work.

Special schools for girls.

The special schools for girls are the Badshah Nawab Razvi Training College and a lace class attached to it, and a training class for women maintained by the Baptist Mission at Bankipore. The former was established in January 1909 with the help of an endowment made by Saiyid Badshah Nawab Razvi of Patna City which yields an approximate income of Rs. 7,267 a year. It is housed in a building near Gulzarbagh, which formerly belonged to the Bettiah estate, but has recently been acquired by Government and improved in many ways. When the college was first established attempts were made to train women with very low qualifications, but this has proved useless; and arrangements are now made to teach the women up to the middle standard before their training begins. The number of women engaged in this preparatory work has averaged more than twenty during the past four years, and last year sixteen women proceeded from the preparatory work to the training class. The college is in charge of a Lady Principal in the Indian Educational Service and there is residential accommodation for all the staff and the students.

Muhammadan education.

The progress of Muhammadan education is shown in the marginal table. As the Muhammadan population of the district is 158,438, out of a total of 1,574,287, or 10 per cent., while the Muhammadan pupils number 7,493 out of 51,489, or nearly 15 per cent., it is plain that the Muhammadans are not behind the general average for the population.

Year.		Number of Muhammadan pupils.
1860-61	...	171
1870-71	...	289
1890-91	...	4,336
1900-01	...	5,000
1910-11	...	7,262
1930-21	...	7,889

Inspecting staff.

The Patna district shares with the other districts in the division an Inspector of Schools, a special Inspecting Officer for Muhammadan education and an Assistant Inspectress. It has also a District Inspector in the Bihar and Orissa Educational Service, 15 sub-inspectors, 2 inspecting maulavis, an inspector of Students' Residences and the Lady Superintendent of *atus* already mentioned.

Hostels.

There are 21 hostels for males in the district with 676 boarders and three for females with 148 boarders.

Libraries and literary societies.

The number of libraries and literary societies officially returned as such is twelve, but the only important institutions are the Oriental Public Library, the Srimati Radhika Institute, and the Rupkala Bhagwan Library at Bankipore, and the Bihar Young Men's Institute. The Oriental Public Library, founded in 1890 by Khan Bahadur Khuda Bakhsh Khan, C.I.E., is accommodated in a building erected by the founder. It contains a unique collection of Persian and Arabic manuscripts and books, a complete catalogue of which has been under preparation for many years at Government expense, as well as a useful collection of works of reference and of literary interest. In this connection should be mentioned also the Srimati Radhika Institute founded by Mr. Sachchidananda Sinha, member of the Governor's Council, in memory of his late wife. The Institute is housed in a fine new building near the Patna-Gaya Road, and contains also a Public Library. The Bihar Young Men's Institute aims at providing social facilities for the students of the different colleges in Bankipore.

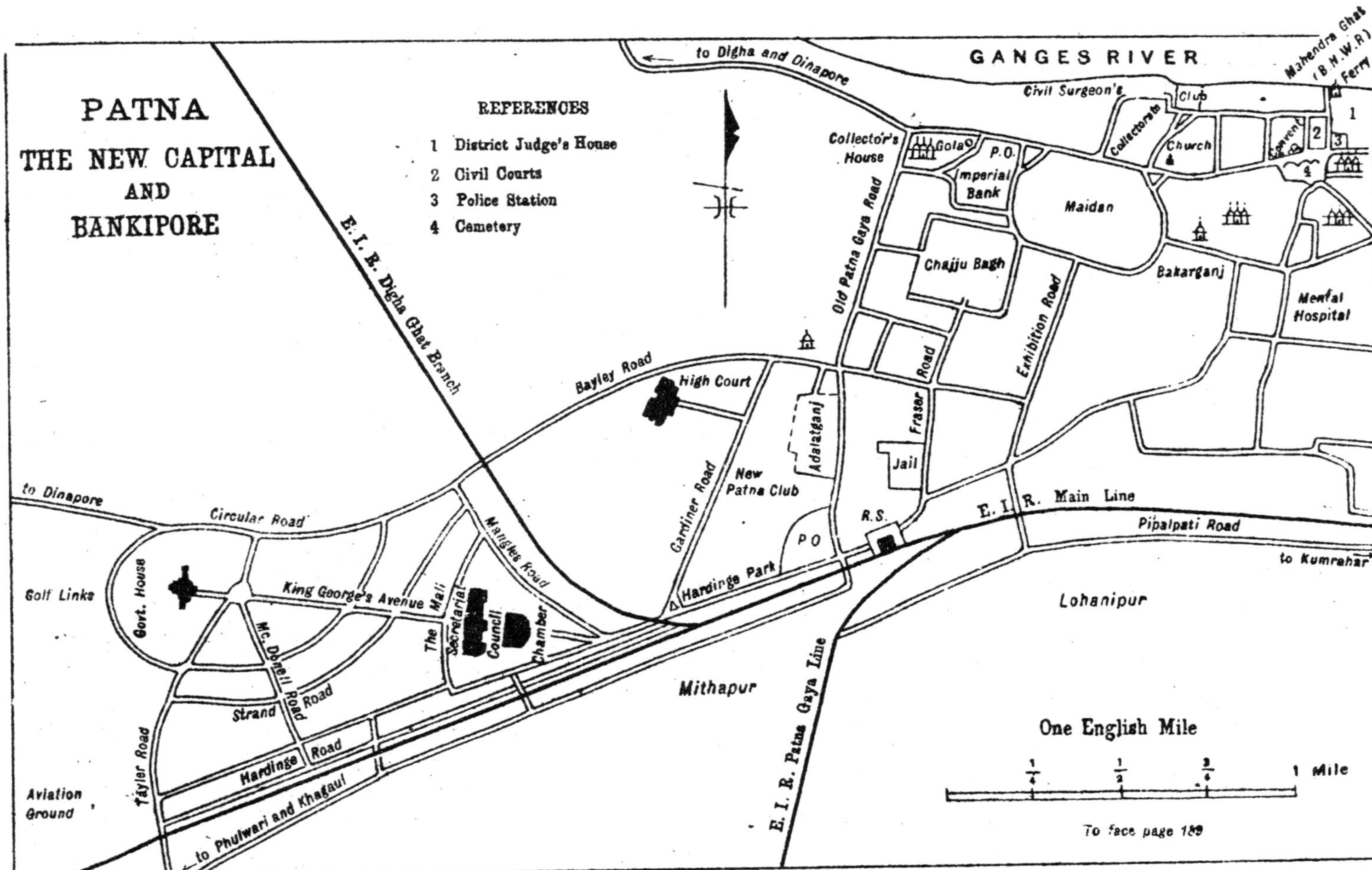

To face page 189

CHAPTER XVI.

THE CAPITAL OF BIHAR AND ORISSA.

PATNA, the capital of Bihar and Orissa, and the head-quarters town of Patna district, is situated on the south bank of the Ganges at 25° 37′N and 85° 10′E. The population is now 119,976, of whom 90,248 are Hindus, and 28,200 Muhammadans. Dr. Buchanan in 1812 estimated the population at 312,000: whatever may be thought of this estimate, William Tayler's figure of 400,000 in 1857 must be regarded as greatly exaggerated. At the census of 1881 the population was 170,654; but since that time it has been steadily declining. In 1911 it was 136,153. In the early nineteenth century Patna was of great commercial importance as the centre of trade between upper India and Bengal; but since the coming of the East Indian Railway the city has been injuriously affected by the decline of the river-borne traffic. This tendency has been accentuated by successive improvements in railway communications in adjoining districts, by the growth of the Tirhut State Railway in the trans-Gangetic districts, the opening of the South Bihar Railway from Kiul to Gaya, the Patna-Gaya Line, and the Grand Chord Line. When these local lines are opened, it is no longer economical to send local produce to Patna for distribution, because rates of booking for short distances are not so low as to make it worth while to unload at Patna, and consignors discover that it is best to book through to the ultimate destination. Population.

Other causes for the decline of the commercial importance of the city, apart from the change in means of communication, were the abandonment of the Company's trade in the early years of the nineteenth century, and in late years the abandonment of the opium trade which had for centuries flourished in

Patna. Apart from these causes for depopulation, plague seriously affected the city in the early years of the present century. But though the population of the city may thus have been steadily decreasing, its importance as an educational and administrative centre is by no means diminishing. For the last sixty years, since Patna College was founded, Patna has been the most important place of education in Bihar; and it is now a university town, the acknowledged headquarters of educational activity in the Province. Moreover, in 1912, with the inauguration of the new Province of Bihar and Orissa, Patna was restored to its old station of a Provincial Capital.

PATALIPUTRA.

Patna stands on the site of one of the ancient cities of the world; but little remains above ground to testify to its early greatness. Various legends exist regarding its origin, of which the most popular ascribes it to Putraka, who named it Pataliputra in honour of his wife Patali. Buddhist accounts place its origin in the reign of Ajatasatru, king of Magadha, describing how the Lord Buddha found the fort in course of building, and halted for a night here on his last journey (*circa* 487 B.C.). A town naturally grew up by the fort, which in the fourth century B.C. became the capital of the Mauryan empire. About 300 B.C., when Chandra Gupta reigned in Pataliputra, Seleukos Nikator sent hither as his ambassador Megasthenes, who wrote an account of the city, of which fragments, quoted by other writers, yet remain.

Megasthenes' account.

Megasthenes describes the municipal government of the city, which was in charge of six boards, each consisting of five members. The first board superintended industries and artisans. The second was concerned with foreign visitors. They found lodging for foreigners who arrived in the city, procured medical attendance for them if they fell sick, buried them if they should die, and forwarded their property to their relatives; and if the foreigner survived the dangers of the city, the board provided an escort for his further journey. The third board was concerned with the registration of births and deaths, not only, says Strabo, for revenue purposes, but also in order that Government might be kept informed of fluctuations of population. The fourth board superintended trade and commerce; they had charge of weights and measures; and it was their duty to see that trade was done in public. The fifth board specially supervised the sale of manufactured articles, which also must be done in public. Each trader had to pay for a license for each kind of commodity in which he dealt. A tenth of the price of articles sold was also exacted, the collection of which was the business of the sixth board. The whole body of thirty councillors was in charge of public buildings and temples, markets and wharves, and the regulation of prices.*

The tradition that Pataliputra had a divine founder did not derive its origin from the magnificence of the buildings subsequently erected by Asoka, since Megasthenes ascribed the foundation of the city to Herakles. The city stood on the tongue of land formed by the confluence of the Ganges and the Son.† Like the modern city under which its remains lie buried Pataliputra was a long and narrow parallelogram, ten miles long and two miles broad. It was defended by a wooden wall, pierced with loopholes, crowned with 570 towers, and having sixty-four gates, protected by a ditch on the landward side, which served for purposes of defence and also as the city sewer. The wooden buttresses supported an earthen rampart; Mr. Manoranjan Ghosh cites Chanakya as authority for the statement that there was a carriage way on the top of the parapet, which has been confirmed by Dr. Spooner's discovery of an ancient chariot wheel actually lying by the rampart.

Excavations at Bulandibagh, etc.

Excavations at Maharaj Khanda and Bulandibagh have disclosed part of this wooden wall. The result of the recent excavations at Bulandibagh was particularly interesting, disclosing the wooden palisade and one of the gateways

*Strabo, XV, 1.

†Erranoboas (Hiranyabahu), then flowing in a bed now partly occupied by the Punpun. See the account of the river Son given in Chapter I above.

of the ancient city, with the chariot wheel lying by the rampart. The wall and tower consist of massive logs of sal wood, fastened together by great wooden pegs. This palisade was apparently at the southern wall of the city. Traces of a similar structure have been also found west of the Kankar Bagh road at Lohanipur.

Excavations at Kumrahar. Chandra Gupta's grandson Asoka, who became an enthusiastic convert to Buddhism, erected a great palace and many stone buildings at Pataliputra, of which the Chinese traveller Fa Hian wrote six centuries later:—"The royal palace and halls in the midst of the city which exist now as of old were all made by spirits at Asoka's bidding, who piled up the stones, reared the walls and gates, and executed the carving and inlaid sculpture, in a way which no human hands could accomplish." Part of a great stone building of Asoka's period was discovered by Dr. Spooner when he excavated at Kumrahar, which was regarded by him as identical in plan with the Hall of a Thousand Pillars at Persepolis. This work of systematic excavation was rendered possible by a liberal donation from the late Sir Ratan Tata; but it was carried on with great difficulty, owing to the water-logged condition of the country. Half of the work consisted of getting rid of the water; and much that had been done was again undone as the monsoon floods annually filled up the trenches.

Buddhist survivals. Colonel Waddell has drawn attention to interesting survivals from Buddhist days which are found at Bhikhnapahari, Bulandibagh, and the Agam Kuan. One such survival may be seen in the worship of a mound called Bhikhna Kunwar, or the mendicant-prince, near the north-eastern base of the Bhikhnapahari mound. "The object", writes Colonel Waddell, "here worshipped under the title of the Bhikhna Kunwar is the image of a many-peaked hill with a pathway leading up from the base along a ledge and climbing a steep valley to a tortuous recess in which the cave was situated. It is, and always has been, without any enclosure and uncovered by any awning or roof. This is clearly the fac-simile in miniature of the hermitage hill built by Asoka for prince Mahendra, who afterwards became the Buddhist Apostle of Ceylon. In Asoka's time objective Buddhism had not yet reached beyond the stage of relic worship; and here we find in the Bhikna Kunwar the practice of that primitive stage of Buddhism still conserved. The prince's hermitage is worshipped under his name. This image is worshipped by the semi-aborigines of the country—the Dusadhs, Ahirs and Goalas—with offerings of flowers, fruits, milk, sweetmeats and silken thread, in the same manner as the remote ancestors of the present generation of worshippers paid homage to the mendicant prince Mahendra in Asoka's day. As the Dusadhs are essentially worshippers of devils and malignant ghosts, they now add to the above offerings their habitual wine libation and an occasional pig sacrifice; but it is remarkable that these are applied to the outer side of the hillock, while all the truly Buddhist offerings of milk, rice, sweetmeats, flowers and fruits are deposited in the recess half-way up the hill, where the cave appears to have been situated, and the outer entrance to which faces eastwards. The higher caste Hindus in the neighbourhood pay the Dusadhs to make offerings on their behalf.

"The history of this image, so far as can be ascertained from the hereditary Dusadh priest in charge of it, is that it existed on the top of the mound of Bhiknapahari, to which it gave its name from time immemorial until Maniruddaula began building his house upon the hill and close to the image. The tradition goes that the building fell down several times and could not be completed until the Muhammadan noble besought the great-grandfather of the present priest to remove the image, and accompanied the request with a present of money. It was then removed to the site where it now is.

"The image is about four and a half feet high and made of clay. As it exists quite in the open and unprotected by any roof, it is partially eroded and washed away during the rains. It is therefore repaired after each rainy season. Its present shape is that which has been handed down in the priest's family as the orthodox shape; but why this particular shape was given it the priest is unable to say. The survival of this image with a well-preserved form during all these centuries is a curious fact in the history of idol-worship, especially when it is remembered that the image is made of perishable plastic material requiring constant renewal, and the worshippers, as well as their priests, are quite unaware that the object which they worship is a hill."*

Two other superstitions have also been observed which appear to date back to Buddhist times. Thus the people of Patna still repeat the legend quoted in the seventh century by Hiuen Tsiang that a stone slab, found in Bulandi Bagh and identified with that on which Buddha last stepped before crossing the Ganges to die at Kapilavastu, always comes back to its old place wherever it may be moved. Equally curious is the legend about the well or pit called Agam Kuan at Patna, which has been identified with the hell of Asoka mentioned by Hiuen Tsiang as having contained fiery cauldrons and ovens for torturing prisoners. According to his account, Asoka was converted to Buddhism through seeing that a Buddhist monk, who had been cast into a furnace in this hell, remained unscathed and was found miraculously seated on a lotus flower. "The very same legend," says Colonel Waddell, "which the Chinese pilgrim records in regard to the torture-chamber, is still related by the Jain priests of the temple adjoining this Agam well. They tell how a monk named Sudarsan was thrown by the king of Pataliputra into a fiery furnace in the neighbourhood; but he remained unscathed and was found seated serenely on a throne of lotuses, to the astonishment of the king, who ordered his release and afterwards patronised him and established him in the immediate neighbourhood. The current popular legend of this Agam well or pit associates the place both with heat and with hell. It is regarded with horror, and though actively venerated, its water is never drunk. It is specially worshipped during the hot weather beginning

*L. A. Waddell, *Discovery of the Exact Site of Asoka's Classic Capital of Pataliputra*, Calcutta, 1892.

with the onset of the hot winds in March and lasting for four months. During these months, and specially on the eighth day of each month, troops of women and children come bringing offerings of money and flowers which they throw into the well, and they especially pray for protection against the disfiguring fever of small-pox. The largest gathering is on the Agri *Mela* on the eighth day of Asarh, at which over 100,000 people attend and goats are sacrificed. The modern legend also associates it with the Indian hell, alleging that the well leads down to hell in the centre of the earth, and that a heavy piece of wood which was lost in the ocean was found by a sage down this well, which, according to the local Brahmanical etymology, means the bottomless pit (*agaham*), though the word is never so pronounced by the people themselves."*

Other reminders of the early Buddhist period are to be seen in the mounds, remains of Buddhist stupas, which are found here and there in the city and its southern suburbs, particularly in the mounds known as Bari Pahari, Chhoti Pahari and the Panch Pahari, south of the Agam Kuan. Two ancient statues which were apparently discovered somewhere in the neighbourhood of Bhikhnapahari, seen by Buchanan in 1812, are now in the Museum at Calcutta. Mr. K. P. Jayaswal considers that they are pre-Mauryan statues of Saisunaka kings; and readers may be referred to his monograph on the subject.† A fine female statue, apparently of the Mauryan period, discovered in 1917 owing to erosion of the river bank at Didarganj on the east of the city, is now in the Patna Museum.‡

Decay of Pataliputra.

With the fall of the Mauryan dynasty the importance of Patna as a capital city ceased; but it apparently continued to exist as a great town until the Hun invasion of the sixth century A.D., which was followed by the invasion of Sasanka, who sacked the city, destroyed its sacred relics, and scattered

*L. A. Waddell. *Report on the excavations at Pataliputra*, Calcutta, 1903.

†Statues of two Saisunaka Emperors (483-509 B.C.). by K. P. Jayaswal, *J. B. O. R. S.*, Vol. V, p. 88.

‡The Didarganj Image now in the Patna Museum, by D. B. Spooner, Ph. D., *J. B. O. R. S.*, Vol. V, p. 107.

the Buddhist monks. When at about 640 A.D. Hiuen Tsiang came to India, he found Pataliputra in ruins. "It is," he says, "an old city but long deserted; now there only remain the old foundation walls. The monasteries, Hindu temples and Buddhist stupas, which lie in ruins, may be counted by hundreds, and only two or three remain entire." All that was left of the ancient city was a small town, containing about 1,000 houses, to the north of the old palace and bordering on the Ganges. For nearly a thousand years Patna remained an inconsiderable town; but that it was not entirely neglected is apparent from the fact that Allauddin Hossain Shah, Sultan of Gaur, built here a mosque at the end of the fifteenth century A.D., which may be seen on the main city street near the Chauk.

Modern Patna.

The city appears to have rapidly grown in importance after Sher Shah built the fort in 1541. Forty-five years later, when Ralph Fitch saw the "lasie lubber" sleeping on a horse at the Chauk, Patna had grown into a great town with a large trade in opium and cotton cloth. The town extended for 1½ miles from the eastern to the western gate, and for three-quarters of a mile from north to south; but it appears from the Sair-ul-Mutakharin that in the early eighteenth century the city had spread beyond the walls.*

* "There was already a city wall, but so neglected and decayed, and withal, so beset by houses, that it could hardly be distinguished from them. He (Zain-ud-din) ordered that a deep ditch should be sunk round, and that the earth dug from it should be thrown behind and upon the old wall, so as both to raise and strengthen the same. But as this was not to be done without ruining the houses already built on the side of the old wall or close to it, it did not fail to occasion much murmuring and much discontent among the owners. But the utility of the undertaking was so apparent, that no regard could be paid to their complaints; and in a little time the wall, rising gradually from the ground, afforded an insurance of future safety. In process of time, whenever the country came to be overrun by Marathas (and it has been so several times), not only vast numbers of people used to retire within the walls, and to find their safety there; but even the numerous houses and habitations which remained without, were effectually protected from plunder by the cannon of the rampart. This work being at last finished, the Governor commenced to live easy in his palace."—*Sair-ul-Mutakharin*, I, 427. The wall, being mainly of mud, required constant repair to keep it effective. It was put in repair in 1772; but from that time it was neglected. It had not completely ceased to be a wall in Buchanan's time: he remarks that it could be easily placed in such repair as to afford a defence against predatory horse (Pindarries, who were actually on the border of Bihar district, causing considerable alarm, while Buchanan was in Patna).

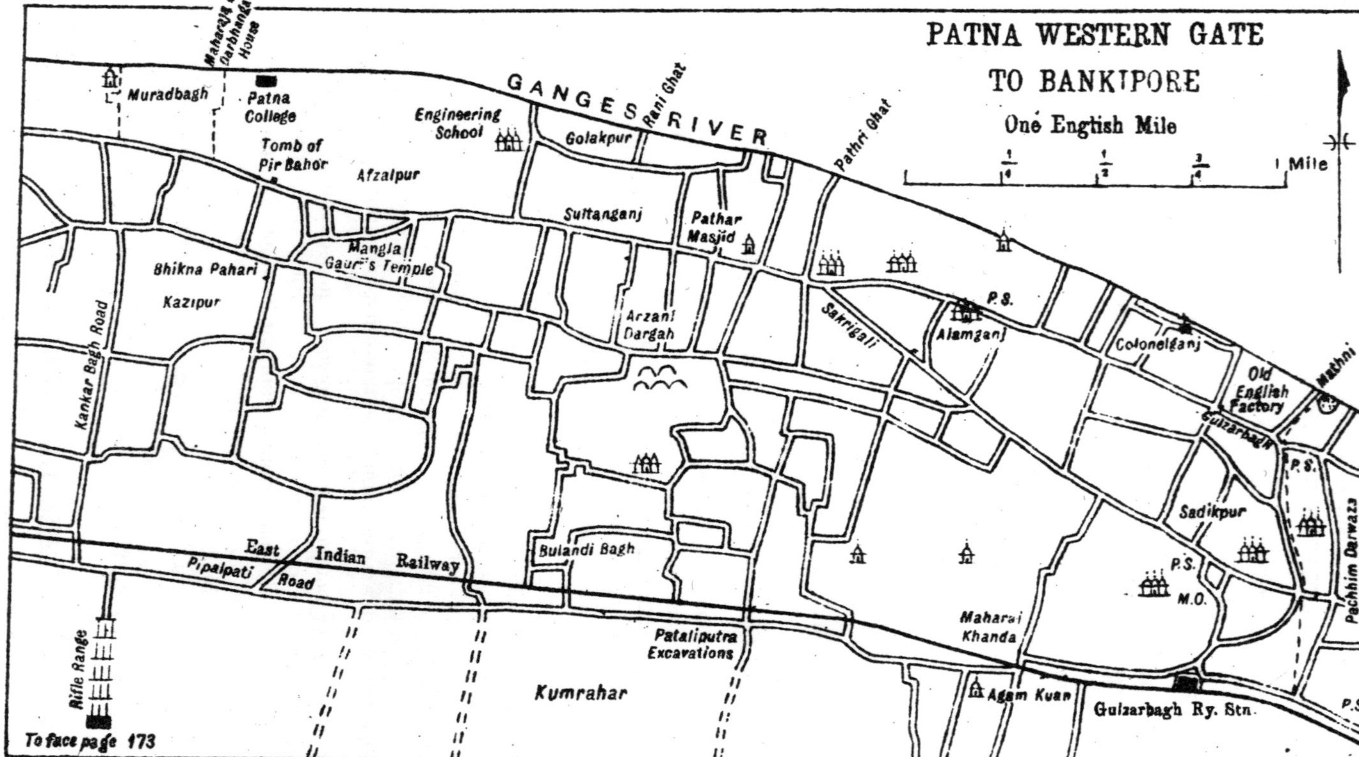

To face page 173

The eastern and western gates, which are now marked by carved blocks of black stone, were sometimes adorned at that period with grim trophies. Thus when Mustafa Khan, the rebellious general of Alivardi Khan, was killed, his body was cut in two and half was suspended at each gate; and a similar fate befell Zain-ud-din after his murder by the Afghans in 1748. The line of the old wall may still be traced without any difficulty. Three of the great towers which marked the four corners of the wall still exist, one east of the fort on the Ganges, another close to Patna City Railway Station, and the third east of Gulzarbagh Railway Station. The fourth, the great bastion which was strengthened in 1763 to command the neighbouring English Factory, was demolished in 1857.

In 1741, as we have seen, the city already extended beyond the walls; great men had their garden houses in the suburbs, and along the river bank as far as Bankipore, where the East India Company had a garden (Company Bagh) on the Ganges. The removal of the factory to this *bagh* (or rather to land on the west of it), and the growth of the bazar which served the needs of the Brigade at Bankipore (Barkerganj), resulted in a great development of the western suburbs. This process of westward extension continued after the Brigade was moved to Dinapore. It is an exaggeration to say that there is a continuous line of houses from Sherpur to Gulzarbagh; but the whole of this long road is suburban in character, though the line of houses is from time to time broken by wooded stretches between Bankipore and Digha. Many of these houses are of mean appearance, ill-built, ill-ventilated, and insanitary; and it cannot be denied that to the casual observer they give an appearance of squalor to the town as a whole.

THE RIVER-FRONT OF PATNA.*

The most pleasing aspect of Patna is that which is to be obtained from the Ganges. The distant prospect of the eastern part of the city is magnificent, though now, as a hundred years

*In this topographical portion of the account of Patna I have followed, with some modifications, the system adopted by Mr. Ram Lal Sinha, in his contributions to Mr. Manoranjan Ghosh's *Pataliputra* to which work I take this opportunity of acknowledging my obligations. Nobody who wishes to explore the highways and by-ways of Patna should do so without that book.

ago, the traveller may be disappointed on a nearer approach by the too common appearance of neglect and dilapidation.* On the Bankipore side, the striking beauty of the scenery, as the morning sun tinges the eastern face of the temples and bungalows lying half-hidden among the great trees which line the southern bank, owes nothing to distance or myopia. The finest views of the Ganges from the land are to be obtained from the lower portion of the city; and the river scenery from the Fort is in its way unequalled.

The gola. The account of the river in the first chapter of this Gazetteer was broken off at the point where Bankipore was reached. From the great bend far to the north of Dinapore a prominent landmark on the Patna side is the *gola*, the huge Bankipore granary, 96 feet high, with walls twelve feet thick at the bottom, built in the shape of a bee-hive, with two staircases on the outside winding to the top. This structure was built by John Garstin in 1786, for the perpetual prevention of famine in these provinces, as its inscription testifies. When John Shore returned to Calcutta from Patna in 1783 he propounded a scheme for the erection of a number of such granaries, to be kept filled in anticipation of scarcity; but this granary was not filled after completion, and no more were built. It stands as a reminder of the scarcity of 1783, and of the alarm which it occasioned while memories of the famine of 1770 were fresh. The building is remarkable for its reverberating echo, and for the view of the surrounding country which is to be obtained from its roof. The two houses north and north-west of the *gola* are occupied by the Bankipore *High School for Girls*, described above in chapter xv.

---

*Compare Bishop Heber's account. (August 20th, 1824.) "We arrived at the south-east extremity of Patna about nine o'clock; it is a very great, and from the water at some little distance, a very striking city, being full of large buildings, with remains of old walls and towers, and bastions projecting into the river, with the advantage of a high rocky shore, and considerable elevation of the ground behind it. On a nearer approach we find indeed, many of the houses whose verandahs and terraces are striking objects at a distance, to be ruinous; but still in this respect, and in apparent prosperity, it as much exceeds Dacca as it falls short of it in the beauty and grandeur of its ruins." *Journey in India*, I, p. 312. The Bishop was mistaken in supposing that the Fort was built on a rock; but the bank certainly gives this impression: and as a description of the appearance of the city, Bishop Heber's account is accurate.

From here to Udho Das's Lane, the silted-up *nala* on the east of the Bankipore Club, we pass the river-front of the old cantonments of the Third Brigade, built under Clive's directions in 1765. In these cantonments occurred the famous mutiny of officers in 1766, occasioned by discontent at the abolition of double batta. Sir Robert Barker, who commanded the Brigade, found on his return from Bettiah in April of 1766 that half of the cantonment bungalows had been destroyed by fire; and it was discovered in the subsequent enquiry that the fire was the result of the overturning of a lamp in a scuffle with an officer who was unwilling to hand over his commission to be returned with those of the rest who proposed to resign. The officers in a body did go to the length of resigning their commissions; but the influence of Sir Robert Barker kept them within bounds, and they did not desert their duty. They submitted when Clive came to Bankipore on the 20th of May.* The old cantonment area.

The present *Commissioner's Bungalow*, altered out of recognition by the restorations of 1923, was built for himself in 1812 by Captain Peach, commandant of the Provincial Battalion then stationed at Bankipore. It stands on the site of an older bungalow, demolished in 1803, wherein probably lived Anne Roberts, buried in the compound, who died in 1768.† Like much land in Bankipore, it has been twice alienated and twice re-acquired by Government. It saved immediate expense to Government to permit an officer to build his own house; but the result was apt to be inconvenient, as happened here in 1819 when Captain Peach proposed to sell his house on transfer to an outsider, and the Magistrate was required to exercise his influence to get the transaction rescinded, so that Captain Peach's successor might purchase it. Indeed it was the alienation of the next house on the east which had compelled Captain Peach himself to build. That house had been built by *Captain Stuart*, Captain Peach's predecessor, in 1803; but on his transfer in 1811, Captain

*See Henry Strachey's *Narrative*, p. 136 and *passim*.

†The lady has not hitherto been identified. The Calcutta registers do not give any account of mufassal burials before 1772.

Stuart sold it to the Collector of Bihar for a local revenue office. Henceforward the house was used as an office of the Revenue Department (in modern times it was the Commissioner's office) until it was again converted into a private residence for Sir Walter Maude, on the constitution of the Bihar and Orissa Board of Revenue.

The house on the east of this building, (now occupied by the Civil Surgeon), and the smaller bungalow which was formerly an appanage of the house, are both old buildings. In the early nineteenth century the house was occupied by the Opium Agents, Campbell and D'Oyly. Here Sir Charles D'Oyly when he was Opium Agent of Bihar entertained Bishop Heber in 1824 ; and Mrs. Fenton, after her first husband's death, lived in the bungalow as guest of Lady D'Oyly. The tomb of Flora Mary Campbell Macnabb, regarding which Mrs. Fenton waxed sentimental, may still be seen by the bungalow.* Beyond the Civil Surgeon's house are the buildings of the *Collectorate*. The portion which faces the river preserves the outward appearance of the old Court of Appeal, built by William Augustus Brooke in 1787, where Bishop Heber preached in 1824 ; but its interior arrangements have been considerably altered. On the east are the buildings of the *Bankipore Club*, suitable for their purpose, but of no special interest.

Company Bagh.

An old and ruinous revetment marks the beginning of the *Company Bagh* of the later eighteenth century. The historic Company Bagh, acquired by the East Indian Company long before 1757, consisted only of the area which now forms the compound of the District Judge's house† ; but the land on the west was used as a camping ground from 1757 by the

---

Journal of Mrs. Fenton, p. 102.

†In 1778, when the Factory Chief complained of encroachments, he discovered to his astonishment that the original *sanad* covered only the compound of his own house in Muradpur. A formal grant was then obtained from the zamindars for the whole occupied area of 86¾ bighas (excepting the ancient *bagh* acquired long before the *Diwani*. (Patna Revenue Consultations, May 22nd, 1778). In 1806, when the occupied area was 133 bighas, complaints of encroachment were again made. The zamindar of Muharrampur (a Collectorate peon who had purchased the estate in a revenue sale), acquiesced in the occupation of the occupied area ; but he naturally declined to give up the so-called "encroachments".

Company's troops, and Factory servants built quarters for themselves immediately outside the garden on the east and south, until in 1778 an area of 87 bighas was known as Company Bagh. The process of encroachment appears to have continued by the occupation of waste land on the west, until at the end of the eighteenth century the area of the garden was 130 bighas. Here Eyre Coote camped with his little force in July of 1757, and here Clive brought his army to rest in the following February, before he moved out to the sandy island which then lay opposite the garden. In 1763 this camping ground (that is to say the land on the west of the temple of Jagannath) was appropriated for the Headquarters Staff, and Captain Thomas Watson began to build, for the Commander-in-Chief, the house which is now used for *Munsifs' Courts.** But in 1765 Monghyr was made the headquarters station of the Commander-in-Chief; and two years later Thomas Rumbold took possession of the military buildings in Company Bagh for the Factory.† Henceforth the staff house became the headquarters of the Company's commercial activities in Patna; after the rest of the trade had been abandoned it became the saltpetre godown (*shora kothi*): and in 1829 when the Commercial Residency was abolished it became the court of the District Judge. After the building of the District Judge's court on the south, the old house was utilised for Munsifs' Courts. West of it is the eighteenth century house of the Commercial Resident's assistant, built originally with a warehouse below and residential quarters on the first floor, which is now utilised as an additional court for Munsifs. Here may be mentioned, though we must leave the river bank to find it, the old *burying ground of Company Bagh*, an ancient and neglected graveyard in the south-east corner of what is now the convent compound. Hither William Billers was carried to burial in June of 1765, but it

*This date, and the name of the builder, with similar details regarding the Court of Appeal at Bankipore and the Diwani Jail at Gulzarbagh, and the date and cost of the Old English Factory at Gulzarbagh, are taken from an official return from the Register of Public Offices at Patna, dated June 11th, 1817.

† Long, p. 479.

can no longer be said that his tomb is a "standing stock for the reflections of his countrymen", since its headstone has perished.* The ancient graves are in ruinous condition; the oldest of which the headstone survives intact is that of Lieutenant William Collins, who died in March, 1766.

East of the Munsifs' courts, overlooking the river, is the *tomb of Randfurlie Knox*, the dulce decus of the Bengal Army. He had served as Quartermaster-General throughout the victorious campaign of 1763, until on the 9th of December, owing to the failing health of Adams, he assumed command of the army, then on the banks of the Karamnasa. His tenure of the chief command was brief; by the end of the month he was so ill that he had to go for treatment to Patna, where he died under the care of Dr. Fullarton. He was buried on the east of the Commander-in-Chief's house, which was then building, where his tomb still stands on the bank of the Ganges.†

Close to Knox's tomb is the *Mahendru Ghat* ferry-station of the Bengal and North-Western Railway, and a temple of Jagannath. The *rath-jatra* festival is celebrated on a small scale by the temple, the car being kept on the raised ground to the east of the lane leading to the river. Here is an image of Buddha three feet high, and a specially fine Hindu Chaturmukha.

Beyond the temple is the old *house of the Factory Chief*, now (1923) occupied by the District Judge. It has already

---

* *See* page 35, above.

† The house could hardly have been completed by January of 1764, since Patna was not reoccupied until the 6th of November, 1763. The inscription on the tomb is worthy of quotation :—

Here Lays Deposited the Earthly Remains
Of the truly Gallant Major Randfurlie Knox
Who after Having
Lived
Many Years in the Military Service
Of the Hon'ble United East India Company
Universally Esteem'd and Belov'd
Died
On the 28th day of January 1764, Aged 34 Years
As Universally Lamented.
Reader
Whatever the Principles of thy Religion may be
Form thy Life after his Examp[le]
So shall the Pious Tear never be wanting to be shed
To thine as to His
Memory.

been mentioned that the compound of this house is the original *Company Bagh*, acquired early in the eighteenth century, the nucleus of British possessions in Bankipore. For a brief period the house was occupied by the President of the Patna Revenue Council, until in February of 1775 it was restored to the Commercial Chief. Here in 1790 lived Mr. C. C. Pote, who collected the oriental manuscripts which are now in the library of Eton College. His successors occupied the house until the abolition of the Commercial Residency in 1829, when it was made over to the Bihar Opium Agent. The old guard-house still stands by the gate, for the military guard which maintained the state of the Commercial Chief.* The Revenue Chief lived at Muradbagh on the east in equal state, which he maintained with some difficulty, lacking the commission on trade which the Commercial Chief enjoyed, as the complaints of the Revenue Chiefs from time to time testified. North-east of the District Judge's house lies a small house which was built for one of the Factory assistants, an encroachment on land adjoining Company Bagh, one of those legalised in 1778. In modern times the house was used for the Patna Law College ; it is now occupied by nurses of the General Hospital.

We now come to *Muradbagh*, where flanked on either side by more modern buildings, the old house of the Chiefs of the Revenue Council still overlooks the river. This house was originally the residence of the second officer of the Patna Factory, and from 1771 to 1775 the residence of the Factory Chief. From 1775 it became the residence of the Chief of the Patna Revenue Council,† and here Ewan Law lived from 1777 until he left India. Mrs. Hastings stayed here in 1781, at the time of Chait Singh's rebellion. The house was subsequently alienated; and later again acquired for the Temple Medical School, which is still housed here, though

* The order of the Governor-General of February 20th, 1775, directed that each Chief should have a military guard, with two sentinels posted at his door, the whole guard to turn out once a day to the Chief with rested arms.

† In 1775 the house was allotted to the Chief of the Revenue Council. It was valued in 1778 at Rs. 15,000, and repaired by Ewan Law in 1779 (Patna Revenue Council Consultations, February 6th, 1775, May, 1778, and May 17th, 1779). While Ewan Law was absent in 1781, on leave from which he did not return, the house appears to have been regarded as his (*Letters of Warren Hastings to his wife*, page 134). The house and compound were sold by auction under orders of the Governor-General in Council, dated January 4th, 1790.

the interesting old building is now under sentence of demolition. South-east of the house is the *tomb of Mirza Murad*, from whom the garden acquired its name. In the bagh are buildings of the Patna General Hospital, erected in 1903 at a cost of a lakh of rupees, and since that time much extended and enlarged. In Chauhatta, beyond Muradbagh, is the new *house of the Maharaja of Darbhanga*, a palatial building standing high above the river, protected by a great revetment, with a flight of steps leading down to the Ganges.

Afzalpur. (Badshahganj).

Next to the Maharaja's mansion is the eighteenth-century building which houses *Patna College*. Buchanan remarks of this house that it would have been a fine piece of architecture if it had not consisted of two orders (the columns of the lower story have Doric capitals and those of the upper Ionic); but it was the best private residence which he saw in Patna. The architecture of this house is in a more ambitious style than that of any other of the old houses of Patna. Sir Charles D'Oyly has given us a picture of it, describing it as Mr. Wilton's house,* but its history before Wilton's occupation is obscure. It was built by a man with generous ideas, as is evident from the fine eastern room which is now used as the Common Room of the College, adorned with friezes which have been attributed to one of the Adam brothers.

The buildings of the *Bihar School of Engineering* may be seen from the river, with the house of the Principal, an old buildings on a bluff overlooking the Ganges. Behind this house is the neglected *tomb of Mir Afzal*, which is now being restored to decent condition, and a small but graceful mosque, bearing an inscription which recounts how the emperor Farrukhsiyar here performed public worship to Almighty God. It was in Mir Afzal's garden that Farrukhsiyar was enthroned,† and later, at the battle of Patna in May of 1763. Carnac's right wing was posted at this place.‡ At about this time the Commander-in-Chief had a house here, one of those taken over by Thomas Rumbold in 1767 (perhaps the house now occupied by the Principal of the Bihar School of Engineering).§ High up on the bank, on the other side of the

* Wilton had been Opium Agent of Bihar, between 1810 and 1818.

†C. R. Wilson, Early Annals of the English in Bengal, Vol. II, page 49.

‡Broome, page 439. A village was levelled in front of the wing, apparently where Ramna mahalla now is.

§Long. Selections from records of the Government of India, page 479.

lane to the east of Afzal Khan's bagh, is the ruined plinth of *Golak Sadih's dargah*, which gives its name to the mahalla of Golakpur. It appears from a pictorial map in the District Judge's record-room that the dargah was standing in Buchanan's time; but only the plinth now remains, with a tree growing from the middle of it. Beyond it, a little way down the river, is *Rani Ghat*, a favourite bathing place, forming with the temples above it a striking picture. A little below this a picturesque house, with a deceptive appearance of age, stands on the foundations of the house of Mir Ashraf, *gumashta* of the English Factory for some years from 1771; but the portion of the house which stands over the river is very modern, owing its ancient appearance to neglect. An old revetment now in ruins, with high and graceful towers, testifies to the magnificence of the eighteenth century house of the *Rajas of Tikari*, to which more modern additions have been made from time to time. At a slight bend in the river stands the *Bettiah House*, now occupied by the Badshah Nawab Razvi Girls' training school. From here until the extended compound of the Opium Factory is reached, there are ruins of ancient revetments, with a picturesque *temple of Siva*. Close to the old Factory compound was the house of the Nawab Baker Ali Khan, which is mentioned by Buchanan, probably the double-storied house east of the Gulzarbagh church, overlooking the river, which is occupied by the Superintendent of the Government Drawing Office. We are now at Colonelganj, the garden of Shaista Khan, and at the outer compound which was acquired for the saw-mill of the Opium Factory.

The English Factory.

Beyond this outer compound, and with its own enclosing well, is the compound of the original *Patna Factory*, which is now occupied by the Government Press. This ground of exceptional historic interest, the Company's cotta (katte) of the early eighteenth century; and the great building above the river is the old English Factory, which received Coote and Clive, wherein the emperor Shah 'Alam was enthroned in the great upper room overlooking the Ganges. The house, which was built early in the eighteenth century by the East India Company at a cost of forty thousand rupees, is essentially a fortified warehouse. Inside the house, by the massive western wall, is an underground passage connecting with the outer well from which water was obtained, so that a supply could be drawn for the Factory without exposure to the fire of an investing force. The existing wall of the Factory compound evidently follows the line of the ancient wall; near its south-western corner is the tomb of Lieutenant Thomas Davies of the Company's Artillery, who died on the 6th of June in 1761. On the other side of the lane which skirts the eastern wall of the Factory enclosure is the ancient city wall; but the great bastion which Mir Kasim erected in 1763 to command the Factory was demolished in 1857. The wicket gate of the city, regarding which there was so much recrimination between Ellis and Mir Kasim, was apparently at the mouth of the Diwan Mahalla lane.

An account of the manner in which the Patna Factory was alternately occupied and abandoned has been given above in chapter II. Mr. Horne thinks that the first permanent English Factory in Patna was built on this site in the middle of the seventeenth century; * but the building substantially in its present form was erected early in the eighteenth century. The remoteness of Patna from the Presidency appears to have offered temptations to the Chiefs to commit embezzlements ; which led to the fall of Samuel Browne in 1719, Robert Eyre in 1750, William Billers in 1765, and Samuel Middleton in 1766. The great embezzlements of Robert Eyre in 1750 resulted in the abandonment of the station for seven years; but the desertion of this important factory gave rise to severe criticism, as may be seen from the comments of Grose, who came to India in 1750.† During the troubled time of 1756-57 there were no covenanted servants of the Company at this Factory. Paul Richard Pearkes reopened it in July of 1757 ; but the building evidently had not been suffered to fall into decay during the period of abandonment, since Eyre Coote on the 26th of July 1757 was able to quarter his whole force here;‡ and here, by timely severity, he was able to restore discipline in his mutinous detachment. Here Clive rested with his army in the following cold weather, before he moved out to Bankipore.

* The First English Factory in Patna, page 4.

† Voyage to the East Indies, Vol. II, page 235.

‡ 'The English Factory, situated on the bank of the river, just without the western wall of the city............was a spacious building. within which the whole of the Europeans and Sipahis were quartered,' Broome, page 172.

From the river terrace, on the morning of the 28th of April in 1760, the Factory officers incredulously sighted the flying column of Randfurlie Knox at the end of his great march from Burdwan; and hence, seven weeks later, Amyatt watched anxiously for signs of the result of the desperate adventure at Birpur on the opposite side of the river, where Knox with his little band engaged and routed the army of Kadm Husain. Here Knox returned with Shitab Rai after the victory, covered with dust and sweat, exclaiming "This is a real Nawab! I never saw such a Nawab in my life." On the tower which crowns the factory house Ellis mounted the light guns with which he vainly endeavoured to withstand the fire of Markar's heavier artillery from the great bastion on the east, until he was driven to abandon the Factory and escape by boats to the Saran bank.

It was perhaps owing to its association with the siege which was the precursor of the Patna massacre that the Factory Chiefs showed a distaste for this site after the recapture of the city. It was at first proposed that the Factory should be removed to the Fort, with which intention building operations were commenced in 1765; but in 1767 Thomas Rumbold moved in the opposite direction, as has been already described. The Gulzarbagh Factory was then utilised for military stores, and was known as the Grand Magazine, until it was ultimately made over to the Opium Agents. Thenceforth the manufacture of Bihar opium was carried on here until 1910.

Most of the other buildings within the compound are comparatively modern; but the old jail may be mentioned, built by General Garstin in 1784, commonly known as the Diwani jail. Buchanan observed of this building that it was not strong enough to confine ruffians, a remark which was justified five years later, when on the evening of the 7th of May in 1817 thirty-nine convicts, by a concerted sally, broke through the weak eastern door of the enclosing wall, and thirty-two were killed in the attempt to check their escape.

Patna City.

The river flowing by the city, augmented by the western branch of the Gandak, is a far livelier stream than the Ganges at Bankipore; and the traffic on it is increased considerably by the boats which come to it from the great tributary. Ruined revetment works are to be seen before the front of the city is reached; but henceforth an almost continuous line of wrecked *poshtas* bears witness to the strength of the stream as it comes down in its annual flood. The manner in which the bank as a whole has withstood erosion during the centuries would indeed be remarkable if it merely consisted of alluvial deposit; but one house and revetment after another has here been built on the ruins of its predecessors, so that when the protective masonry which lined the bank was swept away, it was a very solid bank which stood behind it. Great houses lined the city front during the eighteenth century, of which few traces now remain. A high bare space marks the site of the house of Shitab Rai, which stood until recently, of which some dependent houses still survive, though of the house itself not one stone stands upon another. Massive ruins of the old revetments mark the sites of the eighteenth century houses of Ibrahim Ali Khan and Mir Ashraf, and of the Dutch Factory.* The site of this Factory, which was rebuilt in 1752, may be easily recognised at the place still known as the *Hollandez Poshta*; but nothing now remains of the buildings. It was here that Dr. Fullarton found refuge when he was spared at the Patna massacre; and hence he escaped from Patna by the river. Below the Dutch Factory compound are traces of the *Haveli Begam*, where Khiali Ram was imprisoned in 1781. The *grave of Khwaja Kalan* is near by on the river bank. The most prominent object on the bank here is the large modern house of Sah Radha Kishun. Below this is *Maharaj Ghat*, named after Maharaja Ramnarain, the Governor of Patna, who was put to death by Mir Kasim in 1763. His house, now in a neglected condition, stands on the western side of the ghat. Here is also a fine *temple of Siva*. A little lower down the river, east of Chimni Ghat, is the *Madrasa Mosque*, built in 1039 A.H. (1629-30 A.D.) by the governor Saif Khan, husband of Malik Banu, a sister of the famous Mumtaz Mahal. The mosque had once attached to it a madrasa which is no longer in existence, but enough remains to testify to the magnificence of the original design.

---

* 'The Hollanders.........had a factory at Azimabad, a house of great beauty and vast extent; nor was it even quite destitute of strength, being furnished with cannon and men. This also fell into the hands of the English (in 1781), without the least defence or opposition.' *Sair-ul-mutakharin*, Vol. IV, page 118. M. Raymond adds a note: 'What they call a Factory in India is no less than a fortified palace, where lives a Chief that equals several Princes of Germany by his table and expense, and by much surpasses them in pomp and attendance whenever he appears in public.'

Beyond the Madrasa Mosque is the *Fort*, the old citadel of Patna, standing high on a bluff over the Ganges, which Heber, by a pardonable mistake, took for a great rock. It is not easy now to trace the line of the landward defences, which have been suffered to decay for a century and a half, though a military guard was stationed here until the early years of the nineteenth century. Mrs. Hastings had the Fort put in order to serve as a place of refuge in emergency in August of 1781, when she exercised her steadying influence on the officials of Patna. After her departure, on the night of the 11th of September, a village in the neighbourhood was accidentally set on fire by the torch-bearers of a marriage procession; and the Europeans of Patna, believing that Chait Singh's army was upon them, fled into the Fort pell-mell, in their night attire, to the intense amusement of the people who heard of the incident in Calcutta.* In 1765, when it was proposed to remove the factory from Gulzarbagh to the Fort, Captain Watson built the house on the west of the Fort area. Other buildings which were then in contemplation were apparently not erected. as the project of complete removal to the Fort was abandoned when the Factory was transferred to the Bankipore house in 1767; but the Fort area was shared between the military and commercial departments so long as the commercial activities of the Company in Patna continued. The old house has now been restored and renovated by Rai Bahadur Radha Krishna Jalan, who has converted it into an excellent place of residence, unique in Patna for the magnificent views of the river to be obtained from its terraces. On the west of Rai Bahadur Radha Krishna Jalan's present compound stood the later house of the military commandant, south of which the great well of the ancient fort may still be seen. Farther west stands the old house of the commandant, built by Captain Alexander Hardy, which he was permitted to sell to the Government of Nepal in 1781 for Rs. 1,601. This house (the *Nepali kothi*) was originally acquired to serve as a resting place for pilgrims from Nepal to Gaya, where they might bathe on the banks of the Ganges: and it is still utilised for this, among other purposes, by the Nepal State. As may be imagined, the presence of a number of pilgrims within the fort precincts led to continual bickering between the military authorities and the Nepalese guardians

* Letters of Warren Hastings to his wife, pages 135, 143.

of the house; but the place has remained to the present day the property of the Nepal Government. In the lane behind the Nepali Kothi are two modern temples of Mahadeo. East of it on the river bank is the great *city mound* whereon is the tomb of Pir Maruf, beyond which is the city moat. It was at this corner that Knox made the breach by which the citadel was stormed on the 6th of November, 1763.

A little below this was the *Danish Factory*, founded by Jorgen Hendrich Berner in 1775. Berner died in 1790, and was buried on the east of his house, which is now occupied by the station-master of the Patna Ghat railway station, A hundred yards lower down the river is *Pir Damaria's tomb*, and the great mosque, which is supported by *altamgha* grants dating back over three hundred years. Below this is the *Kadam Rasul* mosque, founded at the beginning of the seventeenth century by Hazrat Saiyid Shah Muhammad Nur Nakse.

THE CITY STREET.

Travellers who have visited Patna have commonly described it as consisting of one long street. The description is not completely accurate; but the most important street of the town is that portion of the ancient Ganges road which passes through it. From Sherpore to Bankipore the road is suburban in character; but from the Barkerganj nala east of the Bankipore maidan to Jafar Khan's Bagh it is definitely a city street, the main highway of Patna. For half a mile from the nala the road runs by *Company Bagh*, of which a great part has long ceased to be a garden in anything but name. Here and there a dilapidated bungalow remains to tell of the building leases by which the extended *bagh* was broken up in the early years of the nineteenth century, until we reach *St. Joseph's Church*, built in 1850, and the convent, with its orphanages and school which have been described in chapter XV. In the south-east corner of the Convent compound is the neglected ancient *graveyard of Company Bagh*. On the opposite side of the road is the *European cemetery* of the middle nineteenth century. Here are the tombs of Henry Douglas, Magistrate of Patna for twenty years from 1792, who died in 1839, and of Dr. Lyell who was killed in 1857. On the same side of the road as the cemetery, a little below it, is the dilapidated house of Christopher Keating, with a mosque in the compound. On the north of the road, after Muradbagh with the hospital buildings, is the *Patna Oriental Library*, in mahalla Chauhatta, founded in 1890 by Khan Bahadur Khoda Bax Khan, sometime Government Pleader of Patna, and afterwards Chief Justice of Hyderabad State, whose tomb is in the Library compound. A volume has been written regarding the treasures of this library; to which the reader may be referred.* Here is a wealth of oriental manuscripts, many exquisitely illuminated, including those saved at the destruction of the University of Cordova when the Moors were expelled from Spain, and a fair supply of more modern literature. The Library is open daily to the public, except on Fridays and gazetted holidays, from 8 to 11 a.m., and from 2-30 to 5 p.m.

We now pass by the road front of Patna College and New College, and the *tomb of Pir Bahor Shah*, under a tamarind tree on the south of the road. A mile down the road is the Stone Mosque (*Pathar ki masjid*) built by a son of Jahangir, Prince Parvez Shah, in 1626 A.D. An inscription on the eastern face of the mosque recounts that it was built from the stone and wood of a fort and temple dismantled at Majhauli. A little beyond the mosque is the *Duchess of Teck Hospital*, maintained by the Zanana Bible and Medical Mission. In a lane running south from the road is the Vaishnavite monastery known as *Bhawani Puri's math*, south of which are the remains of a large Buddhist *stupa*, now converted into a Muhammadan burial ground. A little less than a mile further down the road, the northern side is bounded by the long wall of the old Opium Factory and its saw-mills, opposite which is the house known in the eighteenth century as *Gulzar Bagh*, now known as Bhup Singh's house, wherein Bhup Singh's ancestor, Maharaja Kallian Singh lived, and where Shitab Rai had his garden house conveniently near to the English Factory. The road shortly after this takes a sharp turn south-south-west, following the line of the old city wall, outside which it ran until it entered the city by the western gate. In the Diwan Mahalla stood the riverside house of Shitab Rai, which has completely disappeared, and the *house of Raja Khiali Ram*, built in the troubled years of the early eighteenth century, now in possession of Khiali Ram's descendant Rai Brijraj Krishna, a well-known vakil of Patna. Here we have an example of a Patna family not regardless

* An Eastern Library, by V. C. Scott O'Connor (Glasgow, 1920).

of the monuments of antiquity; the darbar hall of Raja Khiali Ram, wherein he transacted his public business, has been piously preserved exactly as it was in his day, a most interesting survival.

On the main road, passing by the old court of the city magistrate, we come to the *Pachhim Darwaza*, which has been already mentioned, and enter the city proper. On the southern side of the road, adjoining the house of Khan Bahadur Saiyid Muhammad Ismail, is *Mirza Masum's mosque* built in the reign of Jahangir (1025 A.H., about 1616 A.D.), still in a good state of preservation. The steps and gateway leading into the courtyard are of finely carved black basalt, evidently taken from some older building. A little off the road is the house of the late Nawab Vilayat Ali Khan, built sixty years ago on the site of the city house of Nawab Manir-ud-daula, of which a few ruins still remain. In the compound is the *tomb of Manir-ud-daula.*

Immediately east of the lane which leads to Vilayat Ali Khan's house is the *Charitable Dispensary*, beyond which is the *Patna cemetery*, the two compounds occupying the site of the house and compound of Haji Ahmad, brother of Alivardi Khan, and father of Zainuddin. This was the scene of the Patna massacre in 1763. After the recapture of Patna Haji Ahmad's house was acquired and demolished; its site was utilised for a European cemetery, and a memorial obelisk was erected over the well into which the victims had been thrown. The existing obelisk was built in 1880 in place of that erected under Captain Watson's supervision in 1765. Among the tombs in this cemetery are those of Captain Kinloch, who commanded the expedition to Nepal in 1767, William Maxwell, and James Lindsay Ross.

A quarter of a mile beyond the cemetery, on the north of the road, is the old Roman Catholic Church of the Blessed Virgin Mary, commonly known as the *Padri ki Haveli*. It stands on the site of an older church, built in 1713, and destroyed in the disturbances of June the 25th, 1763, when Ellis captured the city and lost it. The building with its Ionian facade does credit to its architect, the well-known Tiretto, who designed it in 1772. The large bell of the church was presented in 1782 by Bahadur Sah, son of Prithwi Narain. Raja of Nepal. A little beyond the church is the *mosque of*

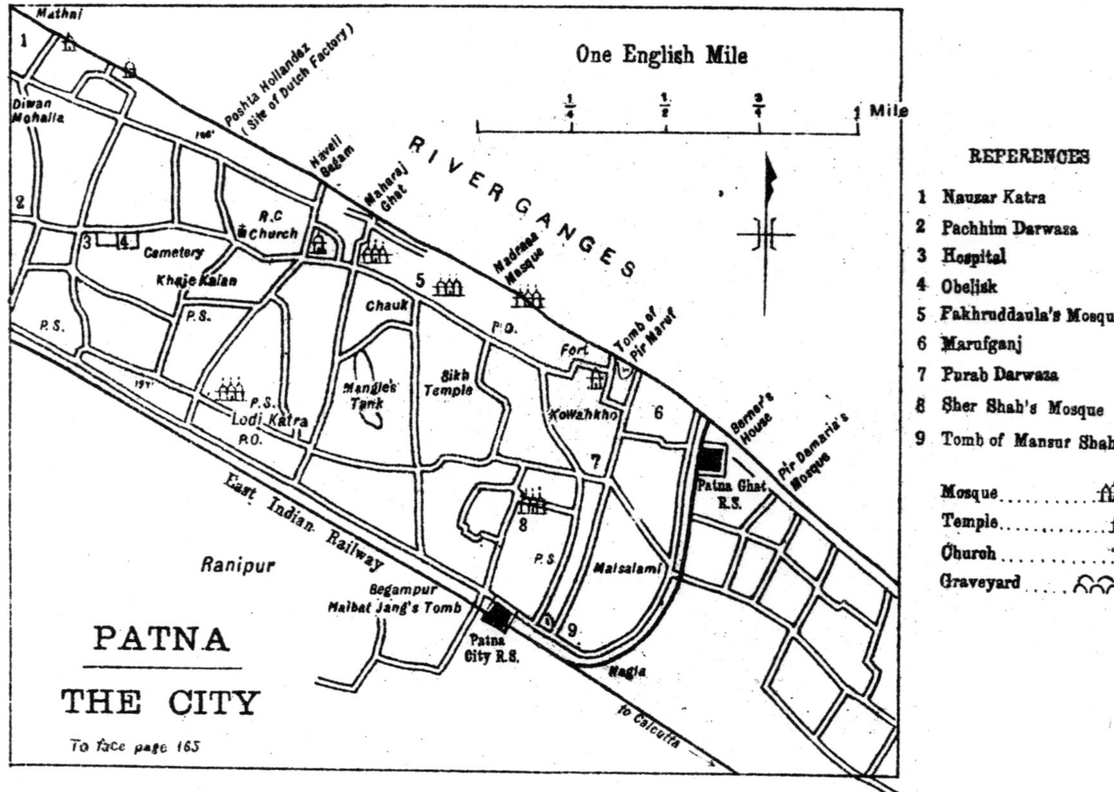

To face page 165

Allauddin Shah, built by the Sultan of Gaur in 1499 A.D., and repaired by Begu Hajjam in 1654. The courtyard of the mosque is paved with glazed tiles of Gaur, and there is a fine carved stone doorway on the south-western side; but it is in a neglected condition. Two hundred yards beyond is the mosque of *Fakhr-ud-daula*, Governor of Patna from 1731 to 1736. This mosque had originally five hemispherical domes; but only three now exist . At the Chauk is *Shaista Khan's mosque and Katra*, built at the close of the seventeenth century, and also the *Ambar Mosque*, built by Shaista Khan's Nazim, Khwaja Ambar, in 1688-89 A.D. In the Harmandir Lane on the south of the road is the *Sikh Temple*, one of the sacred places of the Sikhs, built at the spot where Guru Govind Singh was born. Here are preserved the Guru's cradle, shoes, swords, and arrows, and a beautifully embroidered copy of the holy book of the Sikhs, said to have been presented to the temple by Guru Govind Singh himself. Near the eastern gate is *Sher Shah's mosque*, built by Sher Shah between 1540 and 1545. This is a brick building of plain but massive construction, crowned by a large dome in the centre, with four smaller domes at each corner. Outside the mosque are several tombs, the oldest of which is that of Ashraf Ali Khan, foster-brother of the Emperor Muhammad Shah.

The road passes out of the city by the *Purab darwaza*, past Jafar Khan's garden, the old military camping ground on the east of the city, to Fatuha, whence it runs by the Ganges, through Barh, Mokameh, Monghyr and Bhagalpur to Rajmahal and Bengal.

BANKIPORE.

The name Bankipore, which properly describes only the area west of the maidan, was applied in the eighteenth century to include Muharrampur and Muradpur, wherein lies the greater part of the area now generally known as Bankipore, between the new capital area on the west and Afzalpur on the east. This is the headquarters station of Patna district and division. The whole appearance of the civil station is rendered picturesque by the great *maidan*, the old military camping ground, marking the next stage in the march from Bengal after Jafar Khan's bagh on the east, surrounded by the old race-course and by avenues of noble trees planted over a hundred years ago by Henry Douglas. To the south in Mithapur lies the Bankipore railway station, now known as Patna Junction; whence the Patna-Gaya line branches to the south and the Digha line to the north-west. Close to the railway station is the district jail and the dâk bungalow, whence the road to the civil station is flanked by large modern houses until, as it skirts Chajju Bagh, one of the avenues of Henry Douglas leads to the maidan. *Chajju Bagh* house, now occupied by the Chief Justice of Bihar and Orissa, is said to derive its name from a man whose tomb lies on the western side of the compound. In 1820 an elder brother of Mountstuart Elphinstone lived here, who was then second judge of the Provincial Court of Appeal, whose son, named Mountstuart after his uncle, is buried in the compound. In 1857 William Tayler, Commissioner of the division, was residing here when the Mutiny broke out. Tayler has described* how on the 7th of June, on warning of danger from Dinapore, the European residents of Bankipore came, as had been arranged, to Chajju Bagh, and in what confusion and anxiety the night was passed. The guard consisted of some *najibs*, whose loyalty was doubtful, and of some of Holmes' troopers, who themselves mutinied shortly afterwards; but anxieties were dispelled at 4 A.M., on the morning of the 8th, by the arrival of Captain Rattray with his Sikhs. It was at Chajju Bagh house that Tayler arrested the Maulavis on the 18th of June, as has been described in chapter II above.

The owner of Chajju Bagh was at that time Mr. John Alexander Boilard. Like most of the house property of Bankipore which came into the market in the early years of the nineteenth century, it had passed to Maharaja Mitarjit Singh of Tikari, one of whose sons transferred it to the Boilard family. Mr. Boilard buried his wife in the compound in an unusual fashion, without a coffin and reclining on a couch ; and he left instructions by his will, executed in 1857, that he should be buried by her side in like manner, apparently seeking by this means to make Chajju Bagh, 'our burial place which cannot be sold, ' the inalienable headquarters of his family. The house is however now the property of Government, having been acquired in the time of Sir Andrew Fraser as a Patna residence for the Lieutenant-Governor of Bengal. It was utilised by Sir Charles Bayley as Government House after the creation of the province of Bihar and Orissa while the building on the west of the new capital was being erected. In 1916 it was made over to the Chief Justice; and the compound was divided, two new houses being built in it for Judges of the High Court.

* The Patna Crisis, by W. Tayler, London, 1858.

North of Chajju Bagh, facing the maidan, is the office of the *Imperial Bank*, in the burying ground of Nawab Jahangir Quli Khan,* whose tomb lies on a high mound in the north-western corner of the compound. John Bardoe Elliott, who early in the nineteenth century was a judge of the Provincial Court of Appeal at Patna, built the two-storeyed house and the high enclosing wall. In middle age, after his retirement from the Civil Service, Elliott occupied a prominent position in Bankipore; but in his old age, at the time of the Mutiny, he fell foul of William Tayler, who did not approve of his manner of life: and Tayler attributed his own downfall partly to his feud with the old man. The house was acquired by the Bank of Bengal in 1864. The road which winds round by the Bank wall leads to the Patna-Gaya road, leaving on the right the *Gola*, which has been already described.

The Gaya road still retains its old name; but the road was destroyed by the Patna-Gaya railway line, and anybody who tried to travel to Gaya by it at the present day would soon find himself in difficulties. At the north-east corner of it is the *Collector's house*, an old building of which the early history is obscure. It appears that James Lindsay Ross, afterwards Opium Agent, lived here in 1780, from the inscription on the tomb of John Lowis, Revenue Chief of Purnea, who is buried in the compound. Half a mile down the road, a little away from it on the east, is the *Srimati Radhika Institute*, which Mr. Sachchidananda Sinha has built, close to his own new house, in memory of his late wife. The hall of the institute, which is the largest in Patna, has been designed to serve the purpose of a Town Hall, while the galleries which surround it will house the "Sachchidananda Sinha Public Library," which is being liberally supplied with works of modern literature, chiefly on travel, history, philosophy, sociology, and *belles lettres*.

The road which leads east from the northern end of the Patna-Gaya road, past the Gola, is the old highway by which the main city street is continued to Dinapore, Maner, Koilwar and Buxar. East of the Gola is the new *Commissioner's office*, suitable for its purpose. At the *maidan* the road meets the road from the railway station which passed by Chajju Bagh and the Imperial Bank. The great open space known as the

* Governor of Patna, 1605-07.—*Pataliputra*, page 30.

maidan adds greatly to the amenities of Bankipore; and it has been saved from encroachment because only a comparatively small portion of it can be regarded as a tolerable camping-ground at all seasons, owing to the fact that the western portion becomes flooded after heavy rain. The road passes through one of Henry Douglas's avenues by the old Brigade Cantonment area, of which the river front has been described above. At the farther corner of the *maidan* on the north of the road is the Anglican church of the Holy Saviour, built in 1857. After crossing the silted-up Barkerganj nala, the road becomes the main city street, which has been already described.

On the eastern side of the maidan is *Barkerganj*, commemorating by its name the old military bazar of the 3rd Brigade. Sir Robert Barker's house, occupied as an alternative place of residence by the General commanding the Dinapore Brigade at least as late as 1781, bordered on this bazar.* The road which passes through Barkerganj on the eastern side of the maidan leads to the *Patna mental hospital*, and to *Bhikhnapahari*, where the Nawab Maniruddaula built his garden house, a rambling place which has been considerably extended to house the numerous descendants of this distinguished family. As has been already mentioned, the high mound on which this house was built is probably all that is left of the hermitage hill which Asoka built for Prince Mahendra; and the curious image of the hill, which has been described at page 169, may be seen on the northern side of the road, almost opposite Maniruddaula's house. Near by on the north is the shrine of *Mangala Gauri*†; and a mile down the road, on the site of an ancient Buddhist monastery, is the mausoleum erected over the remains of *Shah Arzani*, an Afghan by birth, who died here in 1623. His shrine is frequented by Muhammadans and Hindus; and in the month of Zikad an annual fair is held at the place, which lasts for three days and attracts five thousand votaries. Adjacent to the tomb is the karbala, where 100,000 persons assemble during the Muharram, and a tank dug by the saint, where

---

* The bungalow, which appears to have been not very large, may have stood on the site now occupied by Christ Church. The Council took possession of it in 1775; but they were compelled to restore it to the General. At the same time, Barkerganj was taken from the military department and made over to the renter of Government gunjes.—Patna Revenue Council Consultations, 28th December, 1775.

† On this shrine and cult, *see* Mr. Manoranjan Ghosh's *Pataliputra*, page 27.

large numbers assemble and bathe once a year. Attached to the shrine is a large Khanqah or monastic institution having endowments granted by Farrukhsiyar and Shah Alam; it possesses landed property in Patna, Saran and Muzaffarpur. According to the canons of the institution, the office of the Sajjada-nashin or superior is elective, the Sajjada-nashins of the various Khanqahs in the district assembling on the fourth day after the death of the last incumbent to elect a successor from among his celibate disciples.

The south-western suburbs.

Most of the important works of archæological exploration of recent years have been made in the south-western suburbs of the city, which are reached from Bankipore by the Pipalpati road, south of the Patna Junction railway station, the end of the old route from Delhi *via* Sasaram, Naubatpur and Phulwari. The name of Lohanipur, where Mir Kasim's father was buried, and where Shuja-ud-daula had his headquarters in April and May of 1764, means according to Mr. Ram Lal Sinha the town of Buddhist monks. About a mile down the road, on the southern side, is *Kankar Bagh*, where Tayler had his experimental farm after he returned to Patna to practise as a vakil. East of the Kankar Bagh Road, north of the railway line, Mr. P. C. Mukherji discovered two ancient columns, apparently of Mauryan times, with a large capital, and the remains of a terrace and wooden palisades. A little over 1¼ miles down the Pipalpati road, north of the railway line, is *Bulandibagh*, where the flat stone is found which has been described at page 170 above. Here the excavations of 1923 were made, which disclosed the gateway of the ancient city, and the chariot-wheel on the parapet.* A quarter of a mile further east, on the south of the road, is *Kumrahar*, where Dr. Spooner discovered the pillared hall. These excavations are now again submerged; but the water does not entirely conceal the pillars which were disclosed. A little over half a mile from Kumrahar, north of the road, is the *Maharaj Khanda*—the Emperor's field, where Colonel Waddell made interesting discoveries in 1895 of ancient beams which he thought were part of the wooden towers of Pataliputra mentioned by Megasthenes. On the opposite side of the road is the *Agam Kuan*, described above at page 170. Away to the south is the group of hillocks known as the

* Page 168 above.

panch pahari, the remains of five Buddhistic stupas, probably the five relic stupas built by Asoka; and the bari and chhoti pahari, identified by Colonel Waddell with the hermitage hill of Upagupta, the saint who converted Asoka to Buddhism. The road crosses the railway line near Gulzarbagh railway station, passing by a mound which indicates the site of an ancient *stupa* at Sadikpur Sanghram, and joining the main city street at the western gateway (*pachhim darwaza*).

Begampur. South of the Patna City railway station is Begampur, where is the tomb of Haibat Jang (Zainuddin, father of Siraj-ud-daula), the Governor of Patna, who was murdered by the Afghans of Darbhanga in 1748. After his remains had been impaled by his murderers, a friend, Saiyid Muhammad Ispahani, took down his head from the eastern gate of the city and buried it with the trunk. A tomb of black stone and white marble was built over his remains, enclosed in an open lattice-work shrine of black hornblende. It is known as the Nawab Shahid-ka-makbara or tomb of the martyr Nawab, and is held in great reverence by the Shias. There are an imambara and mosque in the garden, to which processions with tazias come during the Muharram.

THE NEW CAPITAL. The new capital, the seat of the Provincial Government, occupies an area of a little under three square miles west of the old Patna-Gaya road. This area is now officially known as Patna, as distinct from Patna City which lies far to the east, It is traversed by the main line and the Digha branch line of the East Indian Railway; and an old bed of the Son river meanders through it in a serpentine course, which has considerably affected the laying out of the city. The section to the east of the Digha railway line contains the High Court and clerks' quarters, the Water Tower, the Post and Telegraph Office, the Hardinge Park, and the market. The section west of the Digha line and north of the main railway line contains Government House, the Secretariat, Council Chamber, the principal official residences, and the electric power house. There is a third section south of the main railway line which contains clerks' quarters, a High English school, a dispensary, and a police outpost.

The main feature of the lay-out is the central avenue, nearly a mile long, known as King George's Avenue, which runs east and west between the Secretariat and Government

House, a very fine road two hundred feet wide. The designers of the capital, in laying out the roads, were able to consider the necessities of modern systems of transport; and if the new capital lacks the interest which attaches to ancient cities, its roads have no dangerous turnings caused by old encroachments. The main roads are 150 feet wide, lined with trees which in time will relieve the bare aspect of the area; and the service roads are sixty feet wide. At trijunctions of roads islands have been constructed, which have been fenced and planted with suitable shrubs, which already (1923) have grown considerably. A survey of the capital from the Secretariat Tower will show how admirably it was laid out by the architect Mr. J. F. Munnings and his assistants.

Government House, designed by J. F. Munnings, situated at the western end of the capital site, is a three-storied building with its longitudinal axis running north and south. On the ground floor are the offices and the darbar hall, and on the first floor are the reception rooms, the chief of which are the drawing and dining rooms, each measuring 43 feet by 33. The darbar hall and ball room lies on the west of the main block, measuring 65½ feet by 43, and rising through two floors of the building, overlooked by the colonnaded balconies of the first floor. The floor is of teak planking supported on springs, which give it excellent resilience. The compound of one hundred acres has been well laid out; and it contains a number of excellent lawn-tennis courts which lie between the two main approach drives. Government House.

East of Government House at the other end of King George's Avenue is the Secretariat building, the largest building in the capital, being 716 feet long and 346 feet in breadth. There are 105 rooms on the ground floor and 93 on the first floor, accommodating thirty offices and five hundred clerks. The most prominent feature of the building is the clock tower, 178 feet high, resting on a base fifty feet square. The thickness of the masonry at the base is 3′ 4″, tapering to 1¼ feet at the top. Near the top there is a balcony open on all sides, from which an excellent view can be obtained of the Capital area and of the surrounding country. The Secretariat.

The *Council Chamber*, completed in 1920, lies on the east of the Secretariat. It was designed by Mr. A. M. Millwood in a free Renaissance style, in keeping with the Secretariat The Council Chamber.

building which lies behind it, and is built like the rest of the new city in brick and plaster. The Council Chamber itself, measuring sixty feet by fifty, extends through both floors of the building, with a gallery on the level of the upper floor for visitors and representatives of the Press. In the Council Chamber is a portrait of the King-Emperor by Snowman; and in one of the members' rooms are portraits of the first Lieutenant-Governors of Bihar and Orissa, Sir Charles Bayley and Sir Edward Gait, by H. A. Olivier.

The High Court. The *High Court*, on the Bayley Road, was opened by Lord Hardinge in 1916. It is built on the model of the Allahabad High Court, the only important innovation being the magnificent marble staircase which faces the main entrance.

The Patna Museum. The *Patna Museum*, which was established in 1915, is housed in the northern annexe of the High Court building. Among objects of archæological interest in the museum are the Didarganj statue and articles discovered in the Pataliputra excavations of recent years, which include a fine terra-cotta head ('the laughing girl of Patna'), a terra-cotta votive plaque with a representation of the Bodh-Gaya temple with Kharoshthi legend, glass seals, a good signet ring, and the chariot-wheel discovered at Bulandibagh. There are also antiquities from the excavations at Basarh. In the epigraphic section of the museum there is a fine collection of copper plates of the Bhanja kings of Orissa, while there is a good collection of ancient coins in the numismatic section. The geological section contains a collection of rocks and mineral substances of Bihar and Orissa, arranged by Mr. C. S. Fox of the Geological Survey.

For the rest, the buildings of the New Capital consist almost exclusively of recently-erected official residences. Among the few private buildings may be mentioned the house recently built by Mr. Sultan Ahmad, and the conveniently arranged club-house of the New Patna Club, both situated on the eastern side of the Gardiner Road.

Municipal administration, etc. Patna City Improvement Trust. An account of the educational and medical institutions at Patna has been given in chapters XV and V, and of the trade in the city in chapter X; and it is not necessary to repeat here what has already been written. An account has also been given in chapter XIV of the Patna City Municipality, and of the Patna Administration Committee; but a brief mention should be made of the Patna Improvement Trust. The problem of improving the city of Patna by the opening out of congested areas and widening of roads engaged the attention of the Local Government when the province was created ; and a survey was made, as a result of which some of the most insanitary *bastis* in Bankipore were selected for demolition. Land was acquired at Muharrampur, Kadam Kuan, and Pirthipur for the housing of persons who might be deprived of their habitations by the work of improvement, and this area was made over in 1916 to the Patna City Municipal Commissioners as trustees, together with a grant of Rs. 50,000, to which considerable further grants have since been added. The work of the trust so constituted has not been very successful, owing chiefly to the fact that the body of trustees was too large, and owing also to the fact that they were waiting for protective works to be undertaken by Government to cover the acquired area from liability to flood. Practically nothing was done by the trustees except in the way of making roads running through the acquired areas or giving access to them, until the middle of 1923, when it was at last decided to make permanent settlement for building purposes of the acquired area. The task of clearing Patna City and its western suburbs of insanitary congested areas would be difficult; but it is possible that an effective Patna City Improvement Trust may be able to undertake this work, which is greatly needed.

CHAPTER XVII.

GAZETTEER.

Athmalgola.—A village in the Barh subdivision, on the Patna-Monghyr road, with a station on the main line of the East Indian Railway, 304 miles from Calcutta. Population (1921) 1,011. This was one of the original colonies of invalided sepoys (*thanas*), established in the eighteenth century for the protection of the principal lines of communication.

Azimabad.—A pargana of Patna district, with an area of 139·7 square miles, within which is included the whole of the Patna City subdivision, extending as far as Fatuha. This name was given to Patna in 1704 by the Governor, Prince 'Azim-us-Shan, grandson of Aurangzeb.

Baikanthpur (Baikantpur).—A small pargana in the Barh subdivision, with an area of 2·7 square miles. The name of the pargana is derived from that of the village of Baikanthpur, situated on the banks of the Ganges five miles east of Fatuha and one mile north of Khusrupur railway station. The mother of Raja Man Singh, Akbar's Viceroy, died at this place, and the foundation of the village is traditionally ascribed to the Raja. A locally powerful Bhumihar Brahman, Udwant Singh, was zamindar of the pargana at the time of the Permanent Settlement; but most of the property has now been alienated. An account of the family is given by Rai Bahadur Ramgopal Singh Chaudhuri in his *Further Rambles in Bihar*.

Bakhtiyarpur.—A village in the Barh subdivision, containing a police-station, inspection bungalow, and travellers' sarai. Population (1921) 368. Here is a station on the East Indian Railway, 310 miles from Calcutta, and the terminus of the Bakhtiyarpur-Bihar Light Railway, which runs to Rajgir 32¾ miles to the south.

Ballia pargana.—A pargana situated in Masaurhi thana, with an area of 102½ square miles.

Banka Ghat.—A railway station three miles east of Patna; opened in 1900. A mile north of the station is Jethuli village, which contains two Muhammadan tombs known as the *kachhi dargah* and the *pakki dargah.* The former is the tomb of Shihab-ud-din Jagjaut, father of the saints of Bihar, who was the father of Kamalo Bibi of Kako, father-in-law of Makhdum Yahia of Maner, and grandfather of Makhdum Sharif-ud-din of Bihar. The other *dargah* is the tomb of Shah Adam Sufi. It is a place of pilgrimage; the pious assemble there every Thursday, and an annual fair is held on the 21st day of Zikad.

Bankipore.—See Chapter XVI.

Bankipore (sadr) subdivision.—The subdivision, which has an area of 290¼ square miles and a population of 210,720, is contained by the thanas of Phulwari and Masaurhi, with police-stations at Phulwari, Masaurhi, Digha, Bakarganj, Patna, Punpun and Pabhera. The subdivision is entirely a flat alluvial plain, intersected by the rivers Punpun, Morhar and Dardha.

Bargaon.—Village in the Bihar subdivision, seven miles north of Rajgir. Population (1921) 2,231. See *Nalanda.*

Barh.—Headquarters of the Barh subdivision, situated on the Ganges in 25°29′N. and 85°43′E. Population (1921) 8,464. The town contains the subdivisional offices and munsifi, a sub-jail, sub-registry office, dispensary, dak bungalow and an English cemetery. It has also a station on the East Indian Railway, 299 miles from Calcutta, and is the centre of a considerable trade in country produce, both by rail and river, but its manufactures are of little importance; the manufacture of jessamine oil (*chameli*) is an old but declining industry. The quarter known as old Barh, which lies in the suburbs, contains an old Siva temple called the temple of Amar Nath. The name of the town is derived from the fact that it stands on a spot liable to the flood (*barh*) of the Ganges. The river takes a sharp turn to the north-east here, and when it rises in flood, overflows its banks. Within living memory the place has been so deep under water that residents of two-storied houses have had to step into boats from the upper floor.*

* J. Christian, *Names of Places in Bihar,* Calcutta Review, Vol. XCII, 1891.

Barh is frequently mentioned by the Muhammadan historians in their account of the last days of Muhammadan rule. Some of the battles said to have taken place in the neighbourhood were fought nearer Fatwa, and will be mentioned in the article on that place; but Barh saw the passage of more than one army owing to its position on the line of march from Bengal. The Afghans and Marathas marched here in 1748 to meet Ali Vardi Khan after the sack of Patna, and encamped near the town. Ali Vardi, after halting at Barh, delivered an attack on the flank of their entrenched position, carried it, and sent the Afghans flying. On the following morning the battle of Rabi Sarai, 25 miles from Barh, completed their defeat and ended the campaign. According to the Sair-ul-Mutakharin, the Nawab Mir Kasim Ali stayed at Barh in 1763 on his way from Monghyr to Patna just before the massacre there, and had his prisoners, Jagat Seth and his brother Sarup Chand Seth, the great bankers of Murshidabad, put to death and their bodies exposed to birds and beasts of prey, so as to prevent their being burned according to Hindu custom. When the British army halted at Barh on their march to Patna at the end of 1763, they found the bodies buried in one of the houses there.

Barh subdivision.—North-eastern subdivision of the district, containing the thanas of Fatuha, Barh and Mokameh, with an area of 569 square miles. Population (1921) 354,833. The subdivision contains 576 villages and two towns, Barh and Mokameh. The tract of country comprised by it is an alluvial flat with an uniform level, except for a depressed tract of swampy low-lying land, known as the Mokameh Tal, between the East Indian Railway and the Sakri river, which remains under water for about four months in the year. The subdivision, which is a long and somewhat narrow strip of country, is intersected by a number of streams flowing in a north-easterly direction, the most important of which is the Sakri, which enters the subdivision at its south-western corner and passes out of it in its south-eastern corner.

Bhagwanganj.—Village in the south-east of the Dinapore subdivision, situated a few miles south-east of Bharatpura.

The village contains the remains of a stupa, which has been identified with the Drona stupa mentioned by Hiuen Tsiang. According to his account, eight kings divided the relics of

Buddha after his death, and the Brahman Drona, who distributed them, took the pitcher with which each portion had been measured and returned to his own country. He then scraped the remaining relics from the vessel and built a stupa over them. Afterwards Asoka opened the stupa, took the relics and the pitcher away, and built a new stupa there. The stupa at Bhagwanganj is a low circular mound 30 or 40 feet in diameter and about 20 feet high, built entirely of large bricks set in mud. Not far from the stupa flows the Punpun river. Along its banks, near a small village about two miles from Bhagwanganj, are the remains of a stone and brick temple about 40 feet square; and a mile and a half further north along the Punpun is a large mound, about 45 feet square and 25 feet high, which marks the remains of another shrine. A few misshapen stones and fragments occupy the summit of the mound, and are devoutly worshipped, with libations of milk and other offerings, by the Muhammadans of the adjacent village Bihta (this Bihta should be distinguished from the village with a station on the railway 25 miles to the north). Tradition ascribes these mounds and others close by to a Muhammadan saint named Makhdum Shah. [Reports Arch. Surv. Ind., Vol. VIII.]

Bharatpura.—A village in the Dinapore subdivision, sixteen miles south of Bihta, seat of a branch of the family of Chaudhri Ajab Singh. The village derives its name from Bharath Singh, who is described in the Sair-ul-Mutakharin as zamindar of Arwal and Masaurha, though he was actually uncle and guardian of the minor Raja Bahadur Singh. Bharath Singh here built a fort and palace in the middle of the eighteenth century (see *Dharhara*). [On Bharatpura see an article in the Bankipore *Express* of May 22nd, 1923.]

Bihar pargana.—A large pargana in the south-east of the district, with an area of 209 square miles. This pargana was not transferred to Patna district until 1865; and its records are consequently less complete than those of other parganas since most of them were destroyed at Gaya in 1857.

Bihar sarkar.—One of the districts of Muhammadan days which comprised the present districts of Patna and Gaya, with Japla and Belaunja, which are now in Palamau district, and the parganas lying west of the Kiul river which are now in Monghyr. The district was constituted in the same form in the arrangement of Collectorships in 1787; and for a few years from 1800 it included Ramgarh, which was managed by a joint-magistrate who was stationed at Sherghati. In the early years of the nineteenth century *thaggi* was particularly prevalent in the Barh area, which was inaccessible from Gaya for a great portion of the year. Patna district was accordingly constituted, containing the northern parganas of Bihar district. In 1832 and 1836 the parganas on the extreme east were transferred to Monghyr; and in 1865 Bihar and Rajgir were transferred to Patna.

Bihar subdivision.—Southern subdivision of the district lying between 24° 57′ and 25° 26′N. and between 85° 9′ and 85° 44′E., with an area of 789½ square miles. It consists of the thanas of Bihar, Hilsa and Islampur, with police-stations at Bihar, Hilsa, Islampur, Asthawan, Giriak, Silao, Chandi and Ekangarsarai. Population (1921) 569,635. The subdivision consists of two distinct portions. To the north is an alluvial plain intersected by the Son, Phalgu, Panchana and Sakri, and by numerous small streams. To the south it is separated from the Gaya district by the Rajgir Hills stretching from north-east to south-west which consist of two parallel ridges with a narrow valley between them. These hills, which contain numerous ravines and passes, are rocky and covered with thick low jungle. They seldom exceed a thousand feet in height, but are of great interest as containing some of the earliest memorials of Indian Buddhism.

Bihar town.—Headquarters of the subdivision of the same name situated in 25° 11′N. and 85° 31′E., on the Panchana river. Population (1921) 36,720, of whom 24,177 are Hindus and 12,491 Muhammadans. It is connected with Bakhtiyarpur and Rajgir by a light railway, and contains the usual subdivisional offices. The town has a very ancient history. In the ninth century, A.D., it became the capital of the Pala kings, and Gopala, the founder of that dynasty, built a magnificent *vihara* or monastery there. The present name of the town still preserves the memory of this great Buddhist monastery, but formerly its name appears to have been Udandapura or Otantapur. Tradition states that before the Muhammadan conquest, it was called Dand Bihar or Dandpur Bihar from the great number of *dandis* or religious mendicants who gathered there ; but this name is clearly a corruption of Udandapura Vihara. At the Muhammadan conquest the city was sacked, the monastery burnt, and the Buddhist monks slain by Bakhtiyar Khilji; but Bihar was the place of residence of the Muhammadan Governors until 1541, when Sher Shah rebuilt Patna, which, says the Tarikh-i-Daudi, "was then a small town dependent on Bihar, which was the seat of the local government ....Bihar was from that time deserted and fell to ruins; while Patna became one of the largest cities of the Province". The expression that Bihar fell into ruins seems an hyperbole of the chronicler, for as we shall see later, it continued to be enriched with buildings by the Muhammadans, and its sacred tombs were for many centuries places of pilgrimage. It is rarely mentioned however by the Muhammadan historians until the days of the decline of the Mughals.

It was sacked by the Marathas in the time of Ali Vardi Khan; and in 1757 Mir Jafar Khan paid it a visit, of which an amusing account is given in the *Sair-ul-Mutakharin*. The emperor Shah Alam made Bihar his headquarters in 1763; and it was near here, at Siwan (Bara Khurd) that he was decisively defeated by Carnac.

The town, which is known as Bihar Sharif, owing to its many tombs of Musalman saints, still retains traces of its former importance, though its appearance has been strangely altered by a large sand-bed having formed in the Panchana a few miles to the south, and by the diversion of its water into *pains* or irrigation channels. Several branches of the river still intersect the various *mahallas* and the main stream still flows to the north, but both this and its branches are nearly dry except in the rains, and in the outskirts one finds now a spacious bridge spanning a rice-field or patch of waste, now ruined *ghats* looking down on a wide expanse of arid sand. The town consists principally of one long narrow street with numerous lanes and alleys leading from it. There are two bridges with pointed arches over irrigation channels, the remains of former prosperity; and in all directions are seen Muhammadan tombs, the smaller of brick, the larger of squared and carved stones taken from ruined Buddhist or Brahmanical buildings. To the north-west of the town there is a long isolated hill, called Pir Pahari, having on its northern face a precipitously steep cliff and on its southern face an easy slope in successive ledges of rock.

Bihar contains numerous remains, of which the most ancient is a sandstone pillar, 14 feet high, bearing two inscriptions of the Gupta dynasty. The upper inscription is of Kumara Gupta's time (413—455 A.D.); the lower one apparently belongs to his son and successor Skanda Gupta (455—480 A.D.). This pillar used to lie inside the old fort, but it now stands on a brick pedestal opposite the Court-house. It was placed there, upside down, by Mr. Broadley, a former Subdivisional Officer, who had it inscribed with a list of the local officers and native gentlemen of Bihar.

One of the most interesting monuments of Bihar's past history is the fort, which is now in ruins, though traces of its walls and ramparts still remain. The ground on which it stands is a natural plateau, extending over 312 acres, raised considerably above the level of the surrounding country. In shape, the fort resembles a large irregular pentagon 2,800 feet from north to south and 2,100 feet from east to west; it was surrounded by a cyclopean wall, 18 to 20 feet thick and 25 or 30 feet high, composed of gigantic blocks of stone quarried from the neighbouring hill. Along these ramparts were circular bastions, the northern gate being flanked by tall towers; and the whole site was surrounded by a great moat 400 to 600 feet wide, which has long since been brought under cultivation.

Inside the fort there are many mounds marking the site of old buildings, but for many years excavations were carried on for the sake of the bricks found there. The remains still existing consist of the ruins of a smaller Muhammadan fort and buildings, of Hindu temples, and of the great *vihara* or Buddhist monastery. In the centre is the *dargah* or tomb of Kadir Kumaish, which is of modern date, but is composed almost entirely of the remains of the ancient *vihara*, while its pavement is made up of ancient *chaityas* and pillars. The custodians of the shrine guard them with jealous care, and receive fees for permitting persons suffering from toothache and neuralgia to touch them in the hope of effecting a cure. To the north of the fort, in a plain called Logani, there are traces of another *vihara*; and a little to the east of this plain is the *dargah* of Makhdum Shah Ahmed Charamposh with an ancient gateway, 11 feet high and 7 feet broad, which, tradition says, once served as the entrance to the great *vihara* in the old fort. It is covered with delicate carvings, some of which have been chiselled off, and Persian verses, expressing moral and religious precepts, engraved in their place. A mile away from the fort towards the banks of the Panchana are the remains of several Buddhist buildings, the sites of which are now only marked by heaps of bricks, from which it appears probable that the old city of Bihar lay along the banks of the river and between the fort and the hill.

This hill, which is called Pir Pahari,* is about one mile to the north-west of the town. At its summit is the *dargah* or mausoleum of the great saint of Bihar, Mallik Ibrahim Bayu, round which are ten smaller tombs. It is a brick structure surmounted by a dome and bears inscriptions showing that the saint died in 1353. He was a notable warrior, who overcame a Hindu chief of Rohtasgarh and subdued the warlike tribes of the Province. Another great *dargah* is that of Makhdum Shah Sharif-ud-din, also called Makhdum-ul-Mulk, who died here in 1379; the inscription over the entrance shows that his tomb was built in 1569. This tomb, which stands on the south bank of the river, is held in great veneration by the local Muhammadans, who assemble here on the 5th day of Shawwal to celebrate the anniversary of his death. The Chhoti Dargah is the shrine of Badruddin Badr-i-Alam, a famous saint of Chittagong, who settled in Bihar, and died there in 1440.

The Jama Masjid was built in the time of Akbar by Said Khan, Governor of Bihar from 1595 to 1601. This worthy is said to have had a predilection for eunuchs, and one of the 1,200 whom he possessed, Ikhtiyar Khan, his vakil, was the builder of this mosque. Another mosque, that of Habib Khan, an Afghan of the Sur clan, was built in 1637 almost entirely of Buddhist materials.

Among more modern monuments may be mentioned some Christian tombs outside the northern gate of the old fort. Two of the tombstones with inscriptions in the Armenian character were taken to the Indian Museum in 1891, and examination showed that they bear the dates of 1646 and 1693. In the town itself the most remarkable building is a huge inn (*sarai*), erected about 30 years ago, which is called the Bayley Sarai

* One of the oldest tombs in Bihar is that of Saiyid Ahmed Pir Pahar, with an inscription of the year 1336. Translations of this and other inscriptions will be found in Blochmann's Geography and History of Bengal, J. A. S. B., Vol. XLII, Part I, 1873.

after Sir Steuart Bayley, who was Commissioner of Patna from 1872 to 1877 and afterwards Lieutenant-Governor of Bengal (1887-90). It consists of two large blocks of buildings, enclosing spacious courtyards; and in front of it is an elaborately designed clock tower. The dispensary is housed in this building. Near the Cutchery railway station is a curious structure, formerly a Muhammadan nobleman's summer house, which is called *nauratan* from its containing nine chambers, one in the middle, one at each corner, and one at each side. These chambers are arched with brick, and the inner walls are painted; but the lowness of the roof and the smallness of the doors detract from the general effect. The only other building calling for mention is the Victoria Memorial Hall, opened in 1903, which is used as a reading room. [A. M. Broadley, *The Buddhistic Remains of Bihar*, J.A.S.B., Vol. XLI, 1872; Reports Arch. Surv. India, Vols. I, VIII and XI; Reports Arch. Surv. Bengal for 1901-02.]

Bihta.—Village in the north-west of the Dinapore subdivision, situated nine miles west of Dinapore and five miles south of Maner. It contains an inspection bungalow and a station on the East Indian Railway, and a large annual fair is held there on the 13th of Phagun, in connection with which an agricultural show takes place. There is a village of the same name 25 miles to the south, containing some archæological remains, an account of which is given in the article on Bhagwanganj.

Biswak pargana.—A pargana in the south of the district, in Islampur and Bihar thanas. Area 156 square miles. This pargana formed part of the zamindari of the Mayi family, and after 1781 it was settled with the Nawab Manir-ud-daula for life.

Dharhara.—A village in the Dinapore subdivision, on the Bihta-Paliganj road. This is the seat of a branch of one of the most ancient Bhuinhar Brahman families of the district, descended from Chaudhri Ajab Singh, brother of Raja Kanchand, zamindar of Arwal-Masaurha. The last of the decendants of Raja Kanchand to hold that great estate was Raja Jaswant Singh, who died without heirs, and whose widow*

* The lady is described in *Eastern India* as 'the widow of *Yasamanta*, owing to a misreading of Buchanan's manuscript.

wasted much of the property. After her death what was left of the estate was divided between the sons of Mansaran Singh, (great-grandson of Ajab Singh and ancestor of the Dharhara and Bharatpura branches of the present family), and Dalip Singh, grandson of Ajab Singh, ancestor of the Babus of Sehra.

Digha.—A village on the Ganges, 5¼ miles N.N.W. of Bankipore, on the Dinapore road. Population 2,223. On the west of the village are several houses which were built in the eighteenth century for officers of the Dinapore Brigade. The 'noble habitation erected for the General commanding the station', which roused Lord Valentia's admiration in 1808,* is now in possession of the Maharaja of Hatwa. Below it is the house, also mentioned by Lord Valentia, which was the property of the Nawab Vizier of Oudh Saadat Ali Khan, where he was accustomed hospitably to entertain the officers of Dinapore before his elevation to the *masnad* in 1797. Half a mile from the General's house on the Dinapore side, on the south of the road, is the old building of Digha Farm, which Bishop Heber describes.† It is now the property of Moghal Mian, a grain-dealer of Dinapore.

Digha derives its present importance from the fact that it is the terminus for the large steamers which come up from Goalundo, and the starting place for the smaller steamers of the feeder services to Barhaj and Buxar. Here also connection is established between the East Indian Railway on the south and the Bengal and North-Western Railway on the north of the river by means of a steamer plying between Digha and Pahleza. The river here is constantly shifting its course; and at present (1923) the connection has to be made lower down at Mainpura.

Dinapore.—Headquarters of the Dinapore subdivision, 3½ miles from the Dinapore railway station. The population at the census of 1921 was 30,877, of whom 21,374 were Hindus, 6,201 Muhammadans, and 1,087 Christians. The military force at present stationed here is a battalion of British infantry. The town, with the subdivision, is under a subdivisional officer, while the cantonments are under a special cantonment magistrate. The town is noted for its excellent cabinetware and furniture; it also contains an oil and flour mill and a

* *Voyages and Travels*, Vol. I, page 17.

† *Journeys in India*, Vol. I, page 326.

foundry. The old Ganges road from Patna runs through the town and cantonments, and an excellent road connects it with the New Capital, and thus with Bankipore and Patna. Dinapore contains no buildings of any great interest. St. Luke's Church was built in 1837, and the Roman Catholic Church, St. Stephen's, was built between 1849 and 1854. In the original cantonments, built in 1767, the European lines were in the square which lies 200 yards from the bridge crossing the *nala* which bounds the cantonments on the east. On the northern and western side of the square were officers' quarters, with a large mess-house in the middle of the northern side, which was in ruins in 1811. A second smaller square of officers' quarters adjoined this square on the west. The sepoy lines were on the river bank a mile from the bridge. The road which leads to the south from the old barrack square is one of the original cantonment roads, but it originally ended at the bridge by which it entered the ' Grand Parade '; it now cuts the old Grand Parade in half, running on to the Dinapore railway station at Khagaul. On the eastern side of the Grand Parade four bungalows were built, which still exist. The General lived two miles from the cantonments, on the Digha road; and there were three other large officers' bungalows on that road, immediately east of the sadr bazar, which have long ceased to be included in the cantonments. (See Digha.)

Dinapore subdivision.—North-western subdivision of the district, lying between 25° 31′ and 25° 44′N. and between 84° 48′ and 85° 5′E., contained in the thanas of Maner, Dinapore and Bikram, with an area of 433 square miles, and a population of 326,330. It contains 555 villages and two towns, Dinapore and Khagaul; and has six police-stations, at Dinapore, Maner, Khagaul, Bikram, Naubatpur and Paliganj. The country comprised within it is entirely alluvial and flat, and along the Ganges it is peculiarly fertile.

Fatwa (Fatuha).—Village in the Barh subdivision, at the junction of the Ganges and Punpun, seven miles east of Patna. It contains a station on the East Indian Railway, a police thana and an inspection bungalow, and is a centre of the weaving industry. Tusser silk is manufactured, and table-cloths, towels and handkerchiefs are woven by the Jolahas. Large bathing festivals are held here at the junction of the Punpun and Ganges; at one of these, the Baruni Dawadasi, which commemorates an incarnation of Vishnu in the form of a dwarf, as many as 10,000 persons are said to assemble. The Punpun at this point attains a width of about 100 yards enclosed within high steep banks.

Fatwa, lying on the direct line of march from Bengal, witnessed a good deal of fighting in the last days of Muhammadan rule. In 1748 Ali Vardi Khan defeated the allied force of Marathas and Afghans, numbering over 50,000 men, at Rabi Sarai on the west side of the Punpun near the present railway station. In 1760 another battle took place at Mohsinpur (Masimpore), a village north-west of Fatwa between Shah Alam's army and a force under Ram Narayan and Captain Cochrane, which ended in the complete victory of the former, Dr. Fullarton being the only English officer who escaped.

Close to Fatwa there is a small village called Mari, in which no drums are ever beaten, owing, it is said, to a *fakir* having cursed the place. The *fakir* came here one day thirsty and asked one of the girls at the well to give him water to drink. She contemptuously refused, but one of the village matrons gave him a drink. Thereupon he cursed the place, saying, "may the daughters of the village be husbandless and the daughters-in-law fortunate". Owing to this curse, it is said people do not marry the girls of the village, and if they do, they are sure to die soon ; should any one venture to take one of the villagers' daughters, the marriage takes place without music or processions of any kind. The village girls are so anxious to get husbands that it is said they run away with any one who, by venturing to play on a musical instrument in the village, shows that he is ignorant of the traditional curse.

Gayaspur pargana.—The largest pargana in Patna district, comprising Mokameh thana with the greater part of Barh, with an area of 431½ square miles. This was one of the few parganas settled in 1790 with village maliks ; but adverse seasons made it difficult for the petty proprietors to observe their engagements, and by 1793, when Mr. Vanderheyden made his report, most of them had relinquished their estates. The pargana contained a very large number of jagirs, including the vast so-called *altamgha* estates of Mokameh and Samaia; and the effect of the resumption proceedings was to raise the land-revenue from Rs. 86,145 to Rs. 1,67,345.

Ghosrawan.—Village in the Bihar subdivision situated seven miles south-west of Bihar. The village was the site of an old Buddhist settlement, of which the remains are marked by several mounds. Only two of these are of any interest, one a small but high mound crowned with the temple of Asa Devi, and a great mound close to the village, which is believed to be the ruin of a Buddhist temple called Vajrasana Vihara. An inscription found here records the building of a temple by one Vira Deva, who, it says, was patronized by king Deva Pala and was appointed to govern Nalanda. He then built a *Vihara* for the reception of a Vajrasana or adamantine throne, a building so lofty that the riders in aerial care mistook it for a peak of Kailasa or Mandara. The mention of Deva Pala shows that the temple was erected in the latter half of the ninth century. To the south of the village there is a ruined mud fort with a low mound on its eastern side; and inside the village is an open space called Singh-bahani, where the sculptures found in the great mound have been collected together. The small temple of Asa Devi contains another collection of sculptures, and to the south-east of this a few more have been placed in a small shrine of Durga. A quarter of a mile due west of the great mound there is a large tank 500 feet square called Sahu Pokhar or Seth Pokhar, *i.e.*, the Banker's Tank. The modern village is inhabited almost entirely by Babhans, who distinguished themselves by rising in 1857, an exploit which ended in the burning of the village and the expulsion of a great portion of the insurgents. [Reports Arch. Surv. Ind., Vol. I; The Buddhistic Remains of Bihar, by A. M. Broadley, J. A. S. B. Vol. XLI, 1872.]

Giriak.—Village in the extreme south of the Bihar subdivision, on the Panchana river, 13 miles south of Bihar, with which it is connected by a metalled road. Population (1921) 855. Giriak is a place of special archæological interest, as the rugged hill rising immediately to the west of the village has been identified as the Indrasilaguha mountain of the Chinese Pilgrims, Fa Hian and Hiuen Tsiang, which is sacred to the Buddhists as containing the cave in which Buddha answered the 42 questions of Indra, the lord of the Devas. Opposite the village, on the western side of the Panchana, on the northern range of the Rajgir hills are remains of an ancient stupa, and a little to the west of this tower, on a higher level, is an oblong terrace covered with the ruins of several buildings, the principal of which would appear to have been a Buddhist monastery.

Ascending from the bed of the Panchana river, which washes the eastern foot of the spur, an ancient walled-up road, still traceable in many places along the steep scarp, leads up to the ruined stupa known as Jarasandha's seat or throne (*baithak*), which occupies a commanding position on the eastern end of the ridge, and is visible from a great distance. This structure is a solid cylindrical brick tower 28 feet in diameter and 21 feet in height, which originally stood about 55 feet high when surmounted by a dome; it was erected probably about 500 A.D. The Buddhist legend is that there was formerly a Buddhist monastery on the hill The monks, forbidden by their religion to take animal life, had been for some days without food, when a flock of geese passed overhead. One of the monks cried out—"To-day the brotherhood have no food Oh! noble beings, take pity upon us." Thereupon a goose fell down dead at his feet; and the monks, overcome with pity, built a great stupa on the spot, under which they buried the goose. This memorial stupa was accordingly called the Hansa or goose stupa and their monastery the Hansa Sangharama. Local tradition, however, connects the tower with the name of Jarasandha, the prehistoric king of Magadha, who is said to have used it as a garden-house.

Close to the stupa are the remains of a large water reservoir, and about 100 yards to the south-west the ridge culminates in a small summit, up to which a broad flight of steps leads. This summit was once covered with the buildings of the monastery, and massive terrace walls on the west can be seen through the jungle. The position of these remains corresponds so closely to that indicated by Hiuen Tsiang for the stupa of the goose and the *vihara* behind it, that their identity with the structures seen by the Chinese pilgrim can scarcely be doubted. The ridge, continuing further to the west, gradually rises again and forms at a distance of about 400 yards a second summit covered with large rocks. Descending from this point on the southern face of the ridge towards the valley which separates the two ranges of the Rajgir hills, one reaches the small cave known as Gidhadwari, the position and appearance of which corresponds exactly to the cave which we find mentioned in Hiuen Tsiang's account as the scene of Indra's interrogation of Buddha. The cave itself shows no trace of human workmanship, but at its entrance, which is reached by scrambling over some precipitous ledges of rock, there is a small platform, about 20 feet in length, supported by a wall of old masonry. According to the popular belief this cave, which is 10 feet broad and 17 feet high at the mouth, communicates with Jarasandha's tower, but there is only a natural fissure running upwards for 98 feet.

Among other remains may be mentioned an extensive mound of ruins half a mile long on the east side of the Panchana, with a small mud fort in the middle of it, and the remains of two paved ascents on the river side and of three more on the opposite side of the mound. To the north-west skirting the northern slope of the hills is a long embankment, called the Asurenbandh, enclosing a large sheet of water. This embankment is connected with a curious popular legend. It is said that Jarasandha had a great garden close to this tower, which he built as his *baithak* or throne. One year the garden was nearly destroyed by drought, and Jarasandha therefore promised the hand of his daughter and half his kingdom to any who would water it in a single night from the Ganges. The chief of the Kahars, Chandrawat, undertook the task, and built the great embankment called Asurenbandh to bring the water of the Bawan Ganga to the foot of the hill below the garden : this river, which flows into the Panchana near Giriak, is considered part of the Ganges. The Kahars then began lifting the water with swing baskets in successive stages. The work was all but completed, and Jarasandha was in despair at having to marry his daughter to a Kahar, when a *pipal* tree came to his rescue, and, assuming the form of a cock, crowed loudly. Thereupon, the Kahars thinking it was morning, and fearing the king would take vengeance on them for presuming to seek the hand of his daughter, fled in terror as far as Mokameh. The bread-cakes and balls of rice which they took to sustain them in their work were left behind in their wild flight, and may still be seen on the hill turned to stone. (See *Rajgir.*)

Hilsa.—Village in the Bihar subdivision, on the banks of the Kattar, 13 miles south of Fatuha, with which it is connected by a metalled road, by which runs the Fatwa-Islampur Light Railway. Population (1921) 2,395. Hilsa contains a police-station and inspection bungalow, and has a large market, where trade in grain and oil-seeds is carried on. An annual fair is held here, and it is also a centre for the ceremony of circumcising Muhammadan children. According to local tradition, the name is derived from one Hilsa Deo, a powerful Hindu magician, who was killed by the Muhammadan saint, Shah Juman Madari, commonly known as Juman Jati. After this, the name of the place was changed to Jatinagar, for, when dying, Hilsa asked his conqueror where he should get food, and was told that whoever came to Jatinagar and used the name of Hilsa would receive food. The legend is probably an echo of the struggle between Muhammadans and Hindus; the mosque being avowedly built on the site of a Hindu temple, while Hilsa is said to be buried under the great slabs under the central arch, so that every day he is trodden underfoot by the feet of the faithful.

The *dargah* or shrine of Shah Juman Madari at Hilsa is a place for far-reaching fame. It is a simple, square brick building, covered by one dome, and containing seven tombs, of which the westernmost is said to be that of the saint. An inscription over the gate, the date of which corresponds to 1543 A.D., tells us that in the time of Sher Shah the tomb of Miran Saiyid Juman Madari was repaired by order of Mian Sheikh Alam Adam Shah Juman Madari, at the expense of Daria Khan Zangi, an officer of the body-guard. The original building thus appears to be older than 1543 A.D., but it cannot have been much anterior, as Shah Madar, the founder of the Madari order, to which the saints mentioned in the inscription belonged, is said to have been a contemporary of Ibrahim Shah of Jaunpur, who reigned from 1400 A.D. Another inscription refers to the building of a mosque near the *dargah* by a person called Riza. Its date corresponds to 1604 A.D., and it is of some historical interest as it refers to Jahangir, who is called Shah Salim, as the reigning king. His father Akbar was still alive at that time, but Jahangir was already in open rebellion against him, and had struck coins, with the name Salim, of which numerous specimens exist. The mosque built by Riza is no longer in existence and the present one is an insignificant modern building. [Reports Arch. Surv. Ind., Vols. VIII and XI; Report Arch. Surv., Bengal Circle, for 1901-02.]

Islampur (or Atasari).—Village in the extreme southwest of the Bihar subdivision situated 14 miles south of Hilsa.

Population (1921), 5,073. Islampur is now connected by a light railway with Fatuha, on the main line of the East Indian Railway. The village contains a police-station and inspection bungalow, and is a large market, at which trade in grain and oil-seeds is carried on. It is the centre of the tobacco trade in the south of the district, thousands of maunds being brought annually from Tirhut, stored in large godowns, and thence distributed to various centres. Much of this trade has been diverted from Islampur by the railway, and it is now on the decline. The remains of a large Buddhist monastery or temple exist at the extreme west of the village, and some of the granite columns are still intact. About a mile to the south-west is a small village called Ichhos which was also the site of a great Buddhist temple and monastery. Islampur is the seat of an old zamindari family, whose ancestors obtained settlement of a great part of Shahjahanpur and Bhimpur parganas in 1790.

Jethuli.—See Banka Ghat.

Khagaul.—A municipal town in the Dinapore sub-division, four miles south of Dinapore. Population (1921) 7,195, of whom 5,050 are Hindus, 1,672 Muhammadans, and 453 Christians. The Dinapore railway station is at Khagaul, which has only risen into importance since the opening of the railway. It contains the residences of the local railway staff, and is the headquarters of a Company of the East Indian Railway Regiment (A. F.). The name, says Mr. Christian in "Names of places in Bihar" (Calcutta Review, 1891), indicates that Khagaul was at one time the old bed of a river, which on changing its course left the channel high and dry.

Kurji.—Suburb of Bankipore on the banks of the Ganges, about one mile to the east of Digha Ghat railway station, containing a large European boarding school, called St. Michael's High School. This school, which was founded in 1854, is under the control of a Roman Catholic order known as the Irish Christian Brothers. It is attended by about 200 pupils, and has a Volunteer cadet corps attached to it. Kurji also contains a Roman Catholic Chapel and an orphanage for Europeans and Eurasians.

Malda pargana.—One of the parganas of zila Bihar, with an area of 93½ square miles, which is now in Monghyr district, with the exception of a small area of 1·40 square miles, with revenue of Rs. 567, in the south-eastern corner of Patna district.

Maner.—Village in the extreme north-west of the Dinapore subdivision, ten miles south-west of Dinapore and six miles north of Bihta station on the East Indian Railway. Metalled roads connect it with both places. Maner is a large village with a population of 2,598 souls, and contains a police-station, dispensary and dak bungalow. There is also a camping ground for troops, situated in a large mango tope north-east of the police-station. Maner contains two well-known Muhammadan tombs, that of Shah Daulat or Makhdum Daulat, known as the Choti Dargah, and the other that of Sheikh Yahia Maneri or Makhdum Yahia, called the Bari Dargah. Makhdum Daulat died at Maner in 1608, and the erection of his mausoleum was completed in 1616 by Ibrahim Khan, Governor of Bihar and one of the saint's disciples; the date is recorded in an inscription expressing the pious wish "May it remain for ever safe like Heaven ". The building is an exceptionally fine one, with walls containing carvings of great delicacy and high finish. It stands on a raised platform, and at each corner rises a slender tower of graceful proportions ; it is crowned by a great dome, and the ceiling is covered with carved inscriptions from the Koran. Every detail of it is characteristic of the architecture of Jahangir's reign, and it is by far the finest monument of the Mughals in Bengal. There is a faithful and beautiful illustration of this shrine among Thomas Daniell's drawings, dating from about 1796. Inside the compound is a mosque also built by Ibrahim Khan in 1619, while a fine gateway bearing an older inscription, the date of which corresponds to 1603-04, affords access to the north.

The tomb of Yahia Maneri lies in a mosque to the east of a large tank, with masonry walls and *ghats*, and pillared porticos jutting out into it, which is connected with the old bed of the Son by a tunnel 400 feet long. The tomb is situated in an enclosure half filled with graves and ancient trees, on the north and west of which are a three-domed mosque and some quaint little cloisters built by Ibrahim Khan in 1605-06. Yahia Maneri was born at Maner, and died there in 1290-91 A.D., he was a member of a celebrated family of saints, being the father of Makhdum Sharif-ud-din of Bihar, son-in-law of Sheikh Shihab-ud-din, whose shrine is at Jethuli, and the brother-in-law of Bibi Kamalo, a female saint of the Gaya district. This tomb is not so imposing as Shah Daulat's mausoleum, and there is nothing very remarkable in its structure; but it has been from a very early date a place of pilgrimage, being visited among others by the emperor Babar and Sikandar Lodi; the *pargana* of Maner is sometimes called, after the saint, Maner-i-Sheikh Yahia. The site where the tomb stands was formerly occupied by a Hindu shrine, which the Muhammadans destroyed, purposely, it is said, leaving one of the idols to remind the people of its destruction. This is the figure of a tiger carved in stone called the Sidaul, which lies near the noble gateway to the north.

Of the other monuments none call for special mention except the tomb of Tingur Kuli Khan situated on the bank of the tank to the south-east of the bungalow. Tingur died in 1575, and his tomb is now in a ruinous state, the canopy and pillars lying in broken fragments, but a stone with an inscription still remains. This inscription contains some lines from Sadi which may be translated :—

Alas, that many a year when I am gone,
The rose will bloom, the new spring blossom forth
And those now left behind will tread my dust,
Not knowing and not caring whose it is.

Maner itself is a place of some antiquity, which appears to have come into prominence after the Muhammadan conquest; according to local tradition, its first settler was Sheikh Yahia's grandfather, Iman Tej Fateh, who came here from Arabia. It is mentioned by Ferishta as having been founded in the mythical times of Firoz Rai; in 1529-30 we find it visited by the emperor Babar, who said his noon-day prayers before the shrines. It was formerly situated on the Son, the waters of which were brought into the great tank by the tunnel already mentioned; according to Rennell's map of 1772 that river joined the Ganges here. In 1812 Maner was three miles south of the point of junction; and the Son now joins the Ganges six miles to the north and flows far to the west of the village. Two large fairs are held here every year—one on the anniversary of Makhdum Yahia's death on the 12th Shaban, when his relics and those of his ancestor, Iman Tej Fateh, are exhibited and certain ancient rites and ceremonies are performed; the other is held on the last Sunday in the month of

Jeth in commemoration of the wedding of Ghazi Mian. An interesting account of Maner, with illustrations, by Mr. Arthur Casperz is given in the Journal of the Photographic Society of India, June 1902. See also Report Arch. Surv., Bengal, for 1901-02, and History and Antiquities of Maner by Syed Zahiruddin, Bankipore, 1905.

Maner pargana.—North-western pargana of Patna district, with an area of 199¾ square miles, assessed to revenue in 1790 at Rs. 69,745, which was increased by the resumption proceedings to Rs. 1,15,668.

Masaurha pargana.—Pargana lying immediately south of Maner pargana, in Bikram and Masaurhi thanas, with an area of 173¼ square miles, assessed in 1790 at Rs. 42,128, increased by the resumption proceedings to Rs. 58,066. At the time of the Permanent Settlement this pargana was in the zamindari of Raja Jaswant Singh. (See *Bharatpura* and *Dharhara.*)

Mokameh (Mukama).—Town in the Barh subdivision, situated on the Ganges, with an important station on the East Indian Railway, 283 miles from Calcutta. Population (1921) 15,663, of whom 13,257 are Hindus, and 2,187 Muhammadans. This is the junction for a short branch line, leading to the river, by which passengers from Calcutta to Tirhut join the Bengal and North-Western Railway. A number of European and Anglo-Indian railway servants live in the town, and it is an important centre of trade.

Nalanda.—Site of the most famous of the monasteries of Magadha, on the south of the modern village of Bargaon (q. v.). The place is three miles from the Nalanda station of the B. B. Light Railway, with which it is connected by a road. "Bargaon," wrote Mr. Broadley, who excavated here in the seventies, "has been identified with that Vihara-gram on the outskirts of which, more than 1,000 years ago, flourished the great Nalanda monastery, the most magnificent and most celebrated seat of Buddhist learning in the world. When the caves and temples of Rajagriha were abandoned to the ravages of decay, and when the followers of Tathagata forsook the mountain dwellings of their great teacher, the monastery of Nalanda arose in all its splendour on the banks of the lakes of Bargaon. Successive monarchs vied in its embellishment : lofty pagodas were raised in all directions; halls of disputation and schools of instruction were built between them; shrines, temples and topes were constructed on the side of every tank and encircled the base of every tower; and around the whole mass of religious edifices were grouped the 'four-storied' dwellings of the preachers and teachers of Buddhism." The monastery of Nalanda, the Oxford, as it has been called, of Buddhist India, was a centre from which Buddhist philosophy and teaching were diffused over Southern Asia; and it continued to be a great Buddhist university till the Muhammadan conquest. According to Hiuen Tsiang, the Chinese pilgrim of the seventh century, who himself resided there for some years, it contained numerous temples, pagodas and shrines, and was the home of 10,000 monks, renowned for their learning, who spent their lives in the pursuit of wisdom. There appears to have been a severe kind of Entrance or Matriculation Examination. "If men of other quarters desire to enter," says Hiuen Tsiang, "the keeper of the gate proposes some hard questions; many are unable to answer and retire. One must have studied deeply both old and new books before getting admission. Those students, therefore, who come here as strangers have to show their ability by hard discussion: those who fail, compared with those who succeed, are as seven or eight to ten."

The remains of Nalanda include a range of massive brick ruins, running north and south, of the great stupas attached to the monasteries. A hundred yards east of the stupa mounds, and running parallel to them, is a maze of *viharas*, the original courtyards of which may possibly be traced in the square patches of cultivation set in a debris-strewn area of 1,600 by 400 feet. Detached mounds farther afield mark the sites of temples, while individual sculptures scattered all over the site testify to Nalanda's former greatness. General Cunningham was of opinion that he met with the finest sculptures in India at this site; and it is probable that a considerable portion of the best sculptures now in the Indian Museum at Calcutta came from here. On the south of the monastery, according to Hiuen Tsiang, there was a tank in which the dragon, or Naga Nalanda used to dwell. Cunningham identified this tank with the existing small tank called Kargidya Pokhar, which corresponds in position with the pool of the Naga.

Dr. Spooner in 1916 began systematic exploration of the site, which has been continued in recent years by Mr. J. A. Page of the Archæological Survey. The most important discoveries have been in the opening up of two of the monasteries, one of the stupas, and a temple.

SITE No. 1.—The monastery in which the work of exploration has hitherto (1923) been most completely carried out measures 205 feet by 168, the wall is 6½ feet thick, which is increased by a foot on the western side. Eight different strata have been discerned as the site was cleared, indicating that from time to time, as the monastery was destroyed by fire or collapsed from faulty workmanship, new structures were erected on the ruins of the old.* The lowest stratum cleared, which is probably that of the oldest building on this site, is apparently of the sixth or seventh century A.D. The entrance to this monastery lay through a great portico 50 feet by 24, resting on pillars, the bases of which are still left *in situ.* Facing this portico across the great courtyard was a chapel containing a colossal image of Buddha, of which fragments have been found. The courtyard was surrounded by cloisters, within which were the sleeping chambers of the monks, which have been opened up on the south and east sides of the building. In the north-west corner of the courtyard is a well, seven feet in diameter.

When the original monastery fell down and was rebuilt, the monks, instead of clearing all the debris, smoothed it down and made a new ground level. They had to clear away a certain amount of debris to reach the courtyard well, which appears to have been utilised for every successive building on the site. The wind blowing dust upon the outside debris converted it into a great mound of earth, the height of which must have been increased from time to time as partial clearance was made of the inside of the site. Thus the level of the courtyard came to be below the outer ground level, and a grand staircase was built leading down to the courtyard. In the third or fourth building on the site two structural 'caves' of brick were erected. These chambers have corbelled entrances; but the roofs are vaulted, apparently in imitation of the rock-cut caves at Barabar; the work is certainly pre-Muhammadan, and is one of the earliest arches in India. In the late buildings the great gateway of the chapel or sanctum was blocked in the middle by masonry, on either side of which was left a small door.

* Unmistakable traces of burning are evident, and in places charcoal is lying even now.

In the entrance to the monastery Pandit Hirananda Sastri discovered a copper-plate inscription of Sri Devapaladeva, the third sovereign of the Pala dynasty, bearing a date equivalent to 891 A.D. The inscription records the grant of five villages in the Gaya and Rajagriha districts for the upkeep of the Nalanda monastery and the provision of comforts for monks and *bhikshus* arriving there from all quarters, made at the request of the king of Sumatra, Sri Balaputra Deva, apparently in return for an equivalent grant in that country.

SITE NO. 1A.—Overlapped at its north-eastern corner by the monastery already described is another monastery, which is entered on the north through a pillared portico, of which only the bases of the columns now remain, and a vestibule. The plan of the monastery is a rectangle containing the usual monks' chambers on each side, with the addition of what may possibly have been a shrine in the centre of the south side. An open pillared veranda ran originally round the rectangular panels. In the centre are two parallel rows of hearths, seven in number, connected by a common duct of corbel construction about two feet high. This feature occurs again in the eastern varanda. Pandit Hirananda Sastri thinks that it might have been used for preparing drugs, and that the building may have been a medical seminary or *Bhishak-sala*. In the north-east corner of the court is an octagonal well, which on clearance yielded a number of earthen vases. Heaps of decayed rice and oats were found in two chambers on the east, which appear to have been used as store-rooms. In other rooms on the north several copper and stone images of Tara, Avalokitesvara, Maitreya and Buddha were discovered, perhaps an indication of the saints favoured by individual monks. A flight of steps rises between two of the rooms on the north, probably to afford access to the veranda roof.

THE TEMPLE (SITE NO. 2).—Immediately east of the monastery quadrangle ascribed to Baladitya by Cunningham, the four sides of a ruined stone temple, square in plan, were uncovered during the excavation in 1916. The entrance to the temple was up a low flight of steps on the east. The centre of each facade is relieved by a slight projection; but the feature of special interest is a dado of 211 sculptured panels over the exterior base moulding, showing a great variety of sculpture. It appears that this building was a later structure erected over an older brick building; and as the panels of the plinth are assigned by Dr. Spooner to the sixth or seventh century A.D., it would appear that these materials were taken from an older building and utilised in the decoration of this temple.

SITE No. 3 (STUPA).—The high stupa at the south end of the range of mounds running parallel to the range of monasteries is the *vihara* A of Cunningham, described as being 33 feet high, and about 70 feet thick at the top. This he would identify with the stupa mentioned by Hiuen Tsiang as marking the place where the Lord Buddha dwelt for three months explaining the law of the gods. In the course of excavating the stupa three different integuments of new masonry, each completely enclosing the previous one, were brought to light. It appears that the builders did not wait for the ruin of the older structure before renewing it, but enlarged the stupa by a new masonry facing, leaving intact the Buddhist figures in stucco on the face of the original solid structure. It also appears that the stupa had four towers abutting on to the corners. Each successive addition appears to have followed the original plan; and to give suitable support to the additional masonry to be erected, a square framework of encasing walls was built on each side, the casing then being filled in to form a solid core for the enlarged stupa. (A plan is given in the Report of the Archæological Survey, Eastern Circle, 1919-20.)

The main stupa stands surrounded in the court by a large number of smaller stupas, built one over the other on the same spot, sometimes twice or thrice. As the main stupa increased in size, the level of the original court generally rose, and many smaller stupas are found in several places half or completely buried in the various floors which have been unearthed. At present three distinct levels of the stupa-court can be seen. The first, the existing general level; the second a stratum some three feet higher revealed by two prone fragmentary stone pillars lying where they had fallen to the right of the entrance and almost coincident in level with the very late brick platform on the west; and the third, about four feet below the first, at the south east corner of the stupa. A factor having an important bearing on the chronology of these levels is the existence of a paved drain which originates in the courtyard of monastery No. 1A and enters the stupa court at this latter place, indicating that all the three levels referred to above are later than the monastery No. 1A, which by then had fallen to ruin and was finally deserted; for it is improbable that a domestic drain would be carried through the sacred enclosure of the stupa court, especially when it could without apparent difficulty be diverted clear of it to the south.

From this stupa a long trench running north some 1,500 feet up to the high mound locally known as Autalid-harahar was dug by Dr. Spooner, which brought to light the remains of numerous small stupas, and several shrines and brick pavements. The excavation yielded very few finds, the only thing worth recording being a seated figure of Avalokitesvara, found towards the southern end of the trench. If we may identify them with Hiuen Tsiang's description, the high mounds lying in the middle and at the northern extremity of the range of stupa mounds over which the trench was carried were 200 feet and 300 feet high respectively. The latter of these Cunningham identifies with Baladitya's Temple which, according to the Chinese pilgrim, closely resembled the Temple of Buddh Gaya. This last, in its present form however is actually only about 170 feet high. The colossal statue of the ascetic Buddha called Batuk Bhadrava set up in an enclosure near the foot of this mound was, it would seem, originally enshrined in the Temple itself. Another statue of Buddha in the bhumisparsa attitude has also been set up near by. It is attended by a standing figure on each side, and has two flying figures with garlands overhead. The names of them all are inscribed, the attendants being Arya Vasumitra and Arya Maitreya, and the flying figures Arya Sariputra and Arya Maudgalyana, the two principal disciples of Buddha, who being Arhats, possessed the power of flying through the air. It is to be remarked that an encasing wall on the south side of Baladitya's Temple can still be seen, providing another instance of the practice of enlarging an original structure. On the south and west sides, a little lower than this, a plinth has been disclosed with a dado containing at least two series of panels, one above the other, and originally decorated with low pilasters of well carved pot and foliage design enclosing the representation of a stupa.

Antiquities discovered in the course of excavation are arranged in a museum attached to the Nalanda bungalow.

[Ancient Geography of India by Cunningham, pages 468-471; Beal's Fa Hian and life of Hiuen Tsiang; Arch. Survey Report, Eastern Circle, 1901-2, 1915-16, 1919-20, 1920-21; Nalanda excavations, by J. A. Page (*J.B.O.R.S.* March, 1923).]

Narhat pargana.—An area of 10½ square miles out of Narhat pargana lies in Patna district (in the south-west of the Bihar subdivision), assessed after the completion of resumption proceedings at Rs. 2,274. The whole pargana has an area of 282 square miles, assessed in 1790 at Rs. 64,346, and after the resumption proceedings at Rs. 82,655. This pargana with Samai gave its name to Kamgar Khan's estate which is shown in Rennell's map as Narhat-Samai, as if it were a semi-independent state. The zamindari covered the south-east of zila Bihar, assessed to revenue of Rs. 4,65,188. An area equivalent to three-fourths of Narhat pargana was permanently settled at Thomas Law's mukarrari settlement of 1788.

Okri pargana.—A pargana lying west of the Tilhara pargana, almost wholly in Gaya district, only 1½ square miles being in Patna district, assessed after completion of resumption proceedings at Rs. 3,041. The whole pargana has an area of 105¼ square miles, assessed to revenue after the resumption proceedings at Rs. 82,160.

Patna and Patna City.—See Chapter XVI.

Patna City subdivision.—Subdivision of the district, with an area of 31¾ square miles, consisting of the city of Patna (exclusive of the civil station of Bankipore), and of a few outlying villages. Population (1921) 112,769. The subdivision includes the police-stations of Pirbahor, Chauk Kalan, Malsalami, Alamganj and Khwaja Kalan. Of late years the Additional District Magistrate has ordinarily held charge of the subdivision.

Pawapuri.—Village in the Bihar subdivision, situated three miles north of Giriak, to the east of the road from that place to Bihar. The name is a corruption of Apapapuri, the pure or sinless town. Pawapuri is a sacred place to the Jains, as it was here that Mahavira, the founder of their religion, died; according to another account, he died on Vipulagiri hill at Rajgir, and his body was brought here to be burned. The village is situated a short distance to the north of a great lake in the midst of which stands the holy temple of Jal-Mandar. The lake is a little more than one-quarter of a mile on each side; and there is a bridge on the north side leading to the temple in the middle of an island 104 feet square. The temple is of dazzling whiteness outside, and dismal darkness inside, and is only entered through a low door which forces the visitor to stoop. To the north of the lake there is an old temple called Thal-Mandar, which, according to the priests, is built on the spot where Mahavira died, the Jal-Mandar being the place of his cremation. The lake did not then exist; but such countless crowds of people came to attend the ceremony of burning the body, that the mere act of each taking up a pinch of dust to make the usual *tika* or mark on the forehead is believed to have created a great hollow which now forms the lake.

Between Thal-Mandar and the lake there is a curious circular mound which rises by four successive broad steps or stages, up to a platform 32 feet in diameter. On this there is a small round terrace 8 feet in diameter, surmounted by a miniature temple only 3 feet 4 inches in diameter, containing the footprints of Mahavira. The whole work is called Samosaran, and is said to be the place where Mahavira sat to teach his disciples, who were arranged in concentric circles around him. As usual at all Jain places, where no living thing is killed, there are numerous snakes all about the lake. The fish may eat each other, but they are not molested by man, and when they die, their bodies are carefully brought ashore and buried. [Reports Arch. Surv. Ind., Vols. VIII and XI.]

Phulwari pargana.—A pargana lying between Maner and Azimabad parganas, with an area of 72·38 square miles. The assessment in 1790 was Rs. 42,174, which was increased by the resumption proceedings to Rs. 66,256.

Pilich pargana.—A pargana lying chiefly in Hilsa thana extending into Fatuha, with an area of 140 square miles. This pargana was formerly part of the zamindari of Kamgar Khan and his brothers; and this was one of the parganas in which Thomas Law made his *mukarrari* settlement with village maliks in 1788. Out of 122 estates which he then created, he settled 85 with maliks; and this form of settlement was more successful here than in Gayaspur. The estates then settled are held under covenants by which the proprietor undertakes to maintain irrigation works, to abstain from collecting *abwab*, and to pay additional revenue if it should be necessary for the defence of the country; but the difference between these covenants and those of the Decennial Settlement has not been made a ground for distinguishing these from other permanently settled estates.

Punarak.—A large village on the Patna-Monghyr road, in the Barh subdivision, with a station on the East Indian Railway, 292 miles from Calcutta. Population (1921) 7,339. This was one of the camping grounds on the Ganges road from Bengal to Bihar; here Eyre Coote's European soldiers mutinied on the 24th of July, 1757, in the course of their march to Patna. The principal resident is Chaudhari Bhagwat Prashad Singh, an Honorary Magistrate of Barh. His family possesses a curious *lingam* of which the legend is narrated by Rai Bahadur Ramgopal Singh Chaudhuri in his "*Further Rambles in Bihar*". He also tells an interesting story accounting for the origin of the temple of Sri Surjya Narain in this village, in connection with which an annual festival is held on a Sunday in Sravan.

Punpun.—Village in the sadr subdivision, eight miles south of Bankipore, on the Punpun river. Population (1921) 771. There is a railway station here on the Patna-Gaya line, and the village contains also a police-station and a dispensary. This is the place at which pilgrims to Gaya begin the ceremonies incidental to their pilgrimage. It is incumbent on them to bathe here and shave their heads preparatory to performing funeral rites for their ancestors at Gaya.

Rajgir.—Village in the Bihar subdivision, 13½ miles south-west of Bihar, the terminus of the light railway from Bakhtiarpur. There is an unmetalled road from Bihar bridged throughout and easily passable except after rain. The village contains a dispensary and a good inspection bungalow. Population (1921) 2,693.

Rajgir is one of the most interesting places in the district. It was originally the capital of Jarasandha, a prehistoric king of Magadha and Chedi (Bundelkhand), who is mentioned in the Mahabharata as taking a prominent part in the great war commemorated in the epic. His name still lives in local legend, and remains of his fortress can be seen in the massive walls climbing the neighbouring hills. In historic times Bimbisara (*cir.* 528-500 B.C.) made his capital in the valley between the hills which formed the fortress of Jarasandha; and during his reign Rajgir and the neighbourhood were frequently visited by Buddha. Here Buddha first studied under the Brahmans Alara and Uddaka, and here after the attainment of Buddhahood, or supreme enlightenment, he used to spend his time in retreat, his favourite resorts being the Karanda Veluvana or the Bamboo Grove, close to the northern gap in the hills, and the hill called Gridhrakuta or the Vulture's Peak. At Rajgir he often preached and taught, Bimbisara being among his disciples; here too a Jaina ascetic made a pit of fire and poisoned the rice which Buddha was asked to eat; and it was here that Devadatta attempted to take his life, a crime for which he is punished in the Buddhist hell, where his feet are sunk in burning lime and his head encased in red hot metal, while two red hot iron bars transfix him from back to front and another impales him from head to foot.

After the death of Buddha (*cir.* 487 B.C.), the first great Buddhist council was held here in the Sattapanni cave to fix the tenets of the Buddhist faith; and Ajatasatru, Bimbisara's successor, built a new capital to the north of the old city and erected a stupa over his share of Buddha's ashes. Shortly after this, Rajgir ceased to be the royal residence on the foundation of Pataliputra by Udaya; but it continued to be an important place of pilgrimage. Mahendra, the younger brother of Asoka lived an anchorite's life in a hermitage on the Vulture's Peak, and Asoka himself, we are told, died on one of its holy hills (232 B.C.). In the fifth century A.D. it was visited by the Chinese pilgrim Fa Hian, according to whose account the old city was desolate and without inhabitants, but in the new city there were two monasteries, and the stupa built over the ashes of Buddha was still standing. This site however was also destined to be deserted, for, in the seventh century, Hiuen Tsiang, another Chinese pilgrim (*cir.* 637 B.C.), found that though the inner walls were still standing, the outer walls were in ruins; the sole inhabitants were Brahmans who numbered 1,000 families. The place was still, however, a popular place of pilgrimage, and numerous

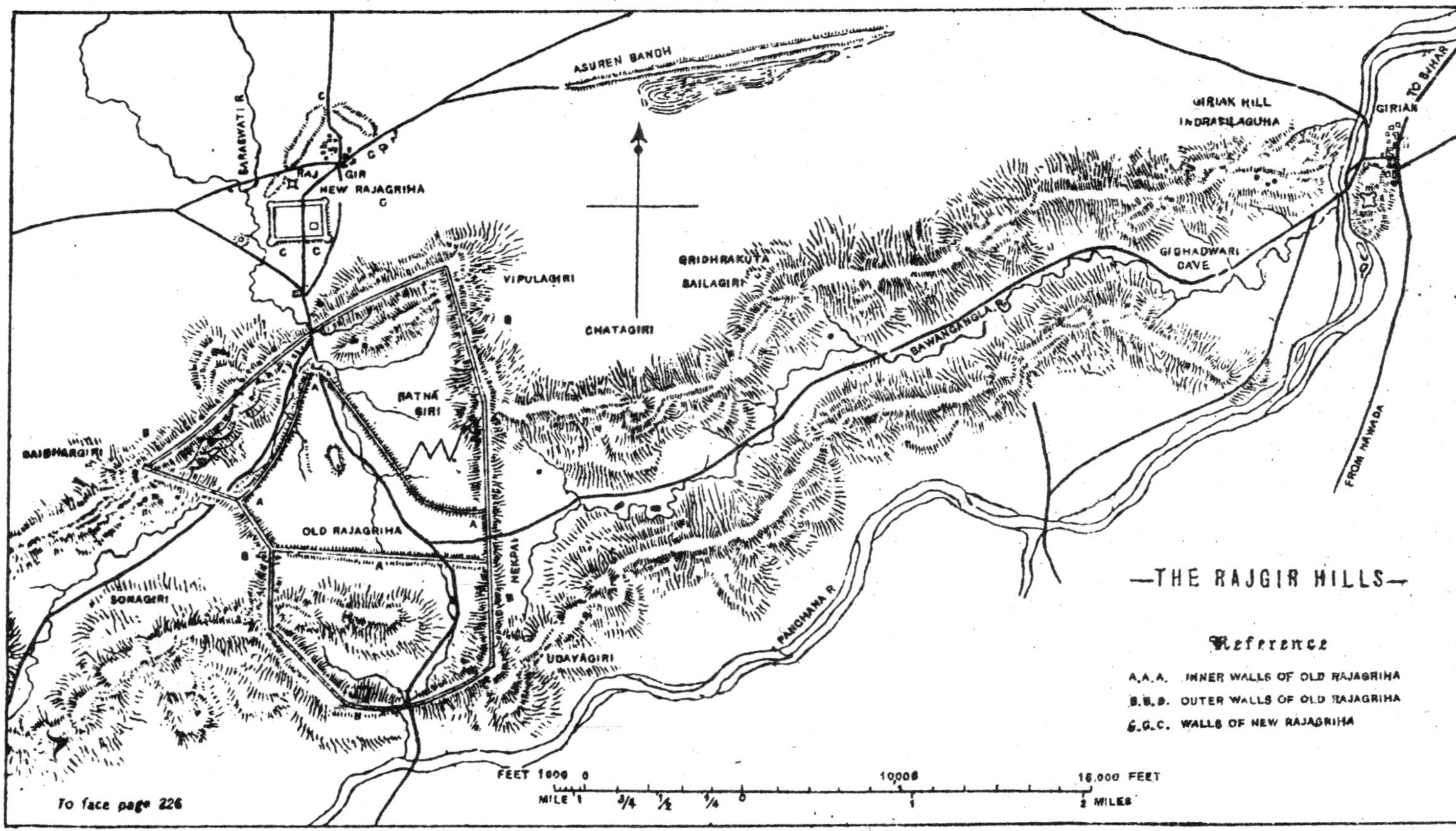

To face page 226

stupas and viharas had been constructed round the sacred springs. Before mentioning the remains still extant, a brief reference may be made to the names by which Rajgir has been known at various times. The name of the old capital of Jarasandha, preserved both in the Ramayana and Mahabharata, was Giribraja, the mountain-girt city or city of many hills. The name Rajagriha or the royal residence was given later when the Saisunaka kings made the place their capital, but the ancient city of Bimbisara was known as Kusagarapura or the city of kusa grass. This is now known as Old Rajgir and the capital of Ajatasatru as New Rajgir—names as old as the days of Fa Hian and Hiuen Tsiang.

The modern village of Rajgir is situated on the site of Ajatasatru's city, to the north of the Rajgir Hills, which consist of two parallel ranges running west-south-west from Giriak, which here broaden out into a fairly extensive valley, in which the original city of Rajagriha was built among the hills. To the east and north of this valley are the peaks of Sailagiri, Chhathagiri, Ratnagiri, Vipulagiri and Baibhargiri, and on the southern side are Udayagiri and Sonagiri.

Old Rajgir.

The oldest remains extant at Rajgir are the prehistoric outer walls of the old city, which are cyclopean in their rude construction and massive proportions. They are usually 17½ feet thick, faced with massive undressed stones set without mortar, usually on the outer edge of the summits of the hills. The walls are in best preservation on the southern ridge on either side of the Bawan Ganga gap; and the inner line, crossing from Udayagiri to Ratnagiri by the Nekpai embankment, over Ratnagiri to Baibhargiri, and thence crossing to Sonagiri by a double wall, is practically continuous throughout. An outer line extends as far as Giriak on the east, making use of any precipices which exist, and it is fully developed on the south-west face of the hills which divide the Rajgir valley from that of Jethian to the S.W., extending as far as the summit of the Handia hill.

Some of these walls were built before Bimbisara's city was founded. The inner ramparts of the city had a circuit of about five miles in the valley, while outside there was another line of circumvallation extending over twenty-five miles along the crests of the hills.

One of the most interesting places at Rajgir, which can easily be identified as Chhathagiri, is the Gridhrakuta hill, with the "Bimbisara road" or stone causeway leading up to it, which still shows traces of the two stupas called "Dismounting from the chariot" and "Sending back the crowd," and of the "vihara on the borders of the precipice at the western end of the mountain," as described by Hiuen Tsiang. It appears that a road led all the way from the eastern gate in the walls of the old city, which crossed a deep moat by a bridge of which the foundations are still visible. No other site connected with the old city itself mentioned by the Chinese pilgrims has been definitely identified, though interesting evidence from the Burmese chronicles has been brought forward by Mr D. N. Sen to show that the garden of Jivaka, the king's physician, was outside the eastern gate, to the north of the road leading to the Gridhrakuta hill. Close to the southern wall of the old city is the ruin of a square stone fort with small circular bastions at the corners, which appears to be very old; and two square wells excavated in the rock, one of which, just outside the original southern gate, still contains water.

New Rajgir. Outside the northern entrance to this valley and about two-thirds of a mile from the old city was situated New Rajgir, which was protected by a wall of massive masonry built of solid blocks of stone. It appears to have resembled an irregular pentagon in shape, and had a circuit of nearly three miles. On the south towards the hills a portion of the interior was cut off to form a citadel, and here portions of the stone walls are still in fair preservation.

Other remains. The existing remains are not numerous, and except for the ramparts there are few above ground. The place, as we have seen, was deserted at a very early date, and has been occupied at different times by Muhammadans and Brahmans, by whom the Buddhist structures were pulled down to furnish materials for tombs, mosques and temples. To the south-west of the modern village is a hollow mound, which probably marks the site of a stupa 60 feet high built by Asoka. In the centre of the valley between the five hills was a brick mound, nearly twenty feet high, on the top of which was a diminutive Jain temple, called Maniar Math, built in 1780. The excavations carried out by Dr. T. Bloch in 1908-9 disclosed a brick structure, which Sir John Marshall is inclined to consider as a colossal *linga.* Round the base were ten stucco images arranged in niches divided by pilasters, which Dr. Bloch assigned to the early Gupta period. These images were in excellent preservation when first unearthed, but have now almost entirely disintegrated. In addition to Siva and Ganesa, Banasura and a linga, there were six *nagis*, which Dr. Bloch supposed to be serpent deities worshipped on the surrounding hills.

The Caves. Inside the valley at the southern foot of the Baibhar hill to the south-west of the gorge leading from New Rajgir to the site of Old Rajgir is an artificial cave called Sonbhandhar, or the treasury of gold, cut out of solid rock, with its interior chiselled to a steely polish, features in which it so closely resembles the Barabar caves that its construction has been attributed to the same period—the third century B.C. Adjoining it to the east is another cave now in ruins. Overlooking the entrance to the valley on the same hill is the small flat-topped stone fort and cavern behind it, identified in 1872 by Cunningham with the Pippala stone house and Asuras' cave. According to Buddhist tradition, Buddha dwelt in the former, which has several small cells in its walls.

The Sattapanni cave. The Sattapanni or Saptaparna cave, in which the first Buddhist Council was held, was identified by General Cunningham with the Sonbhandar cave. It is more likely that the Sonbhandar cave was made by a Jain monk for the use of his own sect. An inscription on the outside of the cave says that Muni Vairadeva made two caves for ascetics desiring to attain Nirvana and that these caves are renowned on account of the Arhats. The two caves referred to can only be the Sonbhandar and the adjoining cave; and the inscription, which is of the third or fourth century A.D., distinctly points to the Jains by its technical terms. Mr. Beglar again conjectured that the Sattapanni cave consisted of a series of fissures of rock forming a natural cavern high up on the north side of the same hill less than a mile to the west of the Pippala stone house; but though the position suggested is more probable, the indications of any cavern are extremely vague.

In 1899 Sir Aurel Stein proposed another site for this famous cave, which he located on the northern scarp of the Baibhar hill, about a hundred feet below the Jain temple of Adinatha. His account is as follows:—"A path, which descends the rugged northern scarp of the ridge to a level of about 100 feet below the temple, leads to a long terrace, which, notwithstanding the luxurious vegetation covering it at the time of my visit, clearly betrayed its artificial origin. The wall, which supports it towards the lower slope, is composed of large unhewn slabs and can be traced for fully 100 feet running in the direction from north-east to south-west along the face of the slope. The average width of the terrace is 25 feet. Where, at the south-west end, the supporting wall is lost in thick jungle, a narrow path strikes off towards a natural cave in the rock face overhanging the terrace. It runs in the direction W.N.W. to E.S.E. and is 40 feet deep in its open portion. The height is about 12 feet at the entrance and 10 feet further in. The cave is widest at the middle, where it is about 16 feet broad. The cave, though undoubtedly due to a natural fissure in the rocks, may have been somewhat enlarged by rough excavations at the sides. At least there is a suggestion of this in the presence of flat low ledges of rock which line the sides. Along the same wall of rocks, at a distance of about 50 feet further to the south-west, is a second and somewhat larger natural cavity. It is 47 feet deep, 25 feet wide at its broadest, and 10 to 11 feet high. Its end is lost in a narrow fissure, which is said to extend much further."

Another reason for regarding this as the real site of the Sattapani cave has been suggested. The stratum of rock overhanging these caves is split vertically into sections, seven of which can be counted. It is possibly these sections (or 'leaves') that gave the cave its name. The debris moreover that has fallen down the hill slope may indicate that at one time a terrace or platform existed in front of the caves.*

Modern pilgrims.

At present Rajgir is a *tirtha* or sacred place of the Jains, who come there in great numbers from different parts of India to visit the shrines on the tops of the five hills: on Baibhar hill alone there are five Jain temples besides the ruins of an old Saiva shrine. The temples are all of recent date and generally contain a stone with the footprints of

---

*Sir John Marshall disagrees with this view, and with the theory that what the Chinese pilgrims saw was a cave, natural or artificial, in the side of the hill. He considers that the 'large stone house' mentioned by Hiuen Tsiang was a structural edifice, and identifies the site with the artificially built up and levelled top of a small spur on the north side of Baibhargiri, nearly half a mile further west of the Venuvana than Stein's site.

some Jain Tirthankara. Older shrines of the middle ages, with numerous Jain images, are also found, but they are no longer used for worship. Rajgir is also a place of pilgrimage among Hindus of all classes. This sanctity is due to the numerous hot springs here, which are worshipped as manifestations of the divine power. These springs are on both banks of the Saraswati rivulet, seven at the foot of Baibhar hill, and six at the foot of Vipulagiri. The names of the former group are Ganga Jamuna, Anant Rikhi, Sapta Rikhi, Byas Kund, Markand Kund, Brahma Kund and Langat Kund. They are surrounded by sacred buildings, and on some days from eight to ten thousand persons will collect to bathe here. The six springs at the bottom of Vipulagiri are called Sita Kund, Suraj Kund, Ganesh Kund, Chandrama Kund, Ram Kund, and Sringi Rikhi Kund. The spring last mentioned, which is about a quarter of a mile east from the others, has been appropriated by the Muhammadans, and is called by them Makhdum Kund, after Makhdum Shah Sheikh Sharif-ud-din Ahmad, a saint who lived at Rajgir and fasted there in a stone cell for forty days. A triennial fair, lasting a month, attracts many thousands of pilgrims to the springs.

The water of the springs is remarkably pure, a recent analysis by Dr. K. N. Bagchi showing not more than 6·8 parts of total solids in 100,000. The maximum temperature of the Baibhar springs, observed since 1909, is 108·3, and that of the water issuing into the kunds on the Vipula side is 106. They are usually hottest about November or December, when the outflow is at its maximum.

Recent excavations.

In the excavations carried out between 1906 and 1909, New Rajgir yielded a large medley of remains of secular buildings, consisting partly of brick, partly of irregular thin flakes of stone. The remains were in three levels, the lowest about eight feet below the surface. At this level two clay seals inscribed in illegible Brahmi characters of the first or second century B.C. were discovered. The rooms in the houses were all small, the largest not more than eight feet square. The old city shows a great number of remains of ancient stone walls, similar to those found round the new city. It was found that these walls were the foundations of buildings, but it is impossible to say whether the buildings were of wood or brick. In one place the pedestal of a large statue was found with an inscription in the characters of the Kushana period (first and second century A.D.). Only the feet of the image remain; but Sir John Marshall considers that it emanated from the Mathura school of sculpture, and that it resembles two similar statues found at Sravasti and Sarnath.

[Report, Arch. Surv. India, Vol. VIII; Report Arch. Surv., Eastern Circle, 1905-6; and Notes of an Archæological Tour in South Bihar and Hazaribagh, by M. A. Stein, Ph. D., Indian Antiquary, Vol. XXX, 1901; Rajagriha and its Remains, by Sir John Marshall, Report, Arch. Survey of India, 1905-6, with map; Notes on Old Rajagriha, by V. H. Jackson, Report, Arch. Survey of India, 1913-14, with plan; Sites in Rajgir associated with Buddha and his disciples, by D. N. Sen, *J.B.O.R.S.*, Vol. IV, part II, June 1918.]

Rajgir pargana.—A pargana in the Bihar subdivision, with an area of 37 square miles. This pargana formerly was part of the zamindari of the Mayi family. After Iqbal Ali Khan's rebellion in 1781 it was permanently settled, with the confiscated estates in Amarthu, on a revenue of Rs. 26,002, with the brother of the soldier Ibrahim Ali Khan (Muhammad Yahia), whose family, commonly known as the Nawabs of Huseinabad, still possess the zamindari.

Samai pargana.—A pargana of *zila* Bihar with an area of 252 square miles, of which 14 square miles lie in Patna district, on the east of Rajgir pargana, assessed to revenue of Rs. 4,773 after the resumption proceedings. Samai was permanently settled at Thomas Law's mukarrari settlement, but almost the whole of it was settled with farmers, as village maliks here would not take settlement.

Sanaut pargana.—A pargana of Gaya district, of which a small detached portion, with an area of 62 acres, assessed to revenue at Rs. 83, lies on the north-west of Rajgir pargana.

Sanda pargana.—A pargana in Masaurhi thana, with an area of 12½ square miles. The pargana was in settlement with a farmer in 1790; but in 1792, when he defaulted in payment of revenue, it was settled with village maliks, with a revenue of Rs. 47,818.

Shahjahanpur pargana.—A pargana lying in Fatuha and Hilsa thanas, with an area of 61½ square miles. The greater part of this pargana was settled in 1790 with the Chaudhris of Islampur, together with their estates in Bhimpur, at a nominal revenue. The revenue after the resumption proceedings was Rs. 65,930.

Silao.—Village in the Bihar subdivision, ten miles south of Bihar, on the Rajgir extension of the Bakhtiyarpur-Bihar Light Railway. The village is a large grain mart, and contains a police-station. It is said that the best *basmati* rice in the district is obtained here, and the place has also a local reputation for the excellence of its parched rice and its sweetmeats, which before the coming of the railway were mainly sold to pilgrims on their way to Rajgir. Silao contains two tombs and a mosque with numerous inscriptions in Persian and Arabic characters. The mosque is of the ordinary kind, without cloisters attached; it is built of stone and mortar, and the floor in front is paved with stone. The whole of the stone was obtained from Hindu or Buddhist buildings. The pavement is indeed one mass of imbedded pillars, and proves that the buildings destroyed to furnish the profusion of materials must have been numerous and extensive. The foundation of Silao is ascribed to Vikramaditya even by the Muhammadans of the place, and the excellence of the sweets and of the parched rice is ascribed to Halwais of consummate skill settled here by him, whose descendants now carry on the trade.

This tradition is explained by the fact that Silao is a contraction of Vikramasila, the name of one of the most famous of the Buddhist monasteries in India. From the Tibetan chronicles we know that this monastery was a great seat of learning in the 11th century when it was ruled over by Atisha or Dipankara Srijnana, who had been proclaimed the Dharmapala or Buddhist hierarch of Magadha. He left it at the invitation of the King of Tibet and succeeded in reforming the debased form of Buddhism then prevalent in that country (1038—53). The monastery of Vikramasila appears to have flourished till the Muhammadan conquest, when it was burnt by the invaders. [Report, Arch. Surv. Ind., Vol. VIII; Sarat Chandra Das, *Life of Atisha*, J. A. S. B., Vol. LX, Part I, 1891.]

Telarha.—Village in the extreme south-west of the Bihar subdivision, situated 13 miles south-east of Masaurhi railway station on a narrow strip of land between the Kattar and Sona, two branches of the Phalgu river. Telarha has been identified with Tailadhaka, the first place visited by Hiuen Tsiang in the seventh century on his journey south from Patna. It contained a great Buddhist monastery, a magnificent pile of buildings in which were four courtyards with numerous arcades and pavilions, lofty towers and pagodas. Here 1,000 monks devoted themselves to study, and the learned from distant countries flocked to its halls. The site of this splendid structure is now marked by a number of mounds, one of which, called the Bulandi or high mound, is literally covered with Muhammadan graves. To the east of the village is a large mosque with a platform composed almost entirely of pillars and stones quarried from the ancient Buddhist buildings. The ancient name of the place, Tailadhaka, is found written in characters of the Pala time (800—1200) in an inscription on one of the stones now used as a lintel over the door. The Sangi Masjid or stone mosque, as it is popularly called, was built on the site of a Buddhist temple, and nearly all the graves dug round it have yielded either figures, pillars, or portions of cornices and mouldings. The Musalmans of Telarha refuse to bury their relations in any tomb from which any idolatrous image or carving has been turned up, and for this reason a grave has sometimes to be dug three or four times over. Outside the doors of the mosque is a second enclosure containing the *dargah* or tomb of Saiyid Yusuf Ekbal, a Muhammadan saint who lived in Telarha about 250 years ago. He and his six brothers are greatly revered by the Musalmans of the neighbourhood; the tombs of the brothers are to be found at the villages of Miawan, Mandaj, Abdalpur, Fatehpur, Parbalpur and Bibipur. Both mosque and *dargah* stand on a high mound, which apparently is the site of some Buddhist building. Some remarkably fine Buddhistic sculptures have been found in the village.

As late as the beginning of the nineteenth century, Telarha was a large town containing about ten thousand inhabitants. The modern village consists of a straggling line of houses and shops running from east to west, but nearly a third of them are unoccupied and falling to decay. It bears the signs of a period of prosperity which has long since passed away. The ruins of a fine bridge of five arches still span the now nearly dried up course of the Sona; a splendid mosque composed entirely of Buddhist materials is falling to decay on the eastern outskirts of the village; and the ruined verandahs, courtyards and tombs, which meet the eye in all directions, serve only to testify to the fact that even during the later days of Muhammadan rule Telarha had not altogether lost its pristine importance..

Telarha (Tilhara) pargana.—A pargana of the Bihar subdivision, with an area of 159 square miles. At the time of the permanent settlement the pargana formed a single estate, which was settled with Muhammad Baqir Khan, son of a sister of Seraj-ud-daula, who was living at Telarha in considerable state when Dr. Buchanan visited the district. Descendants of the family still live at Telarha; but the great estate has long been alienated and split up among a multitude of small proprietors.

Tetrawan.—Village in the south of Bihar subdivision, situated ten miles north-east of Giriak and six miles south-east of Bihar. The village contains several mounds marking the sites of old Buddhist buildings, and there are two great sheets of water—the Dighi Pokhar on the north and the Balam Pokhar on the south. Between the two is a ruined fort surrounded by a moat, standing on a low mound of ruins. Numerous Buddhistic sculptures have been discovered here. "Tetrawan," observes Mr. Broadley, must have been a monastery of no ordinary importance, and its position is even preferable to that of Bargaon. The country around it is well watered and consequently fertile, and groves of trees surround it on all sides. From the towers of the monastery, the hills of Giriak, Bihar and Parvati are distinctly visible, and the banks of the Balam tank are still covered at all times of the year with luxuriant verdure. This lake at sunset would even now charm every lover of the picturesque, and the effect must have been still more striking when thousands of recluses from the stately monastery which rose on its bank left their meditations at evening time to adore and incense the colossal Buddha which they had erected on its northern shore and dedicated "to the greatest of all purposes". [A. M. Broadley, *The Buddhistic Remains of Bihar,* J. A. S. B., Vol. XLI, 1872 ; Reports, Arch. Surv. Ind., Vol. XI.]

Vikramasila.—See Silao.

APPENDIX I.

LIST OF RAILWAY STATIONS.

East Indian Railway, Main Line.

Station.	Miles from Calcutta.	Station.	Miles from Calcutta.
Dumra ...	... 275	Futwah ...	... 325
Mokameh Ghat	... 281	Banka Ghat	... 328
Mokameh ...	... 283	Patna City	... 332
More ...	... 287	(Patna Ghat)	... 333
Pandarak ...	... 292	Gulzarbagh	... 334
Barh ...	... 299	Patna Junction	... 338
Athmal Gola	... 304	(Digha Ghat)	... 343
Bukhtiarpur	... 310	Dinapore ...	... 344
Karowta ...	... 316	Neora ...	... 348
Khusrupur	... 319	Sadisopur ...	... 352
		Bihta ...	... 355

East Indian Railway, Patna-Gaya Branch.

Station.	Miles from Patna Junction.
Poonpoon	8
Taregina	18

Bukhtiarpur-Bihar Light Railway.

Station.	Miles from Bukhtiarpur.	Station.	Miles from Bukhtiarpur.
Chero ...	... 5	Bihar Cutcherry	... 18
Harnaut ...	... 7	Bihar Sharif	... 19
Wena ...	... 10	Dipnagar ...	... 23
Bhagan Bigha	... 13	Nalanda ...	... 26
Pachasa ...	... 15	Silao ...	... 28
Soh ...	... 17	Rajgir Kund	... 33

Fatwah-Islampur Light Railway.

Station.	Miles from Futwah.	Station.	Miles from Futwah.
Daniawan ...	... 5	Kosiawan ...	... 19
Diawan ...	... 9	Ekangar Sarai	... 21
Lohanda Road	... 11	Islampur ...	... 27
Hilsa ...	... 14		

APPENDIX II

POST AND TELEGRAPH OFFICES.

I.—Combined Post and Telegraph offices.

Bakhtiarpur.
Bankipore.
Barh.
Begampur.
Bihar.
Bikram.
Digha.
Dinapore Cantonment.
Dinapore R. S.
Fatwa.
Gulzarbagh.
Khagaul.
Khusrupur,
Lodikatra.
Mahendru.
Masaurhi..
Mokameh.
Patna.
Patna City.
Patna High Court.
Patna Secretariat.
Phulwari Sharif.
Silao.

Note.—All the stations of the East Indian Railway are licensed telegraph offices.

II.—Post offices (other than combined offices).

Abda Chak (Dumrawan).
Asthawan.
Atasarai.
Athmalgola.
Bahpura.
Bain.
Barh R. S.
Beapur.
Bhandari.
Bharatpura.
Bihta.
Chandi
Daudpur.
Digha Ghat.
Dinapore Bazar.
Ekangarsarai.
Giriak.
Gonawan.
Gurhatta.
Harnaut.
Hazrat-Sain.
Hilsa.
Isapur.
Jat Dumri.
Karai-Parsarai.
Kharant.
Lai.
Maner.
Marufganj.
Mirchaiganj.
Mokameh Ghat.
Mor.
Moradpur.
Muhammadpur.
Mukhtarganj.
Nodaul.
Nagar-Nasha.
Nai-Sarai.
Nandlalabad.
Naubatpur.
Neora.
Pachhim Darwaza.
Pabhera.
Paithana.
Paliganj.
Punpun.
Rajgir.
Rambux-Jaitipur.
Sadisopur.
Saidabad.
Saksohra.
Sherpur.
Sohsarai.
Surmaira.

APPENDIX III.

PRINCIPAL ROADS AND BUNGALOWS.

No.	Road.	Class.	Length, miles.	Inspection Bungalows.
1	Dinapore Railway Station to Sadikpore Railway Crossing.	IA	10½	
2	Malsalami-Burhea ...	IA	33	Fatuha. Bakhtiarpur. Barh. Mokameh.
	(Ganges Road) ...	IIA	28¾	
3	Fatuha-Hilsa ...	IA	13¼	Hilsa.
	Hilsa-Lat ...	IIB	17½	Ekangarsarai. Islampur.
4	Bakhtiarpur-Bihar...	IA*	18¾	Bakhtiarpur. Bihar.
5	Fatuha-Bihar ...	IA IIB	7¾** 19½	Fatuha. Chandi. Bihar.
6	Hilsa-Nursarai (7½ miles from Bihar on road No. 5).	IIB	11¼	Hilsa.
7	Bihar-Giriak ...	IA	13¼	Bihar. Giriak.
8	Bihar-Rajgir ...	IIB	13¼	Bihar. Rajgir.
9	Bihar-Asthawan ...	IA	4	
		IIA	2	
10	Bihar-Ekangarsarai.	IIB	18¾	Bihar. Ekangarsarai.

* Spoilt by the Light Railway.
** Including five miles of road No. 3.

No.	Road.	Class.	Length, miles.	Inspection Bungalows.
11	Barh-Sarmera ...	IV	19¾	Barh. Sarmera.
12	Mokameh-Sarmera ..	III	12½	Mokameh. Sarmera.
13	Bankipore Gola-Dinapur viâ Digha.	IA	7	Dinapur.
14	Bankipore Gola-Dinapur viâ New Capital.	IA	8½	Bankipore. Dinapore.
15	Dinapore-Silouribagh.	IA	27¼	Dinapore. Maner. Bihta. Bikram.
16	Maner-Sone Railway Bridge.	IIB	7	Maner.
17	Dinapore-Naubatpur	IA	10¼	Dinapur. Naubatpur.
18	Dinapore-Khagaul (Dinapore R. S.)	IA	4	......
19	Khagaul-Neora ...	IA	4¼	Khagaul.
20	Khagaul-Kanpa ...	IIA	19	Khagaul Naubatpur Bihta.
21	Bihta-Mahabalipur (viâ Kanpa).	IIB	20½	Bihta.
22	Ekangarsarai-Masaurhi.	IIB	15¼	Ekangarsarai. Masaurhi.
23	Masaurhi-Naubatpur	IIA	15	Masaurhi. Naubatpur.
24	Masaurhi-Paliganj...	IIB	14	Masaurhi. Paliganj.

BOOKS TO WHICH REFERENCE IS MADE IN THIS WORK.

Narrative of the transactions in Bengal from the year 1760 to the year 1764, by Henry Vansittart, London, 1766.

A voyage to the East Indies, by Mr. Grose, London, 1772.

Narrative of the Mutiny of the Officers of the Army in Bengal, by Henry Strachey, London, 1773.

A voyage from England to India in the year MDCCLIV, and an historical narrative of the operations of the squadron and army in India in the years 1755, 1756 and 1757, by Edward Ives, London, 1773.

A History of the Military Transactions of the British Nation in Indostan, by Robert Orme, London, 1775.

Life of Robert Lord Clive, by Carracioli, London, 1776.

The Sair-ul-Mutakharin, by Saiyid Ghulam Husain Khan, translated by M. Raymond, Calcutta, 1786.

Travels in India during the years 1780—1783, by William Hodges, R.A., London, 1793.

Voyages and Travels to India etc., by George Viscount Valentia, London, 1811.

Fifth Report from the Select Committee on the affairs of the East India Company, London, 1812.

Analysis of the Bengal Regulations, by J. H. Harington, Calcutta, 1814.

Behar Amateur Lithographic Scrap Book, by Sir Charles D'Oyly, Patna, 1828.

Narrative of a journey through the Upper Provinces of India, by Reginald Heber, D.D., London, 1828.

History, Antiquities, Topography, and Statistics of Eastern India, by Dr. F. Buchanan, edited by Montgomery Martin, Vol. I, London, 1838.

History of the rise and progress of the Bengal Army, by Captain Arthur Broome, Calcutta, 1850.

Selections from the unpublished records of the Government of India (1748—1767), by the Rev. J. Long, Calcutta, 1869.

Travels of Fah Hian and Sun Yun, translated by S. Beal, London, 1869.

The History of India as told by its own historians, by Sir H. M. Elliot, London, 1873.

Annals of Rural Bengal, by W. W. Hunter, 1883.

Buddhist Records of the Western World (Hiuen Tsiang), by S. Beal, London, 1884.

Bihar Peasant Life, by G. A. Grierson, Calcutta, 1885.

History of the Indian Mutiny, by T. R. E. Holmes, London, 1891.

Discovery of the exact site of Asoka's classic capital, by L. A. Waddell, Calcutta, 1892.

Early English Administration of Bihar, by J. R. Hand, Calcutta, 1894.

The Journal of Mrs. Fenton, London, 1901.

Report on the Census of Bengal, by E. A. Gait, I.C.S., Calcutta, 1902.

Report on the excavations at Pataliputra, by L. A. Waddell, Calcutta, 1903.

Riyazus Salatin, by Ghulam Husain Salim, translated by Maulavi Abdus Salam, Calcutta, 1904.

Bengal in 1756-57, by S. C. Hill (Indian Records Series), London, 1905.

Letters of Warren Hastings to his wife, by Sydney C. Grier, London, 1905.

Early History of India, by Vincent A. Smith, Oxford, 1908.

Final Report on the survey and settlement operations in Patna district, Patna, 1914.

Early Annals of the English in Bengal, by C. R. Wilson, Calcutta, 1895—1917.

The First English Factory in Patna, by E. A. Horne, Patna, 1917.

Selections from the correspondence of the Revenue Chief of Bihar, Patna, 1919.

Pataliputra, by Manoranjan Ghosh, Patna, 1919.

Report on the Census of Bihar and Orissa, 1921, by P. C. Tallents, I.C.S.

ABBREVIATIONS.

J.A.S.B.—Journal of the Asiatic Society of Bengal.

J.B.O.R.S.—Journal of the Bihar and Orissa Research Society.

INDEX

A

B